CONTENTS

GRADE 4

CHAPTER 1 • Understanding Numbers and Money

CHAPTER 2 • Using Addition and Subtraction Facts

CHAPTER 3 • Adding and Subtracting Whole Numbers

CHAPTER 4 • Measuring Time, Capacity, and Mass

CHAPTER 5 • Multiplication and Division Facts

CHAPTER 6 • Multiplying by 1-Digit Factors

CHAPTER 7 • Dividing by 1-Digit Divisors

CHAPTER 8 • Geometry

CHAPTER 9 • Understanding Fractions and Mixed Numbers

CHAPTER 10 • Using Fractions

CHAPTER 11 • Decimals and Probability

CHAPTER 12 • Multiplying and Dividing by 2-Digit Numbers

Name

BUILDING TENS AND HUNDREDS

On Your Own Pair and Share In a Group

CARD HOUSES

Emma builds houses with her collection of baseball cards. She uses rubber bands to make sets of 10 and 100 cards. These rubber bands make the card houses stronger.

| = 1 card | = 10 cards | = 100 cards |

How many cards in each house?

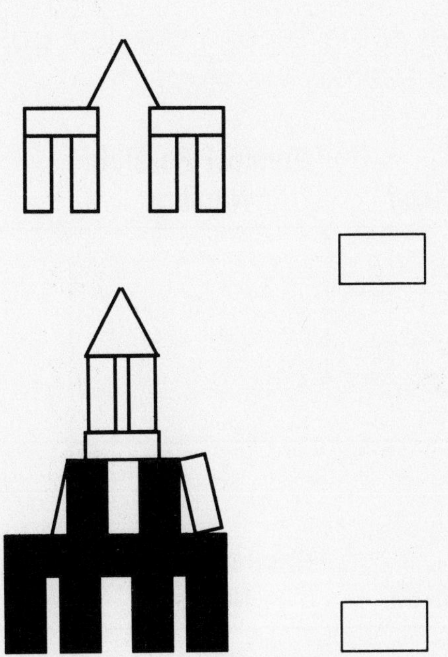

Draw a card house that uses 100 cards.

Draw a card house that uses 343 cards.

Name

THOUSANDS

THE GREATEST GAME

Form two teams. Cut out the markers at the bottom of this page, turn them face down, and mix them up. To play, one person in each team turns one marker over. Another person writes that digit in any one of the boxes for Round 1. Repeat this step using the remaining markers until you have completed the number. Together, look at the digits your team picked and write the greatest possible number you can make using these digits. Turn the markers face down and repeat the process for rounds 2, 3, and 4.

Score 3 points if your team's picked number in each round is the greatest possible number.
Score 1 point if your team's picked number is the second greatest possible number. Count the points to find your total score.

Team	Round	Number Picked	Greatest Possible Number	Score
1	1	☐ ☐ ☐ ☐		
	2	☐ ☐ ☐ ☐		
	3	☐ ☐ ☐ ☐		
	4	☐ ☐ ☐ ☐		
			Total	

Team	Round	Number Picked	Greatest Possible Number	Score
2	1	☐ ☐ ☐ ☐		
	2	☐ ☐ ☐ ☐		
	3	☐ ☐ ☐ ☐		
	4	☐ ☐ ☐ ☐		
			Total	

Name

MILLIONS

On Your Own   Pair and Share   In a Group

ONE PICTURE IS WORTH A HUNDRED THOUSAND WORDS (OR EVEN A MILLION!)

Robby is preparing a social studies report on Europe. He draws a chart to compare populations.

POPULATION OF EUROPE'S FOUR LARGEST CITIES

= 1 million people   = 100,000 people

London, United Kingdom

Paris, France

Essen, W. Germany

Milan, Italy

1. Which city on the chart has the largest population?

2. How many people live in Essen?

3. Do more than 9 million people live in Paris? How can you tell?

4. Do more than 4 million people live in Milan? How can you tell?

5. Manchester is Europe's 5th largest city. It has a population of 4,100,000. How would Robby show this on his chart?

Name

ENRICHMENT-4

PROBLEM SOLVING

On Your Own | Pair and Share | In a Group

SPELLING BY NUMBERS

The words in the list are hidden horizontally, vertically, or diagonally in the puzzle below. But they aren't spelled the same way. Part of each word has been replaced with a number that sounds the same. For example, TUESDAY appears in the puzzle as 2SDAY. Write the new spelling of each word with your partner and circle it in the puzzle. The first one has been done for you.

canine CA9

cartoon ____________

classics ____________

donate ____________

everyone ____________

force ____________

forgotten ____________

fork ____________

great ____________

inflate ____________

once ____________

slate ____________

stewed ____________

straight ____________

stupid ____________

tender ____________

Tuesday ____________

tutu ____________

weighty ____________

wonderful ____________

2 S D A Y 2 N 1 C A 9
W N S O 4 K S L A D E
P D 2 2 U G A 4 R O V
D 4 P 4 S 6 O 8 2 N E
6 T I C T W S 1 N 8 R
1 O D E R W L 7 O R Y
C 4 G R 8 2 8 S 2 D 1
E I N F L 8 1 O 4 C 2
2 S D 1 D E R F U L 8

Name

COUNTING MONEY

On Your Own Pair and Share In a Group

JAN, STAN, FRAN, AND WILBUR

Jan, Stan, Fran, and Wilbur each have the same amount of money. Work with your group to find out which coins each person has.

I have 9 coins.
JAN

I have 5 coins.
STAN

I have 3 coins.
FRAN

I have only 1 coin and it's not a silver dollar.
WILBUR

Jan has: ________ ________ ________

Stan has: ________ ________ ________

Fran has: ________ ________ ________

Wilbur has: ________ ________ ________

Jan, Stan, Fran, and Wilbur each have a different coin.

My coin is worth two of Fran's.

JAN

I have _____ ¢.

STAN

My coin is worth more than anyone else's coin.

I have _____ ¢.

FRAN

If I had 4 more of my coins, I'd have as much as Stan.

I have _____ ¢.

And if I had 4 more of *my* coins, I'd have as much as Fran.

WILBUR

I have _____ ¢.

WILBUR

Would you rather have a quart of pennies or a pint of quarters? Why?

____

____

____

Name

MAKING CHANGE

On Your Own　Pair and Share　In a Group

TAKE-AWAY

Each player starts with 2 quarters, 2 dimes, 2 nickels, and 2 pennies.

Part 1

Players take turns placing one coin in each box until all boxes are filled. Then you flip a coin to see who begins Part Two.

Part 2

Players take turns removing coins. Each turn, you can remove only one type of coin. You can remove coins from any one row or column on the board.

For example, you might remove 2 nickels from the top row. Or you might remove 3 pennies from the right column. You can always remove at least one coin.

The player with the greatest amount of money at the end of the game is the winner.

Answer these questions after you have played the game several times.

1. Which coins are usually taken away first? last?

   Why? ______________________

   ____

   ____

2. Why is it important to play carefully in Part One of this game? ______________________

   ____

   ____

   ____

3. Can you think of any strategies that help you win? ______________________

   ____

   ____

Name

COMPARING AND ORDERING NUMBERS

THE SCALE OF THINGS

Look at the value that each letter represents. Order the letters from least to greatest values in the boxes below.

A. Distance from Earth to Saturn: 887,140,000 miles

B. Number of words in the Encyclopedia Britannica: 44,000,000 words

C. Diameter of Jupiter: 88,846 miles

D. Highest price paid for a diamond: 4,580,000 dollars

E. Weight of the largest ice cream sundae: 33,616 pounds

F. Area of the United States: 3,540,939 square miles

G. Average number of people in the United States watching TV during prime time: 94,900,000 people

H. Greatest speed of the fastest airplane: 2,193 mph

I. Greatest speed of the fastest animal (the peregrine falcon): 217 mph

J. Largest number of pieces in a jigsaw puzzle: 61,752 pieces

K. Amount of food eaten by a wild elephant in one year: 255,500 pounds

Circle the most reasonable value for each. Then use your answers to order the letters from least to greatest values in the boxes below.

L. Length in miles of the Mississippi River

3 3,880 3,880,000

M. Words in the English language

600,000 600 6,000

N. Number of books in a bookstore

100 10,000 1,000,000

Name

ROUNDING NUMBERS

On Your Own Pair and Share In a Group

A SHOCKING SITUATION

The numbers at the left have been rounded. You are given the place to which each number was rounded. Find the original number in the list at the right. Write the letter of the original number next to the rounded number. When you are done, you will have the answer to the riddle.

What did they call Adam after he put his finger in an electric socket?

_____ 1,900 (nearest 10)
_____ $25.50 (nearest $.10)
_____ 2,000 (nearest 1,000)

_____ $15.00 (nearest $1.00)
_____ $14.40 (nearest $.10)
_____ 40 (nearest 10)
_____ 768,200 (nearest 100)
_____ 400 (nearest 100)

_____ 620 (nearest 10)
_____ 2,300,200 (nearest 100)

_____ 2,700 (nearest 10)
_____ 500 (nearest 10)
_____ 3,400 (nearest 100)

_____ $12.00 (nearest $1.00)
_____ $14.00 (nearest $.10)
_____ 3,000 (nearest 1,000)
_____ 56,000 (nearest 1,000)

T. $14.70
O. $14.42
T. 1,897
O. 616
T. $12.35
T. 2,707
I. $26.50
H. $24.46
H. 2,720
T. 377
I. 629
A. 37
G. $12.90
A. $14.21
R. 768,290
E. 3,372
H. 498
E. 2,438
N. 2,300,121
W. 2,600
S. 768,220
N. 55,800
O. $13.96
Y. 56,800
F. 2,300,243

Name ____________________

ENRICHMENT-9

PROBLEM SOLVING

On Your Own | Pair and Share | In a Group

IT'S ALL RELATIVE

Match each item on the left with its correct quantity or best estimate on the right. You don't have to know the answers—just use your common sense. Decide which item in each set is smallest or largest. That will help you choose the correct answers.

_____	1. The weight of a one-day-old kitten	**A.**	3 ½ oz
_____	2. The weight of a one-day-old whale	**B.**	150 lb
_____	3. The weight of a one-day-old giraffe	**C.**	4,000 lb
_____	4. Approximate number of leaves on a tree	**D.**	1,000
_____	5. Approximate number of pages in a dictionary	**E.**	2,500
_____	6. Approximate number of letters on a book page	**F.**	100,000
_____	7. Number of days a 70-year-old has been alive	**G.**	240
_____	8. Average number of heartbeats in an hour	**H.**	3,900
_____	9. Average hours spent sleeping in one month	**I.**	25,000
_____	10. Length of the world's longest river	**J.**	5½ miles
_____	11. Distance around the equator	**K.**	4,180 miles
_____	12. Height of the world's tallest mountain	**L.**	7,927 miles
_____	13. Number of ants in an ant colony	**M.**	100
_____	14. Number of grains of sugar in a sugar bowl	**N.**	4,000
_____	15. Hours of sunlight in one year	**O.**	10,000
_____	16. Number of rainy days in one year	**P.**	100,000
_____	17. Number of people at a concert	**Q.**	2,000
_____	18. Population of Canada	**R.**	600,000
_____	19. Number of women in the world	**S.**	25,900,000
_____	20. Number of doctors in the United States	**T.**	2,500,000,000

Name

USING TABLES

On Your Own Pair and Share In a Group

SCRAMBLED EGGS (AND OTHER THINGS, TOO)

Julio makes banana bread and granola for charity bake sales. He uses the amounts shown in these tables.

Banana Bread			
Batches	Eggs	Flour	Bananas
1	2	1c	3

Granola					
Batches	Oats	Raisins	Bran	Nuts	Apricots
1	4c	2c	2c	1c	1c

He often makes several batches, so he made two charts showing the amounts to use for 1 to 6 batches. Unfortunately, he accidently cut up his charts instead of cutting the bread. Can you and your partner match the pieces at the bottom of this page with their correct position in Julio's charts? (*Hint:* You can cut out the pieces and try rearranging them in the spaces.)

Batches	Eggs	Flour	Bananas
E		B	
L		I	
D		O	

Batches	Oats	Raisins	Bran	Nuts	Apricots
J		K		H	
A		C		M	
G		N		F	

3	12c
4	16c

1c	3
2c	6

6c	6c
8c	8c

5	10
6	12

1	2
2	4

5c	5c
6c	6c

5	20c
6	24c

1c	1c
2c	2c

3c	9
4c	12

1	4c
2	8c

2c	2c
4c	4c

3	6
4	8

3c	3c
4c	4c

10c	10c
12c	12c

5c	15
6c	18

Name

MEANING OF ADDITION AND SUBTRACTION

PATHEMATICS

Follow the path of correct number sentences through this maze. You can enter a box more than once.

Start

7

+	4	=	11	−	2	=	9	+	3	=	5	−
6		10		4		8		3		2		7
=	2	+	5	=	7	+	13	=	10	+	8	=
12		4		8		14		12		8		7
+	12	=	5	−	7	=	4	−	4	=	0	+
6		7		11		8		8		10		1
=	4	−	10	=	10	+	9	=	1	−	6	=
1		5		8		9		4		13		7
+	9	=	10	+	3	=	1	−	8	=	4	+
3		6		7		18		3		5		4
=	7	−	11	=	17	−	9	=	8	+	4	=
6		5		1		8		2		7		11
+	7	=	10	+	10	=	14	+	7	=	8	−
5		11		2		7		2		3		5
=	12	−	5	=	14	+	10	=	8	+	4	=

7

End

Name

ENRICHMENT-12

FACT FAMILIES

On Your Own Pair and Share In a Group

MORRA

Morra is an ancient counting game. There is one way to play. The two players face each other. At a given signal, each player holds up 0 to 5 fingers and says a number between 0 and 10. A player scores one point for correctly stating the sum of both players' fingers. Write each player's score in the boxes.

There is another way to play Morra. Players score one point if they say the sum of the numbers and one point if they say the difference between the numbers. Fill in the correct score in each box.

Fill in the words so that the scores are correct.

1 0 1 1 0 1

Can you describe how a player could score two points in one turn? ______________________

____

____

Now try playing Morra with a friend!

MACMILLAN/McGRAW-HILL

Name

MENTAL MATH: ADDITION FACTS

On Your Own   Pair and Share   In a Group

IT ALL ADDS UP

Use this code for the digits 0–9.

0 1 2 3 4 5 6 7 8 9

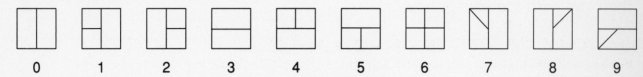

Use two boxes for a 2-digit number. For example:

16

Find each sum. Write the answer in code.

1.

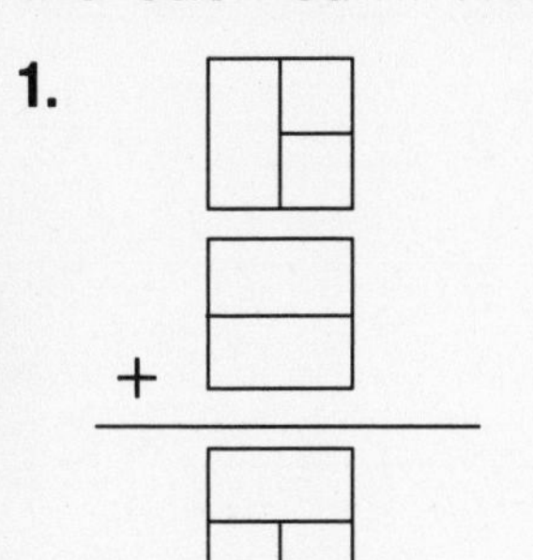

2.

3.

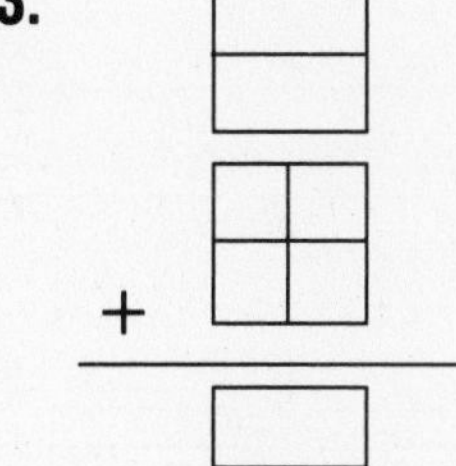

4.

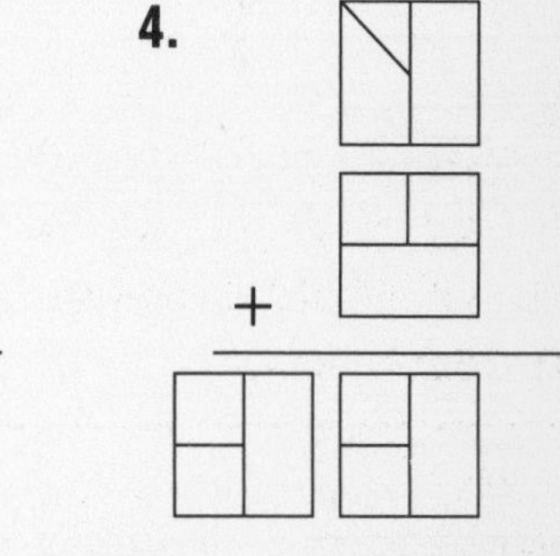

5.

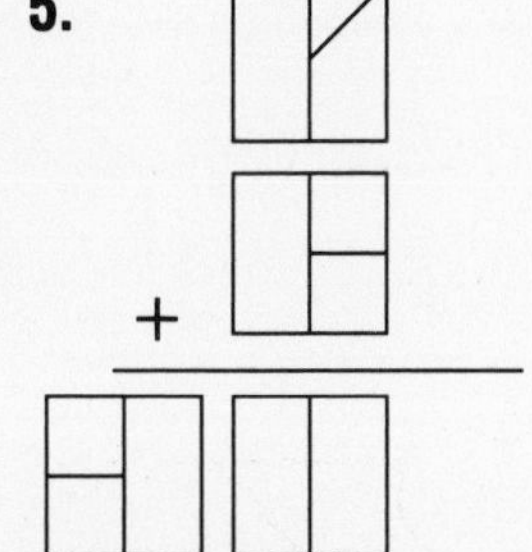

6.

7.

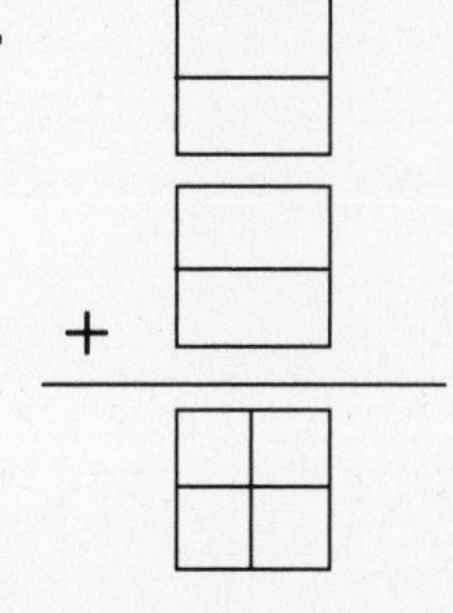

8.

9. Use the code. Show two different ways of getting the sum.

Name

MENTAL MATH: SUBTRACTION FACTS

On Your Own Pair and Share In a Group

COUNTDOWN

Complete this exercise with a classmate. Take turns filling in the blank with the correct answer.

9 − 8 + 7 − 6 + 5 − 4 + 3 − 2 + 1 = _____

Write a + or a − sign in each blank so that the answers shown are correct. You may use a calculator to help you.

9 _____ 8 _____ 7 _____ 6 _____ 5 _____ 4 _____ 3 _____ 2 _____ 1 = 13

9 _____ 8 _____ 7 _____ 6 _____ 5 _____ 4 _____ 3 _____ 2 _____ 1 = 1

9 _____ 8 _____ 7 _____ 6 _____ 5 _____ 4 _____ 3 _____ 2 _____ 1 = 7

9 _____ 8 _____ 7 _____ 6 _____ 5 _____ 4 _____ 3 _____ 2 _____ 1 = 3

What is the greatest sum you can get using 3 − signs?

9 _____ 8 _____ 7 _____ 6 _____ 5 _____ 4 _____ 3 _____ 2 _____ 1 = _____

What is the greatest sum you can get using 4 − signs?

9 _____ 8 _____ 7 _____ 6 _____ 5 _____ 4 _____ 3 _____ 2 _____ 1 = _____

What is the lowest sum you can get using 4 + signs?

9 _____ 8 _____ 7 _____ 6 _____ 5 _____ 4 _____ 3 _____ 2 _____ 1 = _____

Name

MENTAL MATH: THREE OR MORE ADDENDS

On Your Own Pair and Share In a Group

ALL IN A ROW

Fill in the sums for the problems below.

0	1	2	3	4	5
+ 1	+ 2	+ 3	+ 4	+ 5	+ 6

0	1	2	3	4	5
1	2	3	4	5	6
+ 2	+ 3	+ 4	+ 5	+ 6	+ 7

0	1	2	3	4	5
1	2	3	4	5	6
2	3	4	5	6	7
+ 3	+ 4	+ 5	+ 6	+ 7	+ 8

1. Look at the sums of the first row of problems.

How may addends are in each problem? _____

What pattern do the addends follow? ______________________________

What pattern do the sums follow? ______________________________

2. What pattern do the sums of the second row follow? ______________________________

____

3. Based on the pattern you found in question 2, find these sums:

6 + 7 + 8 = _____ 7 + 8 + 9 = _____ 8 + 9 + 10 = _____

4. What pattern do the sums of the third row follow? ______________________________

____

5. Based on the pattern you found in question 4, find these sums:

6 + 7 + 8 + 9 = _____ 7 + 8 + 9 + 10 = _____

6. Can you guess what pattern the sums of these problems will follow?

0 + 1 + 2 + 3 + 4 = _____ The pattern is: ______________________________

1 + 2 + 3 + 4 + 5 = _____ ______________________________

2 + 3 + 4 + 5 + 6 = _____

3 + 4 + 5 + 6 + 7 = _____

Name

PROBLEM SOLVING

On Your Own Pair and Share In a Group

EASIER THAN MEETS THE EYE

These two problems have one thing in common. They seem more difficult than they really are! Just think carefully before you answer, and you'll quickly find the solutions.

The Bus Route

You are the driver of a public bus. There are 9 people on your bus. At the first stop, Zach and Zelda get off; Bob, Brenda, and Billy get on. At the next stop, Alma and Anthony get on and Kyle and Keith get off. Hal, Hank, Hannah, and Henry get off at the next stop. A group of 12 gets on at the stop after that, while Alma and Anthony get off. Mark and Melba get on the bus two stops later, but Timothy, Tara, Talbot, and Tillie leave the bus. At the next-to-last stop, Paula, Peter, Phil, and Paulo leave through the side door. Martin and Martha leave with the rest of the riders at the last stop.

What is the name of the bus driver?

____

DIVIDING EVENLY

These figures have each been divided into four equal parts.

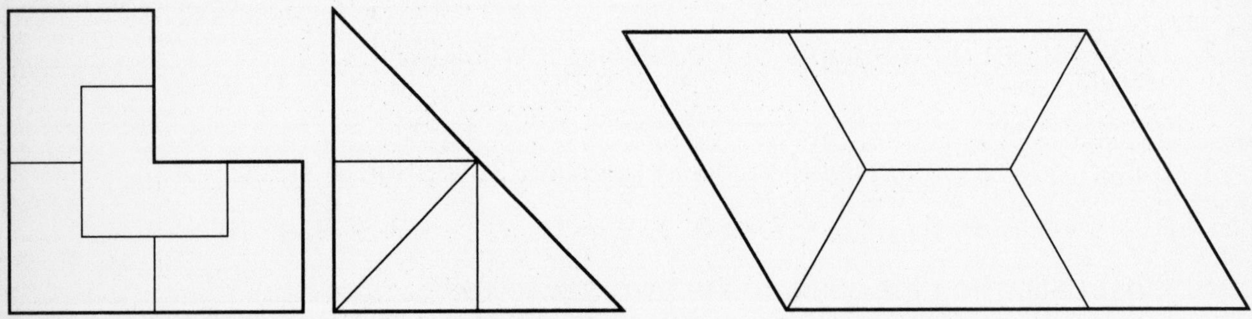

Can you divide this shape into five equal parts?

MACMILLAN/McGRAW-HILL

Name

MEASURING LENGTH: METRIC UNITS

ART FROM MEASUREMENT

You can create beautiful designs with a ruler! Experimenting with measurements can produce amazing results.

Measure the box below. What is the length of each side? ______

On the top line, draw dots 2 cm from each corner.
On the side lines, draw dots 2 cm from each corner.
Draw a dot in the middle of the bottom line.
Now connect every dot to every other dot on the box.
You can color the design to make it more vivid!

Now experiment with the boxes below. Where will you place the dots?

You can try this pattern for the first box, or invent your own: On the top and bottom lines, draw 4 dots spaced equally apart. On each side line, draw 2 dots spaced equally apart. Then connect all the dots.

Below each drawing, explain how you created it. Tell how you placed each dot.

Name

ESTIMATING LENGTH: METRIC UNITS

NATURE'S LITTLE SECRET

Circle the best estimate for each length. Then find the number next to the correct answer in the drawing below and color in that area. When you are done, you will find the answer to the riddle below.

A. The height of a tree	**1.** 60 cm	**2.** 60 m	**3.** 60 km
B. The length of an alligator	**4.** 130 dm	**5.** 130 m	**6.** 130 km
C. The height of an acorn	**7.** 2 cm	**8.** 2 dm	**9.** 2 m
D. The length of a forest	**10.** 50 cm	**11.** 50 dm	**12.** 50 km
E. The height of a bear	**13.** 250 cm	**14.** 250 dm	**15.** 250 m
F. The distance a leaf falls	**16.** 8 cm	**17.** 8 m	**18.** 8 km
G. The distance across a lake	**19.** 20 cm	**20.** 20 dm	**21.** 20 km
H. The length of a rattlesnake	**22.** 4 cm	**23.** 4 m	**24.** 4 km
I. The height of a rose bush	**25.** 5 dm	**26.** 50 cm	**27.** 500 dm
J. The length of a centipede	**28.** 4 cm	**29.** 40 cm	**30.** 400 cm

What kind of room is impossible to enter?

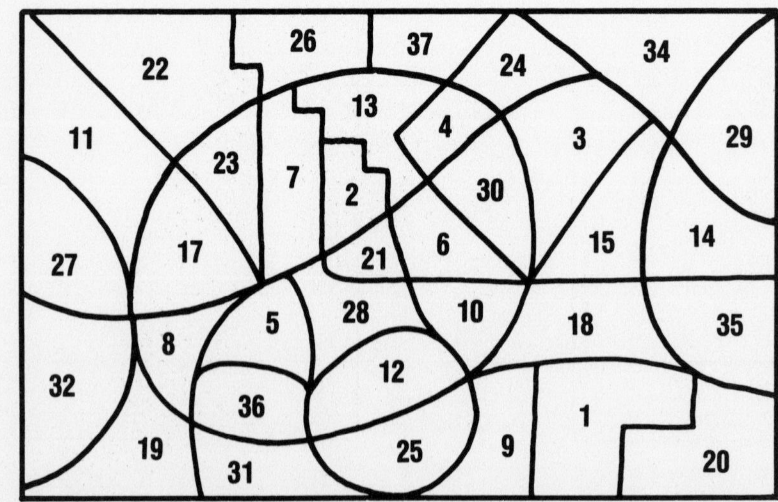

MACMILLAN/McGRAW-HILL

Name

PROBLEM SOLVING

FORM ONE LINE, PLEASE

Can you draw each of these designs using only one line? Each member of your group can try. Do not lift your pen from the paper or go over a part more than once. But be warned! One of these problems is impossible! Which one? Circle it when you find it.

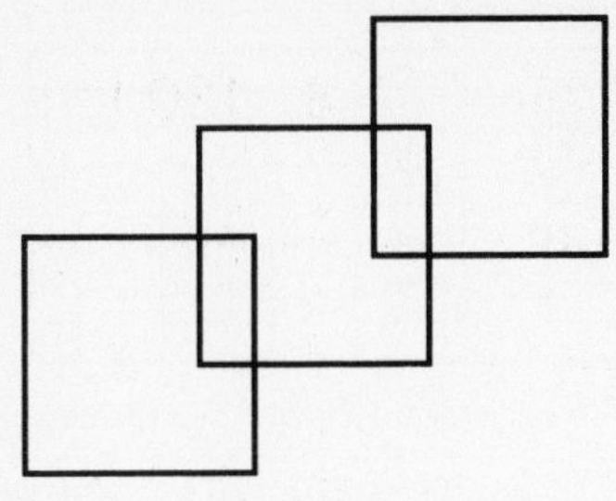

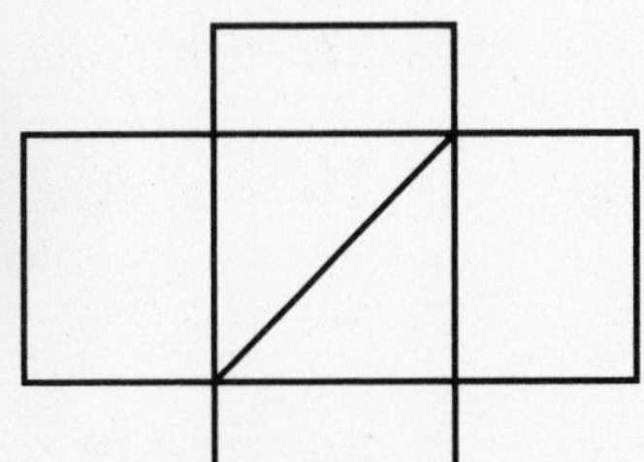

Now create two designs of your own that can be drawn using only one line. Then exchange papers with a classmate and try to draw his or her new designs.

Name

MAKING BAR GRAPHS

On Your Own Pair and Share In a Group

AND THE SURVEY SAYS...

Stacy polled her fellow students about their favorite sports. The bar graph below shows the results of her poll.

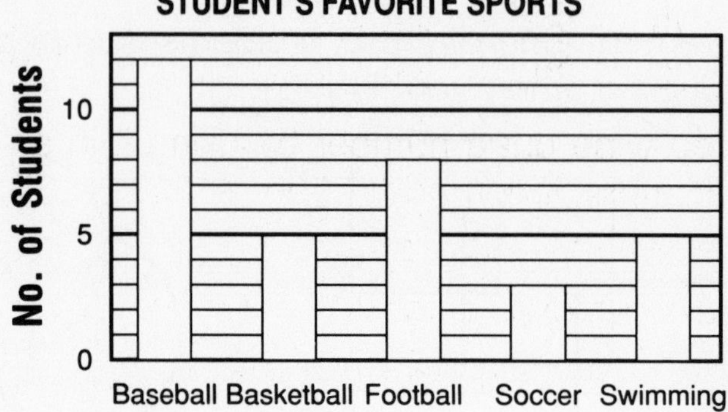

1. Which sport was most popular in Stacy's class? ________________
2. Which two sports did the same number of people vote for?

   ____
3. How many more people voted for football than soccer? __________

Now conduct your own poll. Ask your fellow students about one of these topics, or choose one or your own:

favorite sport	favorite TV show	favorite movie
favorite food	favorite animal	

To conduct your own poll, make a chart and keep track of everyone's answer on a separate sheet of paper. Label each heading. For example, if you are asking people about their favorite animal, the first might be labeled "cat." Then, each time someone answers "cat," put a mark in that box.

Now make a bar graph showing the information in your poll. Remember to label and draw each bar carefully.

Name

MENTAL MATH: ADDING 10s; 100s; 1000s

On Your Own Pair and Share In a Group

WIPE OUT!

The object of this game is to wipe out every number on this list.

10	100	1,000	40	400	4,000	70	700	7,000
20	200	2,000	50	500	5,000	80	800	8,000
30	300	3,000	60	600	6,000	90	900	9,000

You wipe out a number by using it in an addition fact. For example, if you add 7,000 + 200 + 300, you wipe out those three numbers.

You can use up to four numbers in each addition fact.

The sum of your numbers must be less than 10,000.

1. Here is a set of sums that will wipe out the list. Can you find the addition facts that were used?

Sum Addition Facts

9,990 _____ + _____ + _____

9,880 _____ + _____ + _____ + _____

7,780 _____ + _____ + _____ + _____

6,760 _____ + _____ + _____ + _____

5,570 _____ + _____ + _____ + _____

5,230 _____ + _____ + _____ + _____

4,740 _____ + _____ + _____ + _____

2. Now create your own set of sums. Show your addition facts as well. Can you wipe out the set with seven sums that each total less than 10,000? (*Remember,* use no more than four numbers for each sum.)

Sum Addition facts

_____ ______________________________

_____ ______________________________

_____ ______________________________

_____ ______________________________

_____ ______________________________

Name

ENRICHMENT-22

ESTIMATING SUMS BY ROUNDING

On Your Own Pair and Share In a Group

THE CAT'S MEOW

Estimate each sum by rounding. Then find the letter that goes with each answer. Fill in the blanks to answer this riddle:

"What is a cat's favorite breakfast food?"

1. 420 + 380 + 187

2. $7.35 + 1.18 + 3.75

3. $8.89 + 3.98 + 2.66

4. 81 + 407 + 15

5. $10.66 + 4.23 + 16.44

6. 485 + 243 + 68

7. $2.75 + 4.45 + 5.48

8. $7.72 + 6.72 + 4.72

9. 355 + 432 + 189 + 74

10. $3.32 + 3.67 + 3.49 + 2.26

11. 76 + 59 + 188 + 92

12. $1.53 + 7.07 + 10.59 + 0.40

1,400	$30.00	500	$12.00	1,000	$11.00	1,100	800	$20.00	700	$16.00
A	C	E	I	M	N	P	R	S	T	C

The answer to the riddle is

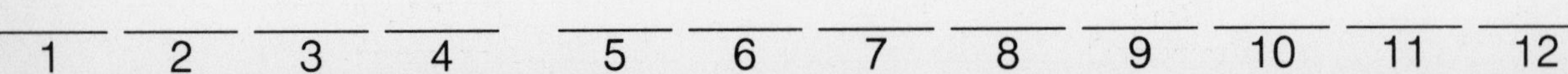

___ ___ ___ ___   ___ ___ ___ ___ ___ ___ ___ ___
1 2 3 4   5 6 7 8 9 10 11 12

Name

FRONT-END ESTIMATION

On Your Own Pair and Share In a Group

GREAT ESTIMATIONS

1. Use front-end estimation with adjustment to find an estimated value for the three paths shown (—— , -- -- , and —-—). Write your estimates at the end of the paths. Then find a new path that follows these rules.

   The path begins at START.

   The path can go from one circle to any circle next to it.

   The path travels through 7 circles (including the START circle).

   The path ends at any circle on the outside.

2. Can you find the path with the highest possible total? Use front-end estimation with adjustment to help. Draw your path using a dashed line (-----).

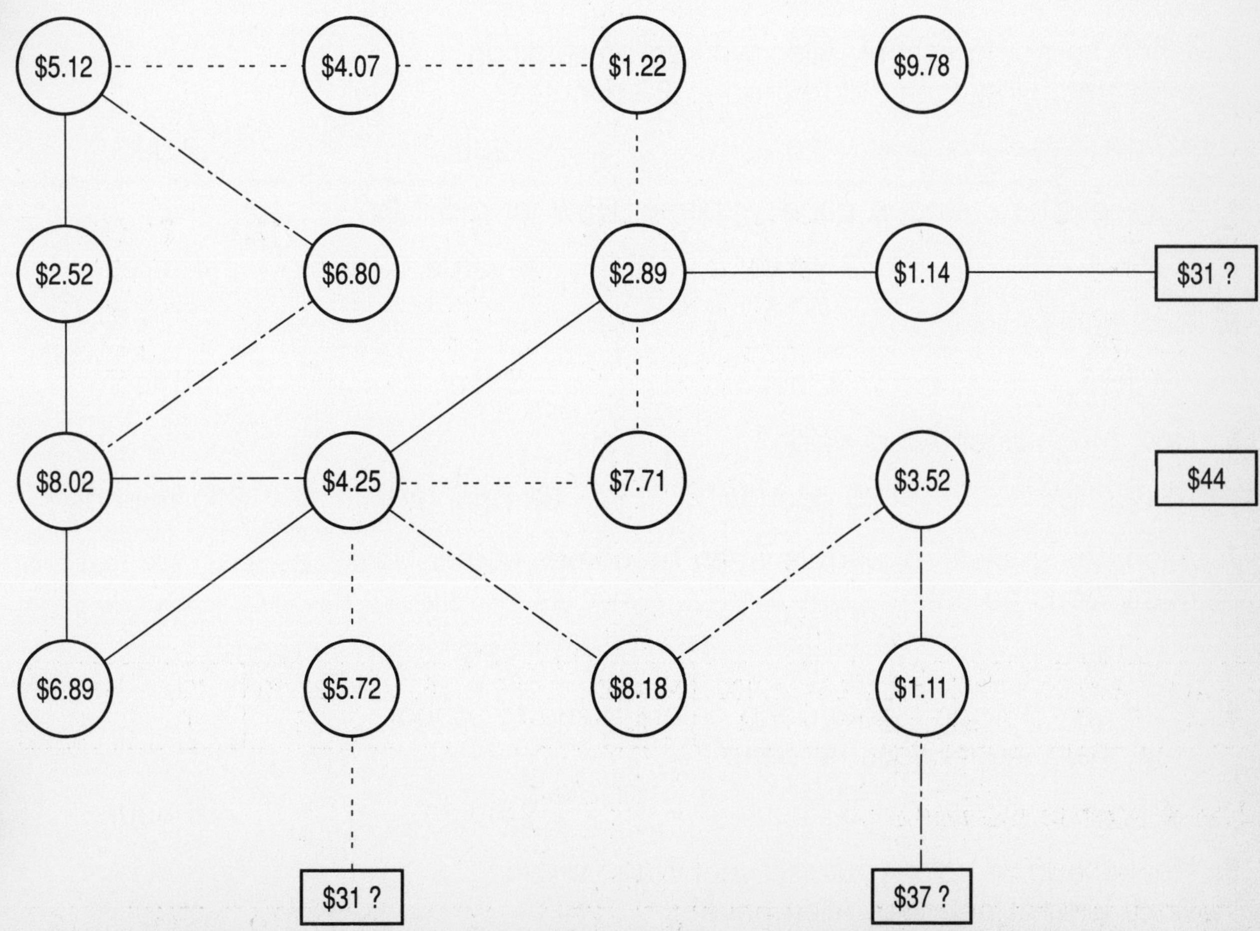

Name

PROBLEM SOLVING

On Your Own Pair and Share In a Group

MATH WITHOUT MATH

You don't have to do any calculations on this worksheet! Just circle *every* answer that seems reasonable. Some questions have more than one possible answer that is reasonable. Circle all of them. Then shade or color the shapes that show your answers. You'll find a hidden picture.

18 hours
15 feet
4 miles
3
1
20
4 feet
2,000
15 hours
15 seconds
8 hours
35
2
10 pounds
4 yards
70 pounds
2 yards
200
9 hours
5 feet
350
10
80 pounds
25
1 foot
1 inch
4 hours
15 minutes
800 pounds

1. Allen ran 1 mile on his way to school this morning. How long did it take him?

   15 seconds 15 minutes 15 hours

2. Allen delivers newspapers in the morning. His route takes about half an hour. How many papers does he deliver?

   3 25 35 350

3. When he got to school, Allen worked on addition problems. How many did he do in 20 minutes?

   10 20 200 2,000

4. At recess he cut out a paper airplane. How far did it fly?

   1 inch 2 yards 4 yards 4 miles

5. How tall is Allen?

   1 foot 4 feet 5 feet 15 feet

6. How much does Allen weigh?

   10 pounds 70 pounds 80 pounds 800 pounds

7. Allen has a snack of carrots when he comes home. How many does he eat?

   1 2 25 200

8. Allen gets a good night's sleep before going to school. How many hours does he sleep?

   4 hours 8 hours 9 hours 18 hours

9. Now shade or color your answers in the drawing. What kind of pet does Allen have?

Name

ADDING WHOLE NUMBERS

CLUNK!

Play this game with another student. First cut out the circles and triangles on this page. Then turn them upside down.

At each turn, a player can take one triangle or two circles. Write down your scores. Keep a running total as you play. Take turns choosing shapes until they are all gone. The player with the highest total is the winner.

But watch out for the CLUNKS! If you pick one, you lose all the points you have gained so far!

Think about your strategy.

1. What is the most you can score in a single turn? _____
2. What is the least you can score in one turn? _____
3. How will your strategy change as pieces are taken? ____________________

____

____

100	170	240	310	380	440
110	180	250	320	390	450
120	190	260	330	400	460
130	200	270	340	410	470
140	210	280	350	420	480
150	220	290	360	430	490
160	230	300	370	CLUNK!	CLUNK!
CLUNK!	CLUNK!	CLUNK!	CLUNK!		

Name

COLUMN ADDITION

On Your Own Pair and Share In a Group

SLOW-POKE JOE

"Joe is the slowest person I know. In fact, he's so slow that. . ."

To find out how slow Joe is, circle the sets of numbers that add up to the sums given. Each set will be together in a column.

When you have finished, write the letters in the numbered blanks. The first one has been done for you.

1. 2 numbers that add up to 187

2. 2 numbers that add up to 43

3. 3 numbers that add up to 323

4. 3 numbers that add up to 271

5. 3 numbers that add up to 181

6. 4 numbers that add up to 35

7. 4 numbers that add up to 204

8. 4 numbers that add up to 1,307

10	T (3)	205	L (14)	16	E (23)
20	H (12)	14	M (5)	111	R (17)
108	E (2)	360	V (25)	12	A (6)
109	A (15)	172	A (4)	7	M (16)
106	O (23)	15	N (19)	4	D (25)
50	C (7)	70	P (17)	12	A (11)
201	D (24)	77	H (10)	24	S (20)
318	H (1)	82	I (18)	19	T (9)
593	R (3)	22	E (17)	101	I (15)
295	D (13)	20	Y (14)	20	A (8)
101	C (22)	80	N (24)	42	C (14)
567	W (1)	92	E (21)	80	N (5)
390	O (6)	99	B (7)	62	N (12)

Joe is so slow that

___ ___ ___ ___ ___ ___ ___ ___ ___ ___
1 2 3 4 5 6 7 8 9 10

___ ___ ___ ___ ___ ___ ___ ___ ___
11 12 13 14 15 16 17 18 19

___ ___ ___ ___ ___ ___
20 21 22 23 24 25

Name

MENTAL MATH: SUBTRACTING 10s; 100s; 1000s

JUST THE FACTS

Make subtraction facts by matching two numbers from the first two columns with a difference in the third column. Use each number in each group only once. Write the number sentence in the blank at the right. One has been done for you.

1.	100	20	10	100 − 90 = 10
2.	60	90	20	________
3.	80	10	40	________
4.	30	30	50	________
5.	400	200	100	________
6.	200	300	200	________
7.	800	100	300	________
8.	700	400	500	________
9.	7,000	5,000	1,000	________
10.	9,000	4,000	2,000	________
11.	10,000	3,000	6,000	________
12.	4,000	2,000	7,000	________

Name

ESTIMATING DIFFERENCES

ADDITIONAL SUBTRACTION

1. The arrow points to the number being subtracted. Estimate the difference between each pair of boxes connected by a horizontal, vertical, or diagonal line. Use rounding. Write your estimate on the line.

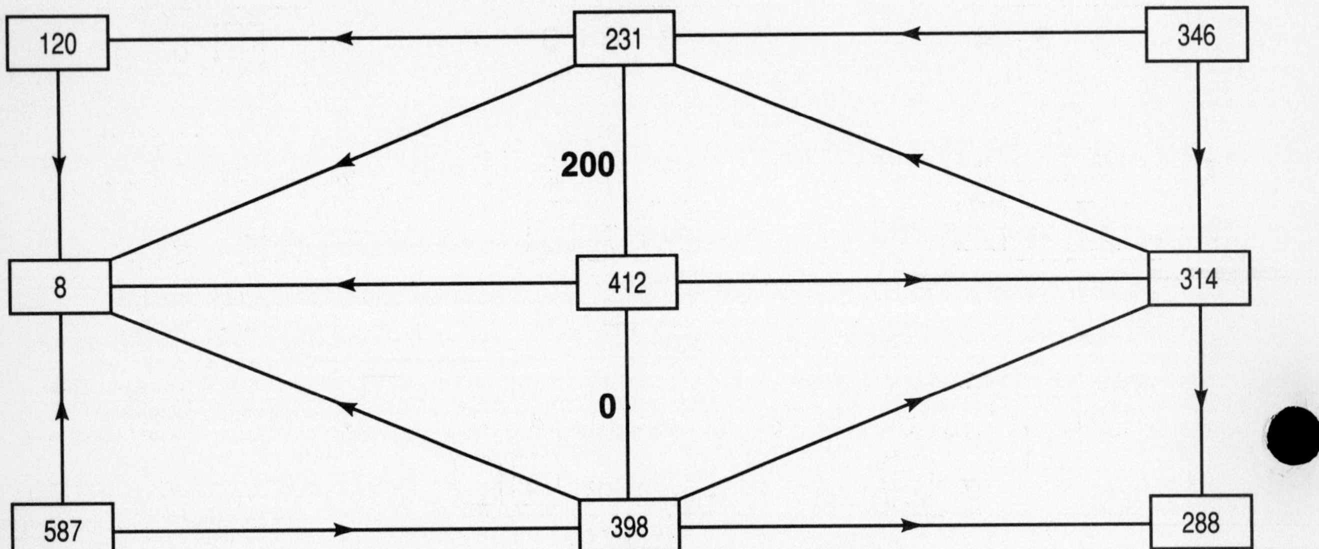

2. The numbers on the lines show the difference between each pair of boxes. The arrow points to the number being subtracted. Can you fill in every box in this puzzle? (*Hint:* Using addition may help.)

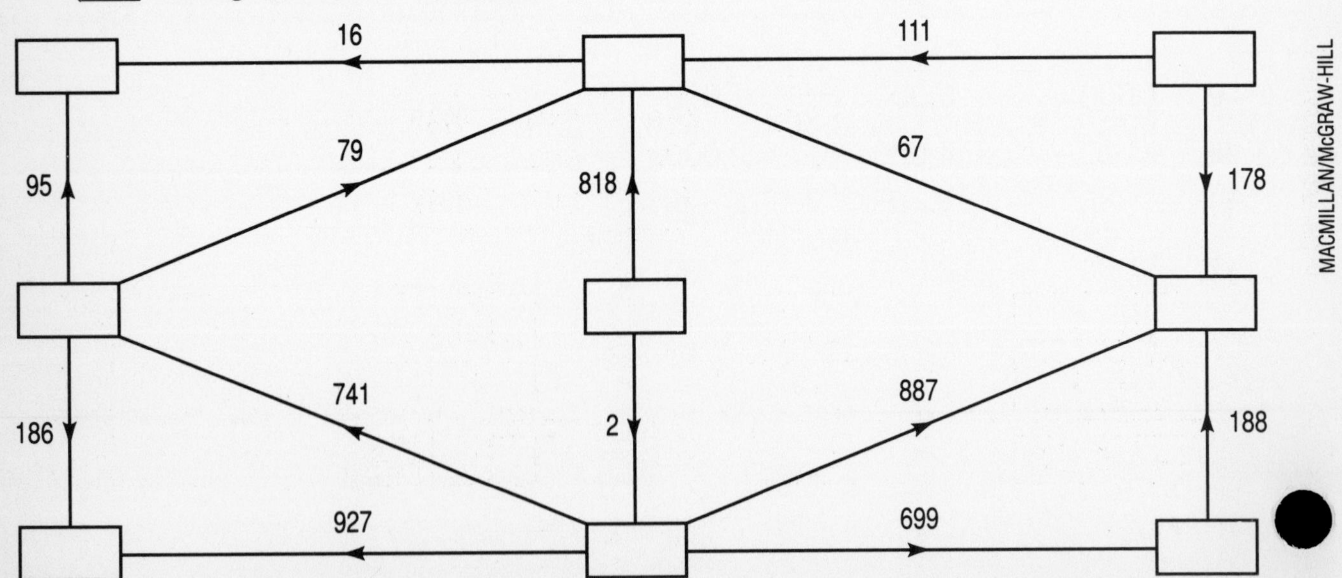

Name

ENRICHMENT-29

SUBTRACTING WHOLE NUMBERS

On Your Own | Pair and Share | In a Group

LESS AND LESS

Find the missing digits.

1. □ 2 1 − □ □ = 2 3 4

2. □ 6 □ − □ 2 = 8 5 0

3. 5 1 □ − □ 2 = □ 2 3

4. 7 □ 6 − □ 0 □ = 1 2 3

5. 3 1 2 − □ 7 □ = □ 5

6. 5 □ □ − □ 8 5 = 1 7 7

7. □, 1 □ 5 − 7 □ = 2, □ 9 3

8. 8, 4 4 4 − 8 □ □ = □, □ 8 3

9. 7, □ □ □ − 3, 5 2 2 = □, 7 4 6

10. Use the numbers in the box to complete the problems. Use each number only once.

363	458	519	882
403	476	584	954
409	478	867	987

□ □ □ − □ □ □ = 4 0 3

□ □ □ − □ □ 8 = 4 □ □

□ 6 □ − □ □ □ = □ 5 □

8 □ □ − □ □ □ = □ □ □

Name

SUBTRACTING ACROSS ZEROS

On Your Own Pair and Share In a Group

NUMBER SHRINKING

Find the pattern of each subtraction series below. Write the missing numbers in each series and find the final value. Use a calculator to help you.

1. 10,000 − 999 − 888 − 777 − ______ − ______ − ______ − ______ − ______ − ______ = ______

2. 10,000 − 987 − 876 − 765 − ______ − ______ − ______ − ______ = ______

3. 10,000 − 919 − 818 − 717 − ______ − ______ − ______ − ______ − ______ − ______ = ______

4. 10,000 − 90 − 80 − 70 − 60 − ______ − ______ − ______ − ______ − ______ = ______

5. 100,000 − 9,955 − 8,844 − ______ − ______ − ______ − ______ = ______

6. 100,000 − 9,079 − 8,068 − 7,057 − 6,046 − ______ − ______ − ______ = ______

7. 100,000 − 1,213 − 2,324 − 3,435 − 4,546 − ______ − ______ − ______ = ______

8. 100,000 − 135 − 246 − 357 − ______ − ______ = ______

Name

PROBLEM SOLVING

On Your Own Pair and Share In a Group

HOW LOW CAN YOU GO?

Cut out the shapes at the bottom of this page. The numbers are in squares □, and the operation signs are in triangles △. Place the numbers and operation signs in this pattern.

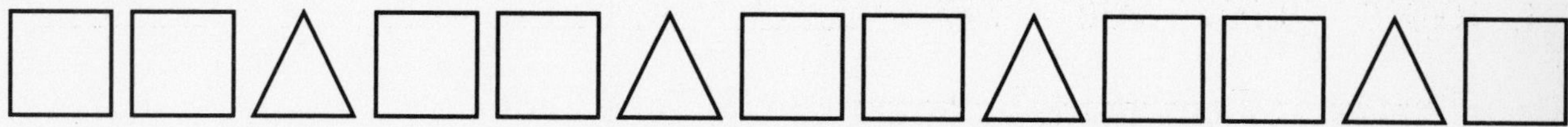

1. What is the greatest value you can get?

____

2. What is the least value you can get?

____

Now place the shapes in any pattern to find new values. For example, you might find 321 + 7 − 8 + 904 − 56, which equals 1,168.

3. What is the greatest value you can get when you use all the numbers and operation signs? Write the pattern as a number sentence.

____

4. What is the least value you can get when you use all the numbers and operation signs? Write the pattern as a number sentence.

____

____

5. Form a pattern that uses every shape and that equals 100. Write the pattern as a number sentence.

____

____

1 2 3 4 5 6 7 8 9 + + - -

Name

FINDING PERIMETER

On Your Own Pair and Share In a Group

TWO BUGS TO BUG YOU

Play this game with a classmate.

Doug Bug and Barney Beetle both crawled from the rock to the flower. They crawled on the grid shown below. They never crawled on the same line twice and they never crossed each other's path.

Doug crawled 36 cm. Barney crawled 46 cm. Take turns measuring the lengths of the lines. Use your metric ruler to measure. Then draw the paths Doug and Barney might have taken. One player should use ▬ ▬ for Doug's path and the other player should use ▮▮▮▮▮▮ for Barney's path. Then compare each other's paths.

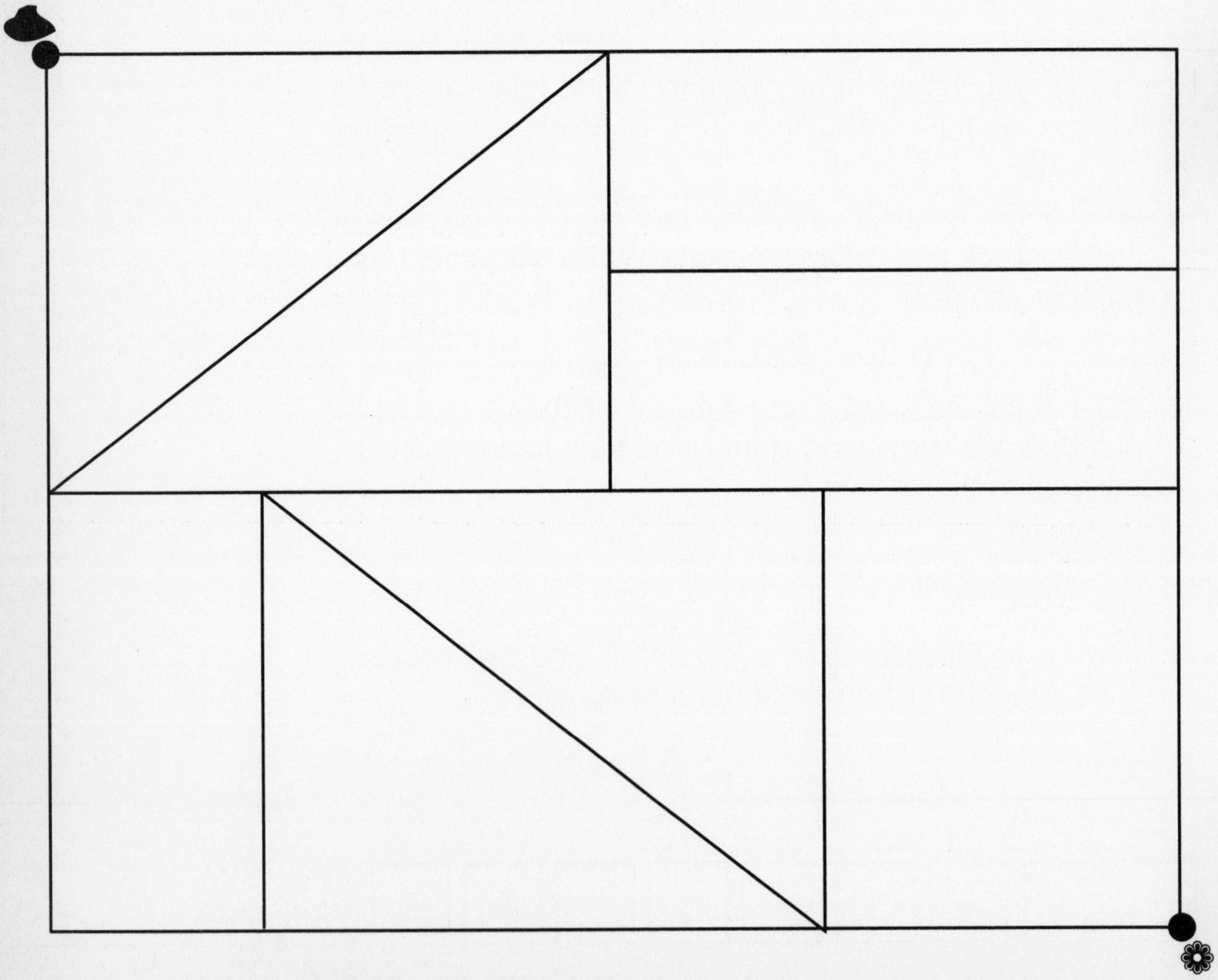

Name

Estimating Time

HOW THE TIME FLIES

Fill in each box with one or more examples of an event or activity that could take that amount of time. Compare and discuss what you wrote in a group. Pick one box and draw a picture for it.

30 seconds	4 minutes	50 minutes
2 hours	12 hours	1 day
5 days	1 year	100 years

Name

TELLING TIME

On Your Own Pair and Share In a Group

CLOCK JUMBLES

The nine clocks on this page are missing their numbers. They have also been turned so that the number 12 is not always at the top.

The clocks show these times:

1:00	2:00	3:00	4:00	5:00	6:00
7:00	8:00	9:00	10:00	11:00	12:00

Try to match each of the times above with a clock below. Then mark a 12 on each clock to show which way is up!

1.

2.

3.

4.

5.

6.

7.

8.

9.

Name

ELAPSED TIME

On Your Own Pair and Share In a Group

FROM TIME TO TIME

Cut out the digits at the bottom of this page. Place them in the digital clock displays. Compare your answers with another student.

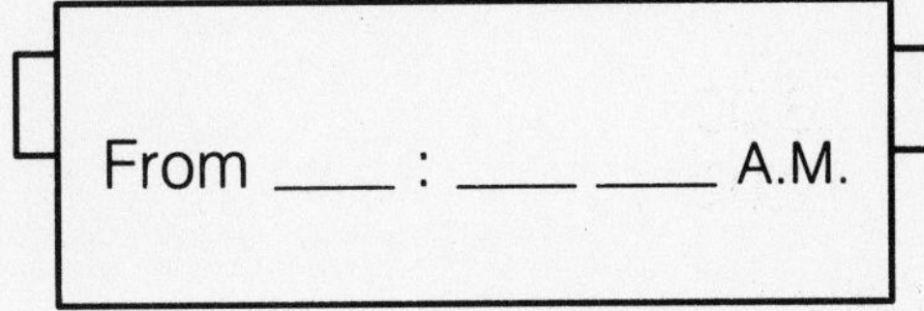

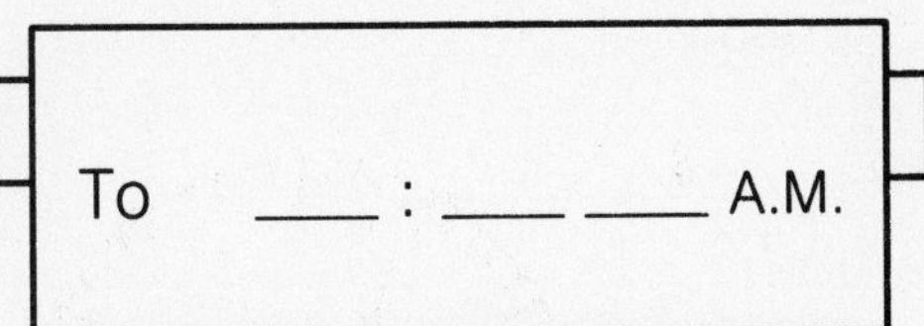

1. How close can you get to showing one hour of elapsed time?

___

2. How close can you get to showing three hours of elapsed time?

___

3. What is the shortest period of time you can form using the digits?

___

4. Can you find a way to show more than 10 hours of elapsed time?

___

5. What is the longest period of time you can form using the digits?

___

Macmillan/McGraw-Hill, MATHEMATICS IN ACTION
Grade 4, Chapter 4, Lesson 3, pages 138–139

Name

PROBLEM SOLVING

On Your Own Pair and Share In a Group

HOW OLD ARE YOU? I'M 3,728!

When someone asks how old you are, you probably respond in *years.* But you can measure your age in any unit of time. Use this worksheet to help you find your age in days.

1. Use a calculator to multiply your age in years by 365. Press 365 × [your age in years] = ☐ Write the answer at the right. ___ ___ ___ ___

2. Don't forget about leap years! Every four years we add one day to our calendars. For example, 1972, 1976, 1980, 1984, 1988, and 1992 are all leap years. How many leap years have occurred *since* you were born? Write this number at the right. ___

3. Now you have to find out how many days have passed since your last birthday. You may want to use a calendar to help you count. Start by counting the number of days from your birth date to the end of that month. Write the number at the right. ___ ___

4. Now add the number of days in complete months that have passed. ___ ___

5. Finally, add today's date. ___ ___

6. Add all of the columns, and that's how many days you've been alive! ___ ___ ___ ___

7. For another challenge, try to find how old you will be in days on your next birthday.

Name

ENRICHMENT-37

ORDERED PAIRS

On Your Own Pair and Share In a Group

MAKING CONNECTIONS

A. First, circle the dot at (8,4). Then, connect the dots described by each ordered pair below. You will find a secret drawing.

1. (0,0)	**2.** (2,3)	**3.** (4,1)	**4.** (3,0)
5. (6,1)	**6.** (8,2)	**7.** (9,3)	**8.** (8,5)
9. (7,6)	**10.** (5,7)	**11.** (3,8)	**12.** (4,7)
13. (2,5)	**14.** (0,8)	**15.** (1,4)	**16.** (0,0)

B. Now Create your own connect-the-dots game. Draw a picture and list the ordered pairs you used. Then have a friend try to follow your list of ordered pairs. Did your friend get the same drawing?

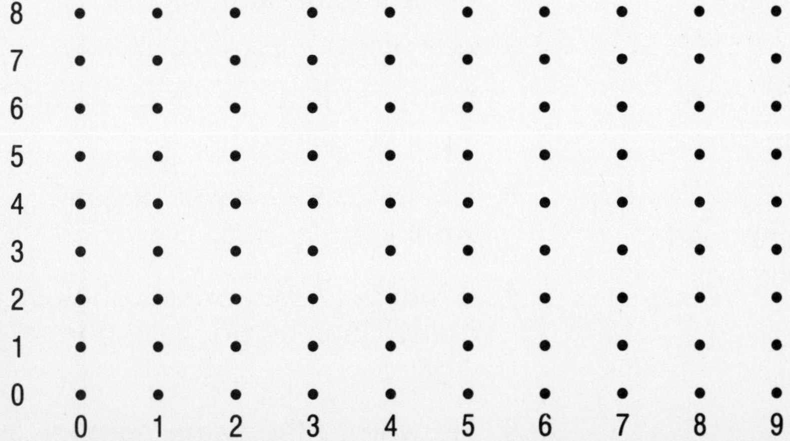

Name

MAKING LINE GRAPHS

On Your Own Pair and Share In a Group

GRAPHIC LOGIC

Use the clues and the points given on the graphs to help you complete each line graph.

A. Ray shampoos dogs at a pet beauty shop. This graph shows how many dog shampoos he gave from Monday to Friday last week.

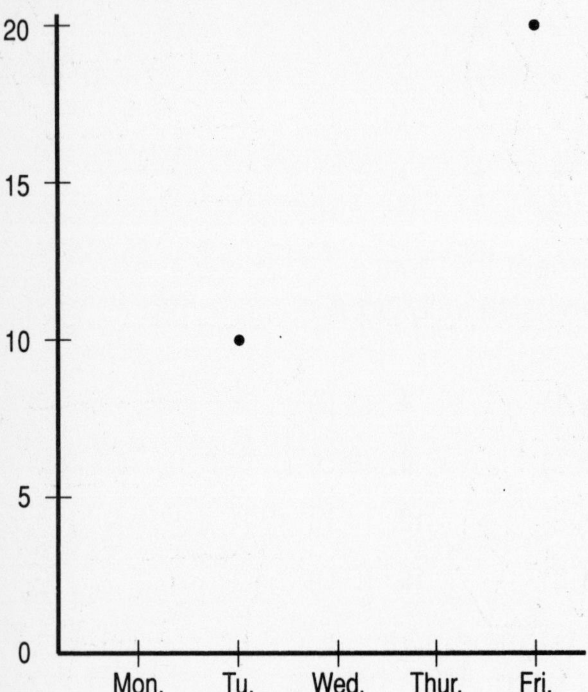

1. Ray shampooed 5 fewer dogs on Monday than he did on Tuesday.
2. He shampooed twice as many dogs on Wednesday as on Monday.
3. On Thursday, Ray shampooed three times as many dogs as on Monday.

B. Ray also walks dogs. This graph shows how many dogs Ray walked each month from January to June.

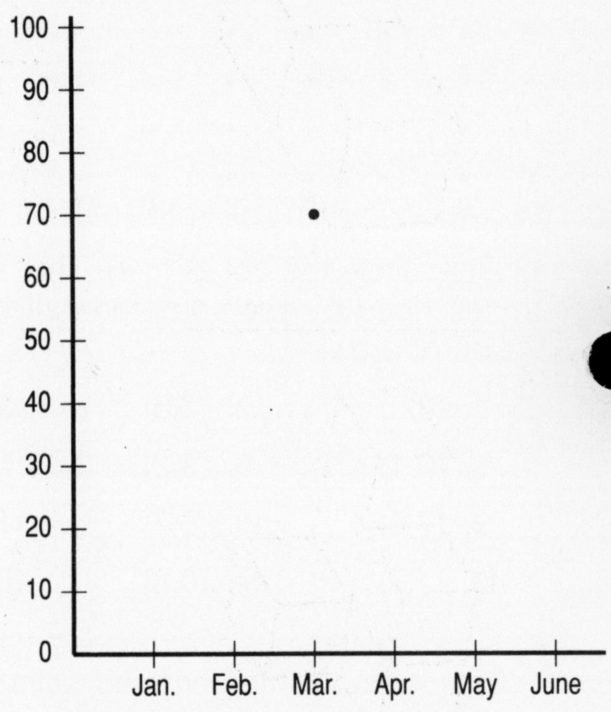

1. Ray walked 10 more dogs in June than in March.
2. In February, Ray walked as many dogs as in January and April combined.
3. He walked 20 fewer dogs in April than in June.
4. In January, Ray walked half as many dogs as he walked in April.
5. He walked the same number of dogs in February and May.

Name

CAPACITY

On Your Own Pair and Share In a Group

HOLDING PATTERNS

Imagine that this cube can hold one liter of water. 

How many liters of water could each of these shapes hold?

1. 

____

2. 

____

3. 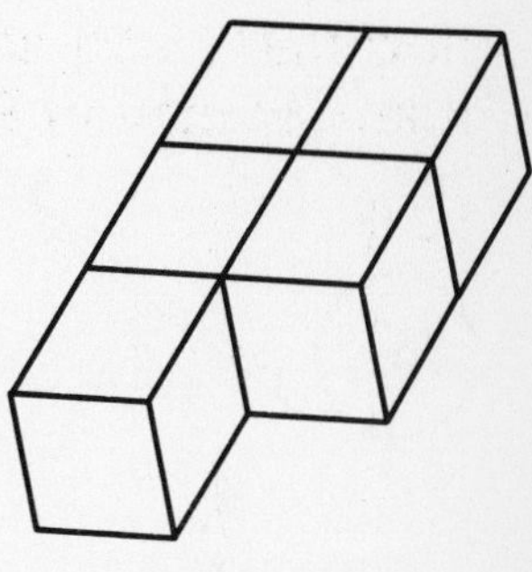

____

4. 

____

5. 

____

6. 

____

7. 

____

8. 

____

9. 

____

Name

MASS

On Your Own Pair and Share In a Group

BALANCING ACT

Cut out the weights at the bottom of this page. Place one or more weights on the empty end or ends of each seesaw to balance the seesaw. Use each weight only once. Move the weights around until you are able to balance the seesaw.

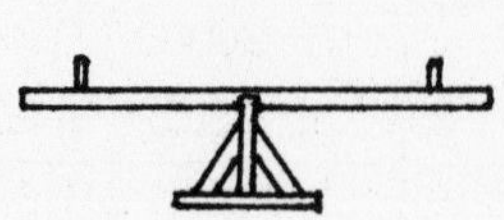

1,000 g	40 g	7 g	1,500 g	4 kg	11 g
50 g	8 g	500 g	5 kg	25 g	2,000 g
10 g	3,000 g	2 g	18 g	4,000 g	12 g

Name

PROBLEM SOLVING

On Your Own Pair and Share In a Group

TILE TEST

Jan plans to tile a floor with black and white tiles. She will use small squares and small triangles. She will use this pattern in this exact size.

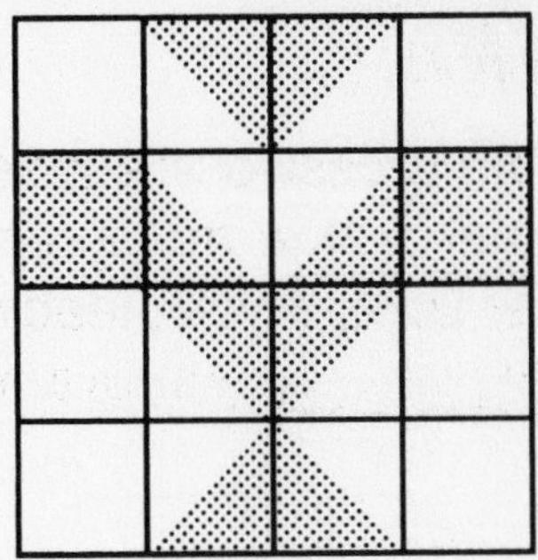

Work with a partner to answer these questions. Use a calculator.

1. How many of each shape does she need to complete the pattern?

   small black squares _____ small white squares _____

   small black triangles _____ small white triangles _____

2. Use a ruler to find each measurement.

   The width of a small square: _____

   The width of the whole pattern: _____

3. What will the floor look like when Jan places four of the complete patterns together? Use this grid to show your answer.

4. Jan will use the complete pattern 8 times to cover her floor. How many of each shape will she use in all? Use a calculator to help you.

   small black squares _____

   small black triangles _____

   small white squares _____

   small white triangles _____

5. How should Jan place the 8 complete patterns so that they cover an area 16 cm wide and 32 cm long? Make a sketch.

Name

ENRICHMENT-42

TEMPERATURE

On Your Own Pair and Share In a Group

UNITS TO FIT

Complete the crossword puzzle below. The words that appear in the puzzle are printed upside down at the bottom of the page. Look if you need help.

ACROSS

2. 60 minutes in 1 ____

4. 1,000 ____ in 1 liter

8. What grams measure

10. 100 ____ in 1 meter

12. What liters measure

14. 60 seconds in 1 ____

15. Water boils at 100 degrees ____

DOWN

1. 1,000 ____ in 1 kilogram

3. 1 ____ equals 1,000 grams

5. What a thermometer measures

6. 10 centimeters in 1 ____

7. 1,000 milliliters equals 1 ____

9. What meters measure

11. 10 decimeters in 1 ____

13. 100 years equal 1 ____

capacity
Centigrade
centimeter
century
decimeter
gram
hour
kilogram
length
liter
mass
meter
milliliter
minute
temperature

Name

THE MEANING OF MULTIPLICATION

On Your Own Pair and Share In a Group

DOTS THE POINT

You know that you can represent 3 × 5 with this dot drawing:

These nine multiplication sets can be found in the drawing below:

3 × 3	2 × 14	4 × 4
5 × 5	3 × 9	2 × 5
5 × 6	4 × 6	2 × 15

Can you find them all? Each dot is used only once.
No sets overlap. There is only one complete solution!

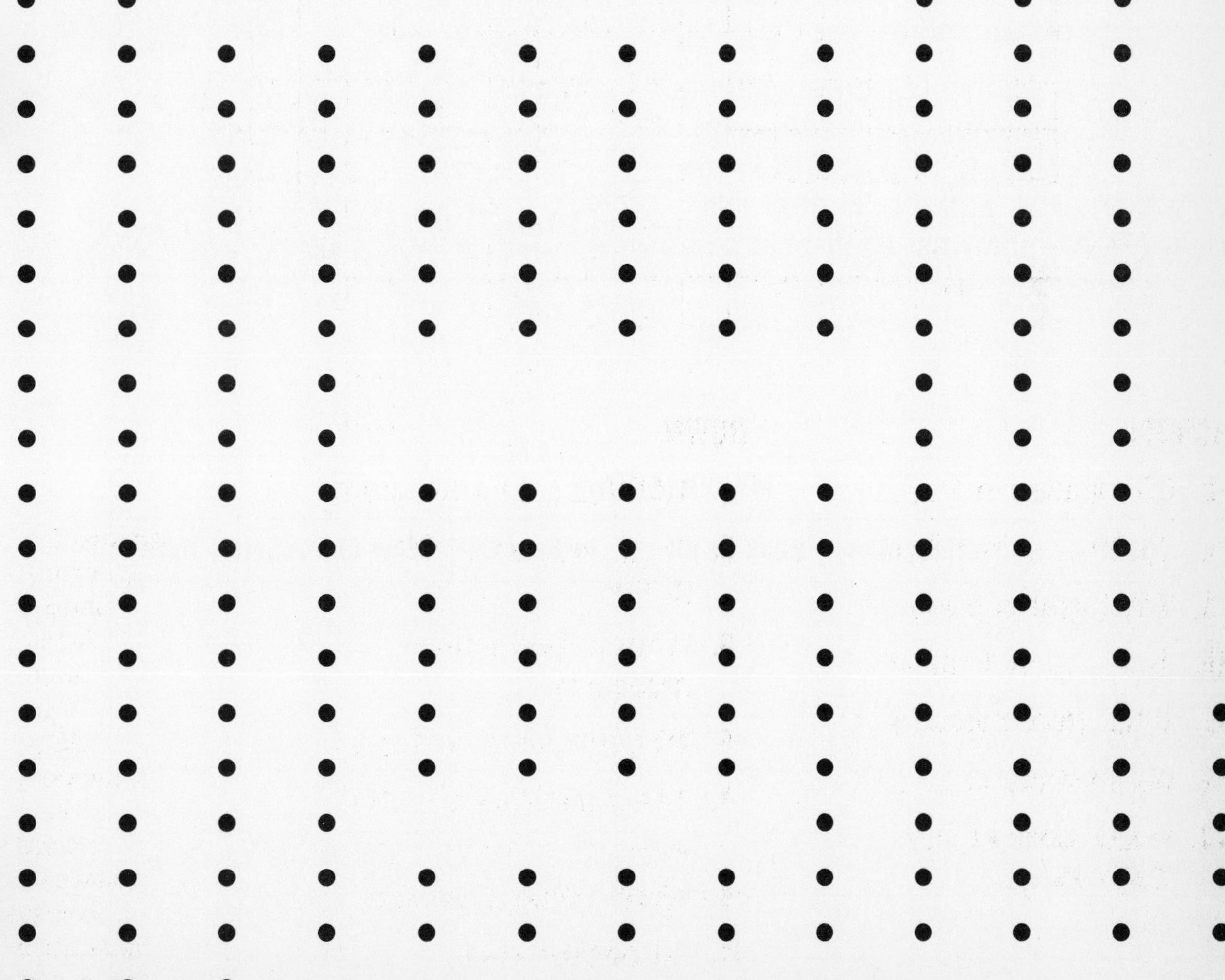

Name

THE MEANING OF DIVISION

On Your Own Pair and Share In a Group

STEFFI'S STUFF

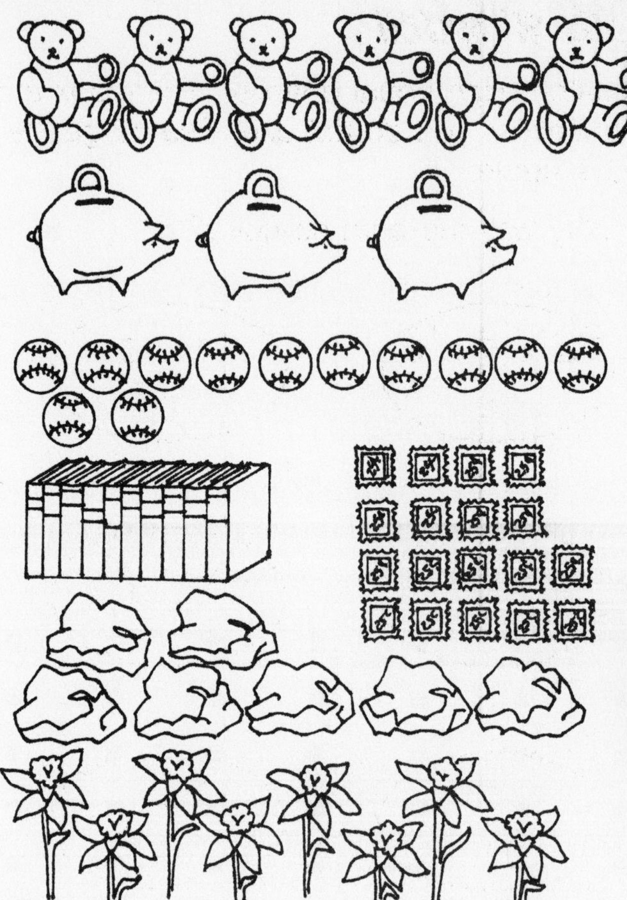

Steffi collects objects in sets.
She collects:

stamps flowers books
rocks piggy banks
teddy bears baseballs

Steffi collects in sets of twos, threes, fours, fives, sixes, sevens, and eights. She uses a different number for each object.

For example, she collects teddy bears in sets of twos. As you can see in the drawing, Steffi has six teddy bears, or three sets of two bears.

Work with a partner. Discuss what you see in the drawing. Use the drawing of Steffi's collection to help you fill in her collection chart at the bottom of this page. Remember that each object has a different-sized set.

MY COLLECTION			
Item	**How Many I Have In All**	**In Sets Of**	**How Many Sets I Have**
Teddy Bears	6	2	3
Piggy Banks			
Baseballs			
Books			
Stamps			
Rocks			
Flowers			

Name

MULTIPLICATION AND DIVISION PROPERTIES

On Your Own Pair and Share In a Group

MIX 'N' MATCH

Match each equal quantity. Then look at the letters under the quantities you do not use. Rearrange the letters to answer this riddle:

"Why was the barn so noisy?"

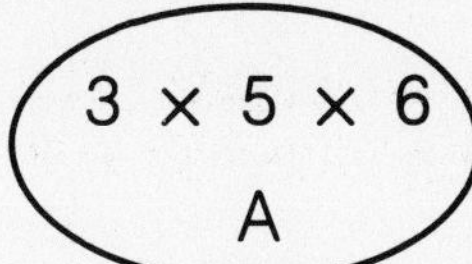

3 × 5 × 6 A	9 × 2 D	4 × 7 × 8 C	8 U
8 × 7 × 4 E	3 ÷ 1 R	2 ÷ 2 I	
1 T	3 M	5 × 6 × 3 N	2 × 8 H
7 × 8 × 4 W	8 ÷ 1 H	4 × 5 N	2 × 9 Y
8 × 3 O	7 ÷ 1 K	7 × 2 × 10 N	10 × 7 × 3 R
	5 × 8 S	3 × 6 × 5 T	7 I

Because the cows had _____ _____ _____ _____ _____.

Macmillan/McGraw-Hill, MATHEMATICS IN ACTION
Grade 4, Chapter 5, Lesson 3, pages 180–181

Name

FACT FAMILIES

On Your Own Pair and Share In a Group

BOXED IN

Can you find the numbers that complete each multiplication box? All the information you need is in the boxes.

1.

×	4	7	8	2	5
6					
7					
3					
4					

2.

×			6		
			54		
			6		
2	6	16	12	4	8
			48		

3.

×	9		7	6	
5					
7		7			
			42		24
0				0	

4.

×					
		0			0
				15	24
	2			5	8
	8	0	36		

Name

2 THROUGH 9 AS FACTORS

On Your Own Pair and Share In a Group

SOME PRODUCTS!

A. Work with a group of friends. Take turns reading the riddles below to the group.

Can you find each pair of numbers described?

I'm thinking of two numbers that . . .

. . . have a sum of 5 and a product of 6. _____

. . . have a sum of 6 and a product of 9. _____

. . . have a sum of 12 and a product of 32. _____

. . . have a sum of 13 and a product of 40. _____

. . . have a difference of 1 and a product of 42. _____

. . . have a difference of 2 and a product of 24. _____

. . . are equal and have a product of 81. _____

. . . have a difference of 5 and a product of 14. _____

. . . have a difference of 7 and a product of 18. _____

. . . are less than 6 and have a product of 12. _____

. . . have a sum of 15 and a product of 56. _____

. . . have the same number of letters in their names and a product of 21. _____

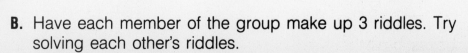

B. Have each member of the group make up 3 riddles. Try solving each other's riddles.

Name

DIVIDING BY 2 THROUGH 9

SORTING CENTS

Ray has a coin collection. Here are the coins in his collection.

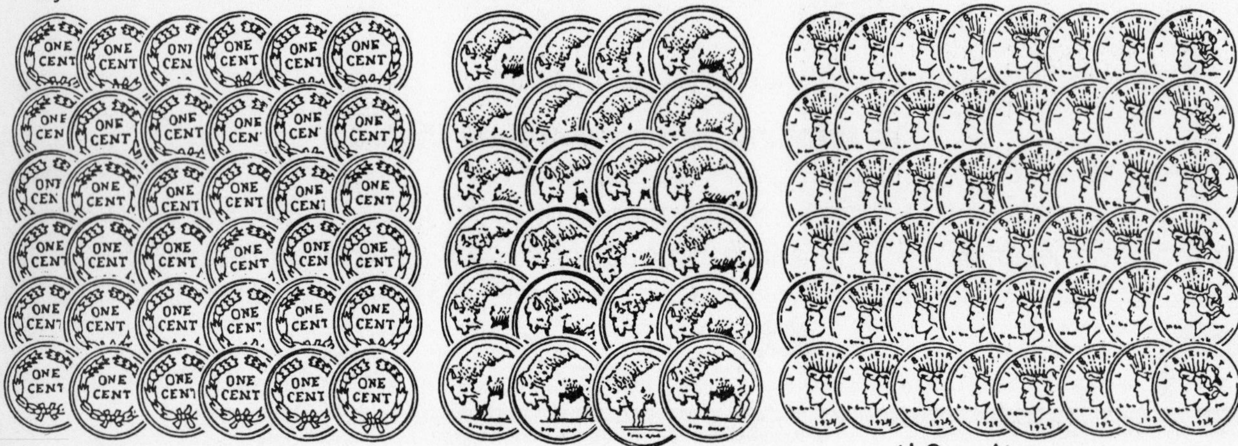

Ray wants to sort his collection. He plans to choose from envelopes, sacks, and boxes. He will put the same kinds of coins in each container.

- Each envelope can hold 3 coins.
- Each sack can hold 4 coins.
- Each box can hold 6 coins.

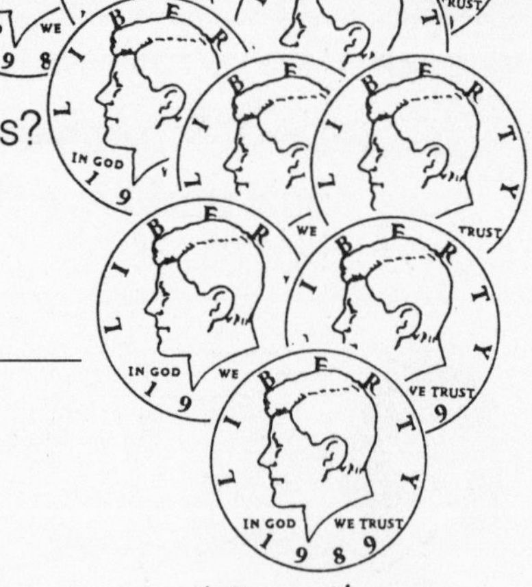

How will he divide his collection if he uses only envelopes? sacks? boxes?

If Ray uses only envelopes:

1. He will fill _____ with pennies, _____ with nickels, _____ with dimes, and _____ with silver dollars.
2. He will use _____ envelopes in all.

If he uses only sacks:

3. He will fill _____ with pennies, _____ with nickels, _____ with dimes, and _____ with silver dollars.
4. He will use _____ sacks in all.

If he uses only boxes:

5. He will fill _____ with pennies, _____ with nickels, _____ with dimes, and _____ with silver dollars.
6. He will use _____ boxes in all.

Name

PROBLEM SOLVING

On Your Own Pair and Share In a Group

LUCKY SEVEN

Answers will vary.

Fill in each box with a −, ×, or ÷ sign to make the number sentence true. Use your calculator to help. You may use an operation sign more than once in each sentence.

1. 7 ☐ 7 ☐ 7 ☐ 7 = 0
2. 7 ☐ 7 ☐ 7 ☐ 7 = 1
3. 7 ☐ 7 ☐ 7 ☐ 7 = 3
4. (7 ☐ 7) ☐ 7 ☐ 7 = 9
5. 7 ☐ 7 ☐ 7 ☐ 7 = 14
6. 7 ☐ 7 ☐ 7 ☐ 7 = 15
7. 7 ☐ 7 ☐ 7 ☐ 7 = 28
8. 7 ☐ 7 ☐ 7 ☐ 7 = 35
9. (7 ☐ 7) ☐ (7 ☐ 7) = 50
10. 7 ☐ 7 ☐ 7 ☐ 7 = 63
11. (7 ☐ 7) ☐ 7 ☐ 7 = 91
12. (7 ☐ 7) ☐ 7 ☐ 7 = 105

Name

ENRICHMENT-50

MISSING FACTORS

On Your Own Pair and Share In a Group

PRODUCT PYRAMIDS

In these pyramids, each number is the product of the two numbers directly below it. Can you complete all of the pyramids?

1.

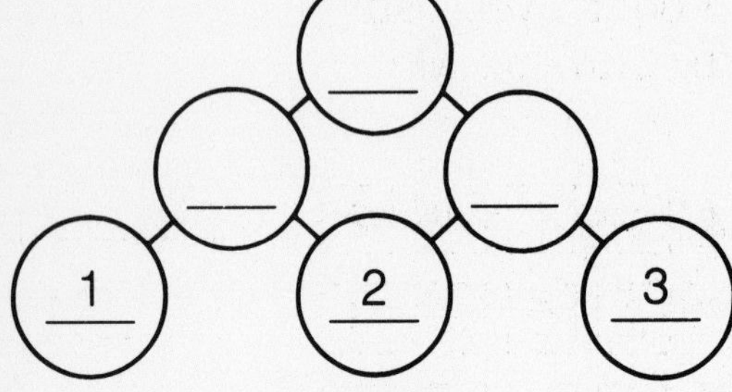

2.

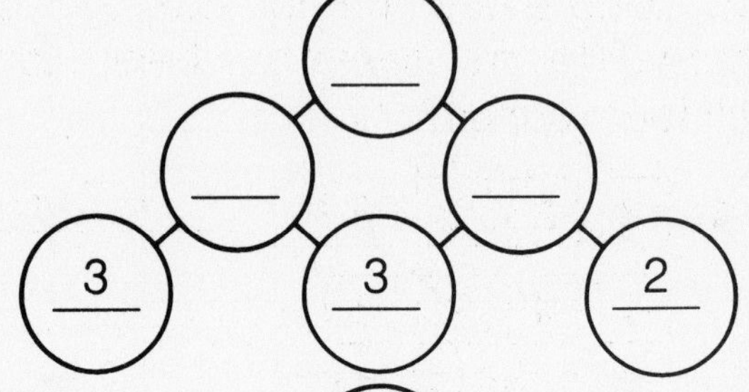

3.

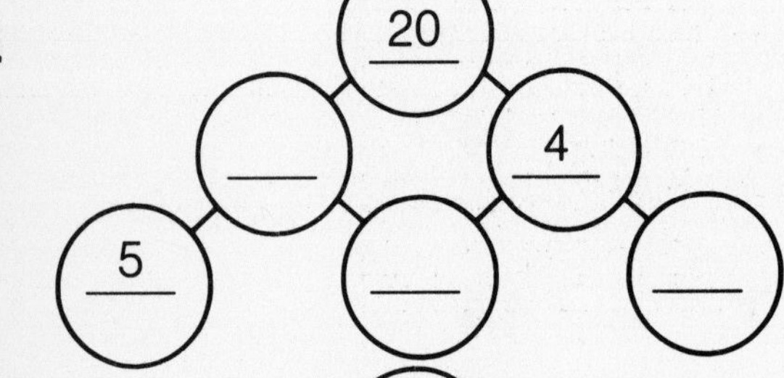

4.

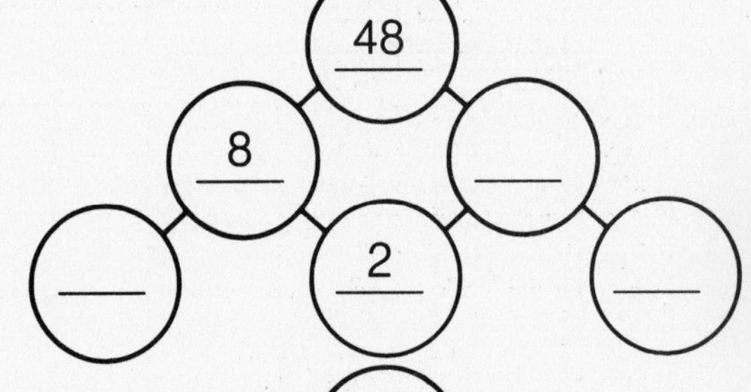

5.

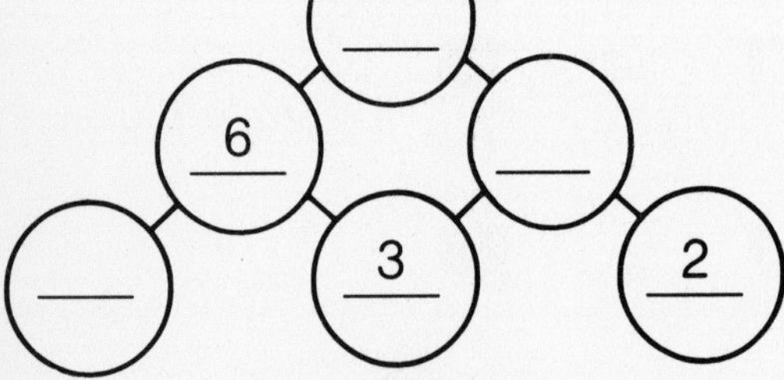

6.

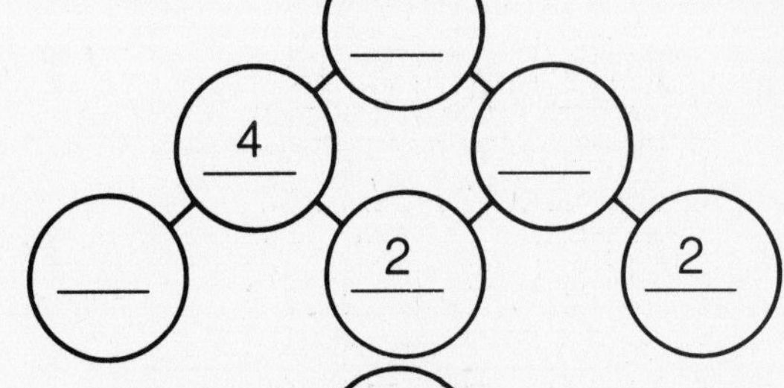

7.

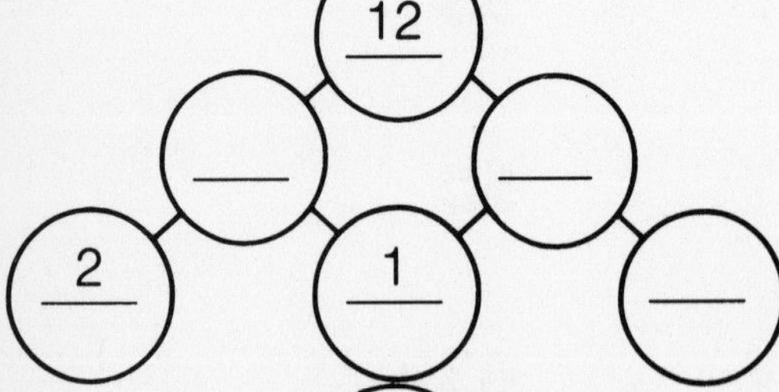

8.

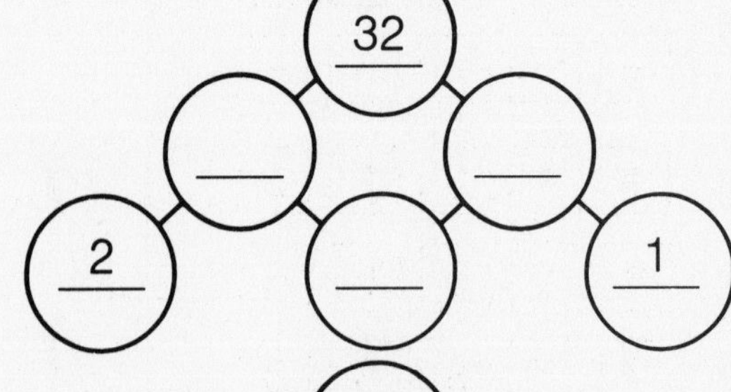

9.

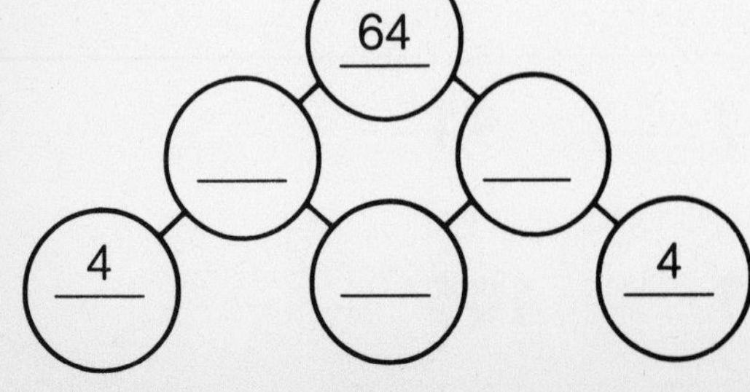

10.

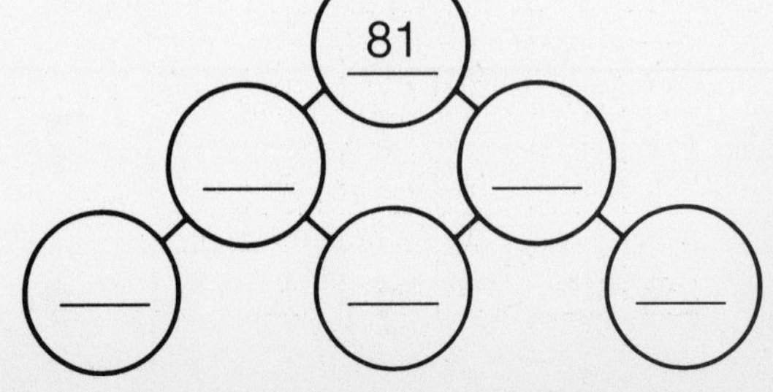

Name

OTHER FACT STRATEGIES

On Your Own Pair and Share In a Group

FACTMAKER

To play Factmaker, use the numbers and signs below to make multiplication and division facts. Use each number or sign only once. You win a round if you can clear the board by using every number and sign. Cross them out as you use them. The first game has been started for you. Can you win all four rounds?

1.

2	2	3	3
4	4	~~4~~	5
5	6	~~7~~	~~7~~
7	7	8	~~9~~
~~×~~	×	÷	÷
~~=~~	=	=	=

7 × 7 = 49

______

______

______

2.

1	1	1	2
2	3	4	4
4	5	6	6
6	6	8	9
×	÷	÷	÷
=	=	=	=

______

______

______

______

3.

0	0	1	2	2
3	3	4	5	5
5	5	5	5	5
5	5	6	7	9
×	×	÷	÷	÷
=	=	=	=	=

______

______

______

______

______

4.

1	1	2	2	3
3	4	5	6	6
7	7	8	8	8
9	9	9	9	9
×	×	×	÷	÷
=	=	=	=	=

______

______

______

______

______

Macmillan/McGraw-Hill, MATHEMATICS IN ACTION
Grade 4, Chapter 5, Lesson 10, pages 194–195

Name

FACTORS AND MULTIPLES

On Your Own Pair and Share In a Group

SALTWATER TOUGHIE

Use the numbers below to complete the problems. When you find a number, write it in the space and cross it and its letter out. Be sure to do the problems in order! When you are done, the remaining letters, written in order from left to right and top to bottom, will spell out the answer to this riddle:

"What do you use to cut through the ocean?"

1. Factors of 12: _____, _____, _____, _____, _____, _____
2. Multiples of 3 that are less than 30: _____, _____, _____, _____
3. Multiples of 5 that are greater than 30: _____, _____, _____
4. Multiples of 2 that are also multiples of 4: _____, _____, _____, _____, _____, _____
5. Multiples of 7 that are greater than 40: _____, _____, _____
6. Multiples of 9: _____

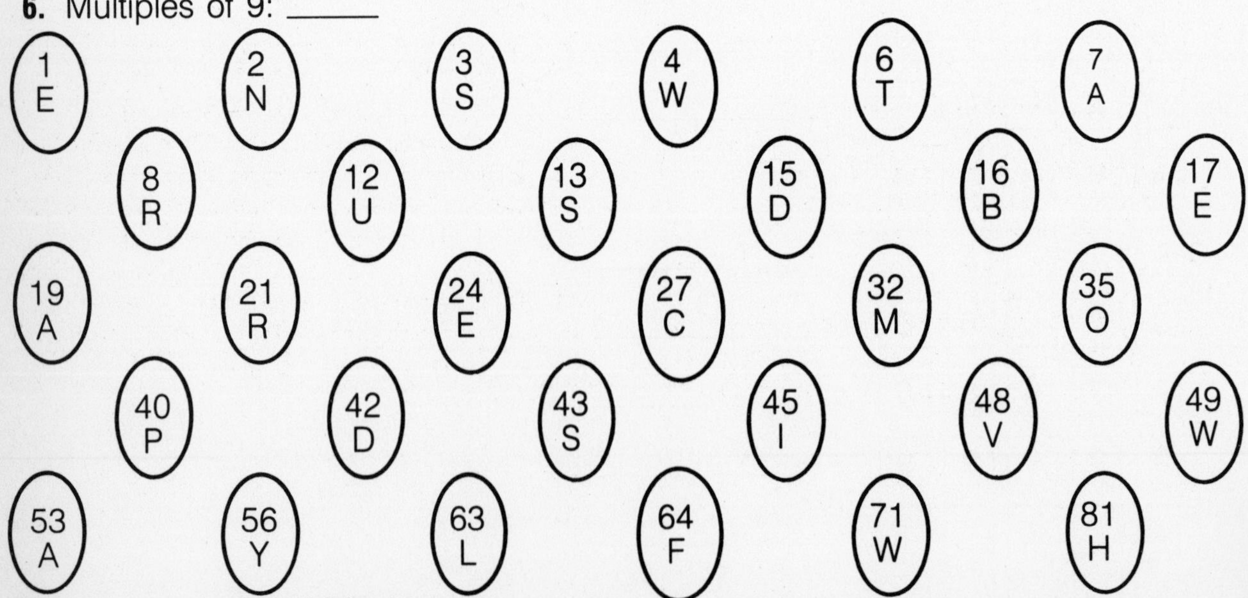

The answer to the riddle is:

_____ _____ _____ _____ – _____ _____ _____

Name

PROBLEM SOLVING

On Your Own Pair and Share In a Group

PATTERN MAZES

Each of the mazes below has a hidden pattern. The pattern will travel through each circle in the maze once and only once. The arrows show you where the pattern begins and ends. Can you find the ways out? In each maze, your path should touch every circle and should never cross itself.

1.

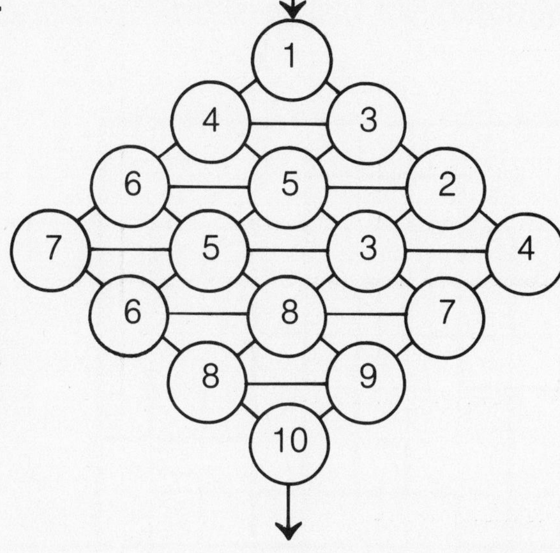

2.

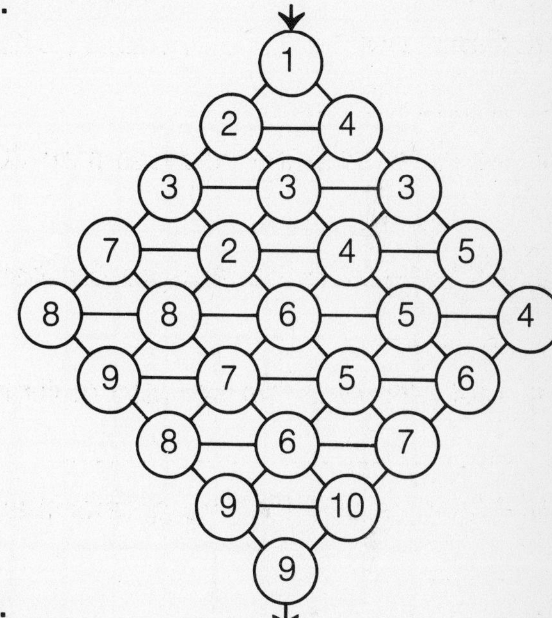

3.

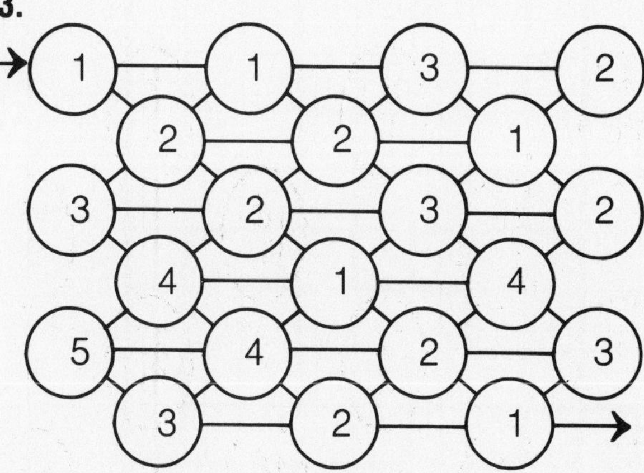

4.

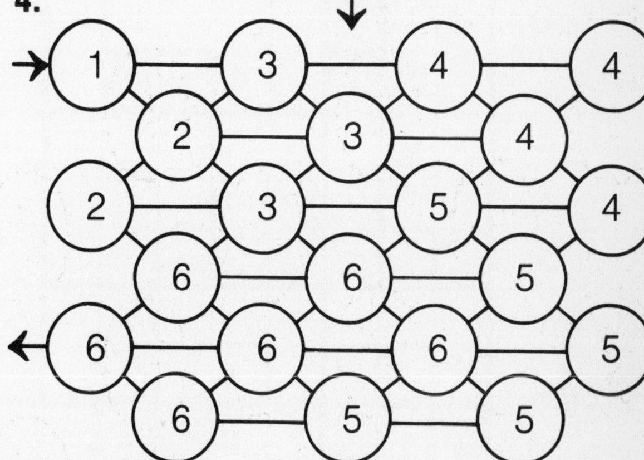

MACMILLAN/McGRAW-HILL

Macmillan/McGraw-Hill, MATHEMATICS IN ACTION
Grade 4, Chapter 5, Lesson 12, pages 198-199

Name

AREA

COLOR-BY-AREA

Follow this chart to color each shape in the grid below.

Key: One □ = one square centimeter	
If the shape has an area of:	**Color it:**
1 sq cm	black
7 sq cm	brown
8 sq cm	red

If the shape has an area of:	Color it:
9 sq cm	blue
10 sq cm or greater	green

What does your picture show? ___________

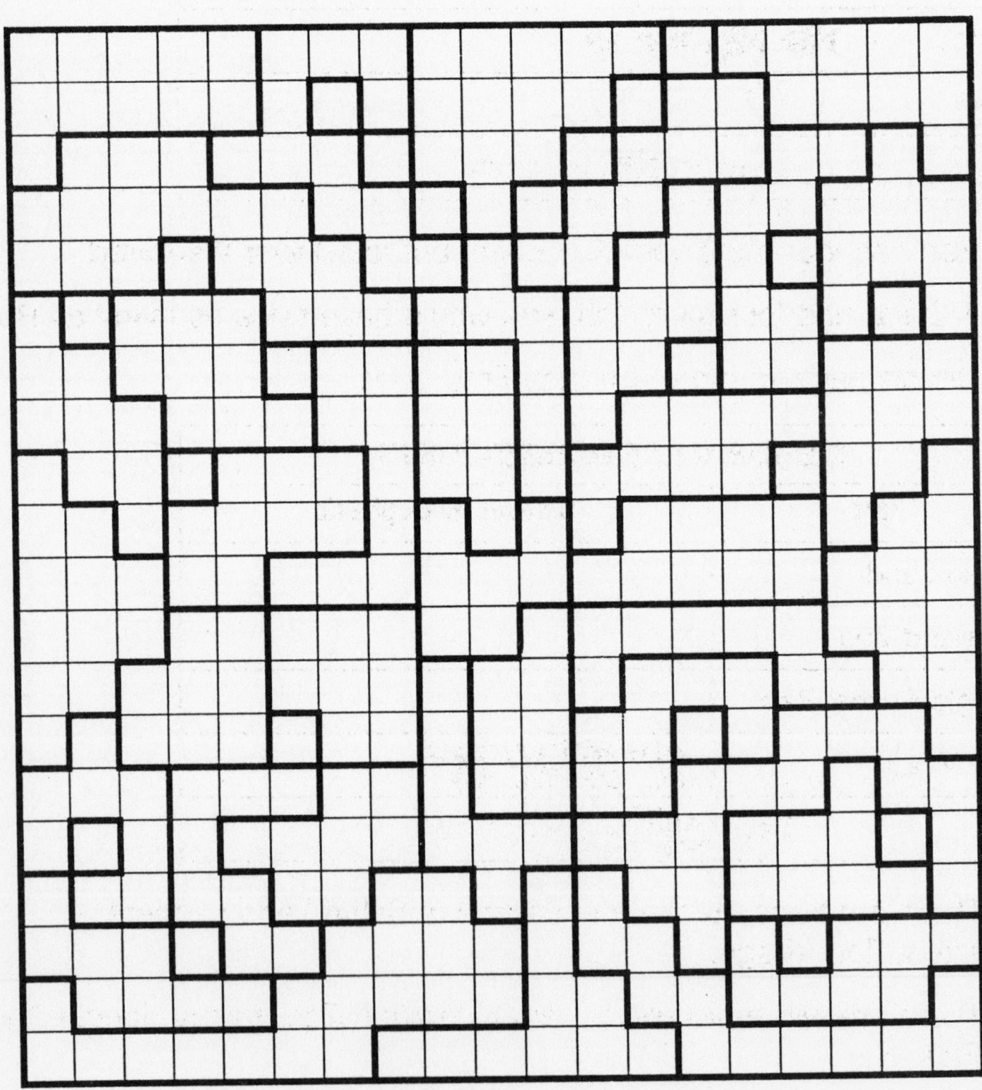

MACMILLAN/McGRAW-HILL

Name

MAKING PICTOGRAPHS

On Your Own | Pair and Share | In a Group

WHICH FISH?

Work with a partner. Use the clues to complete each pictograph.

1.

FISH IN FIVE STUDENTS' AQUARIUMS	
Student	**Number of Fish**
Bob	
Claire	
Dennis	
Edith	🐟 🐟 🐟 (half fish)
Fred	
Each 🐟 = 4 fish	

Clue 1 Bob has four more fish than Edith, but four fewer than Fred.

Clue 2 If Claire had four more fish, she would have twice as many as Bob.

Clue 3 Dennis has two more fish than Fred does.

1.

ELEPHANTS AT FIVE ANIMAL PARKS	
Park	**Number of Elephants**
Safari Land	
Newland Zoo	
Jungle Animal Park	
Zoo Village	🐘 🐘 🐘 🐘
Each 🐘 = 2 elephants	

Clue 1 There are twice as many elephants at Safari Land as there are at Zoo Village.

Clue 2 There are two more elephants at Newland Zoo than at Jungle Animal Park.

Clue 3 Newland Zoo and Zoo Village have the same number of elephants.

Name

MENTAL MATH: MULTIPLYING BY 10s AND 100s

On Your Own   Pair and Share   In a Group

GEOGRAPHY GROANERS

Fill in each box. Then find the letter in the grid that matches each answer. Write the letter that goes with each exercise number and solve the riddles.

1. 300 × ☐ = 2,700
2. 600 × ☐ = 4,800
3. ☐00 × 4 = 2,400
4. ☐00 × 9 = 1,800
5. 700 × ☐ = 4,200
6. 800 × 5 = 4,☐00
7. ☐,000 × 2 = 8,000
8. ☐,000 x 7 = 49,000
9. 4 × 8,000 = 3,☐00
10. ☐,000 × 6 = 6,000
11. ☐00 × 3 = 900
12. ☐ × 500 = 2,000
13. ☐,000 × 5 = 25,000
14. 8,000 × ☐ = 16,000

Answer	0	1	2	3	4	5	6	7	8	9
Letter	A	C	E	H	I	L	M	N	O	R

What city likes to wander? _____ _____ _____ _____
1. 2. 3. 4.

What state reminds you of part of a lion? _____ _____ _____ _____ _____
5. 6. 7. 8. 9.

What country is always cold? _____ _____ _____ _____ _____
10. 11. 12. 13. 14.

Name ____________________

ESTIMATING PRODUCTS

On Your Own   Pair and Share   In a Group

BOOK NOOKS

Imagine that you belong to a Science Club. Your club has decided to buy new bookcases. Work with a group of friends to decide which bookcases to buy.

Here are some things to consider:

- Your club has 1,000 books.
- You may buy more books in the future.
- You want to use as little floor space as possible.

You can purchase any combination of these bookcase styles:

A — 3 ft

B — 4 ft

C — 6 ft

Answer these questions to help you estimate how many books each case will hold:

1. About how many books will fit on 1 ft of shelf space?

 ____

2. How many feet of shelf space are in each case?

 ____

 Bookcase A: ______ Bookcase B: ______ Bookcase C: ______

3. About how many books will each case hold?

 ____

 Bookcase A: ________ Bookcase B: ________ Bookcase C: ________

4. Which bookcases will your club order? Why?

 ____

Name

PROBLEM SOLVING

On Your Own Pair and Share In a Group

PATH PATTERNS

You can use a +, −, or × in any box. Find a path of correct number sentences through the maze. There is a pattern that can help you. What is the pattern?

ENTER

3	□	7	=	10	□	170	=	190	□	210	=	400
□				□				=				□
2				2				10				300
=				=				□				=
4	=	2	□	8	□	3	=	19	□	72	=	100
□				□				=				□
5				10				16				50
=				=				□				=
180	=	10	□	18	=	4	□	3	□	151	=	150
□				□				=				□
5				105				224				2
=				=				□				=
185	□	25	=	220	□	7	=	227	=	6	□	300
□				=				□				□
175				20				20				12
=				□				=				=
10	□	1	=	11	□	5	=	5	□	40	=	312

LEAVE

Name

MULTIPLYING 2-DIGIT NUMBERS: REGROUPING ONCE

On Your Own Pair and Share In a Group

NUMBER JUMBLES

For each problem, use the numbers in the box to complete the multiplication problem. Use a calculator to help you check your answers.

1.
```
    1 □      [0 6 8]
×     □
  1 □ 8
```

2.
```
    □ □      [1 2 8]
×     4
  3 □ 4
```

3.
```
    9 □      [2 3 6]
×     □
  2 7 □
```

4.
```
    6 □      [1 8 8 8]
×     □
  4 □ □
```

5.
```
    □ 9      [1 5 5 9]
×     □
    □ □
```

6.
```
    □ □      [1 2 7 8]
×     3
    □ □
```

7.
```
    □ □      [2 2 4 6 9]
×     □
    □ □
```

8.
```
    □ □      [1 2 3 5 5 6]
×     □
  □ □ □
```

9.
```
    □ □      [1 2 8 9 9 9]
×     □
  □ □ □
```

Name

MULTIPLYING 2-DIGIT NUMBERS: REGROUPING TWICE

JOIN THE CLUB

Work with a partner to complete this page. The Gleeful Club chose this design for their new T-shirts:

They will cut each shape out of felt and then glue the shapes onto the shirts.

1. Complete this chart to show how many of each shape they will have to cut to make each number of T-shirts:

Number of T-shirts	Diamonds	Hearts	Stars
10			
16			
25			
48			
67			
89			

2. The club has enough felt to cut 161 diamonds, 244 hearts, and 322 stars. What is the greatest number of T-shirts they can make with this felt?

____

3. How might they change their design to be able to make more T-shirts?

____

____

4. Draw and color your new design on another sheet of paper. Work with your partner to make up a chart like the one above. Decide on several numbers for the first column (Number of T-shirts). Ask some friends to complete the other columns based on the shapes in your design.

Name

MULTIPLYING 3-DIGIT NUMBERS

On Your Own Pair and Share In a Group

HIGH OR LOW

Play this game with a partner. One player is High, the other is Low. Cut out the cards along the side of this page and turn them upside down. You may combine two sets of cards. Players take turns picking a card and placing it on the board. When the board is filled, find the product by multiplying. If the product is greater than 2,500, High wins a point. If the product is less than 2,500, Low wins a point. The player with the most points at the end of 10 rounds is the winner. If the score is tied, play another tie-breaking round.

1 2 3 4 5 6 7 8 9

Gameboard

□ □ □
× □

SCORESHEET

	Problem	Product	High	Low
Sample	672 × 3	2,016		1
Round 1				
Round 2				
Round 3				
Round 4				
Round 5				
Round 6				
Round 7				
Round 8				
Round 9				
Round 10				
		Total		

Name

Multiplying Money

On Your Own   Pair and Share   In a Group

MONEY MAZES

Can you find the path from top to bottom of each maze that results in the greatest amount of money? You may only travel downward in each maze. Use estimation to help you.

1.

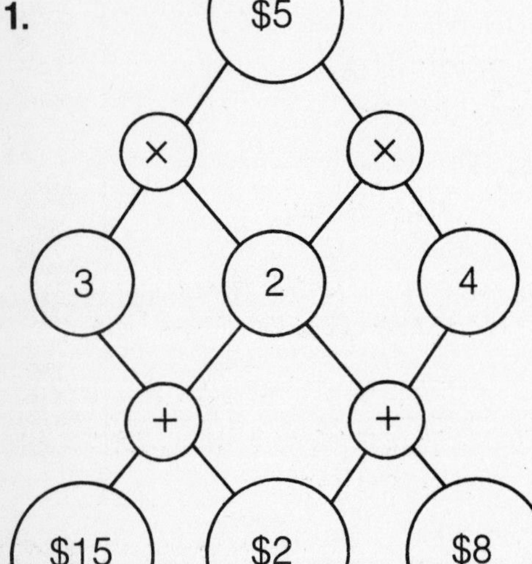

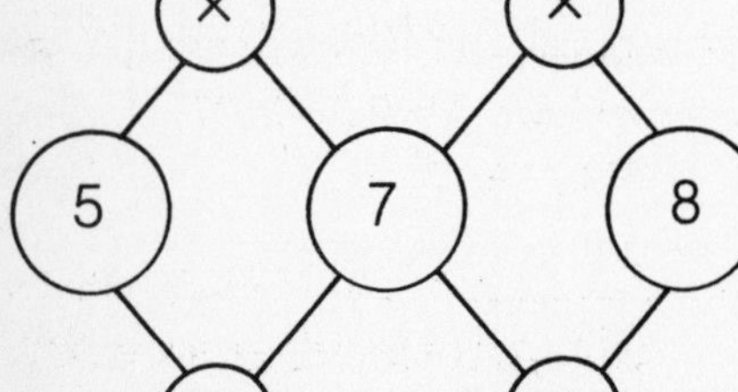

Total ________

2.

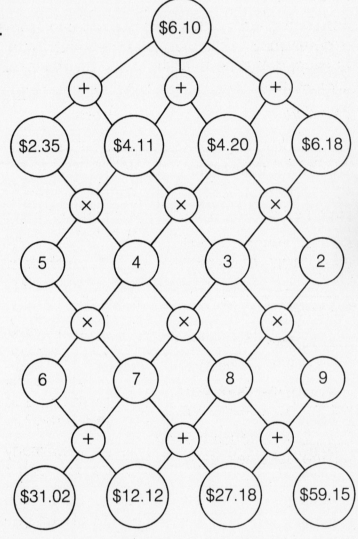

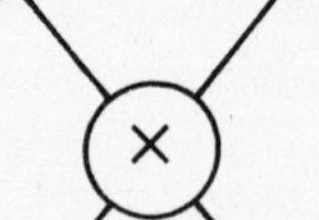

Total ________

Name

PROBLEM SOLVING

On Your Own Pair and Share In a Group

FUN FUND RAISING

Imagine that your class has decided to raise some money for a school or class trip. Choose one of the activities below and work with your group to estimate how much money you will be able to earn.

For each quantity, decide if you will overestimate, underestimate, or find an exact amount. Write over, under, or exact in the blank to the left of each item. Be prepared to give reasons.

Bake Sale

_____ How many products will you sell?

_____ How much will you charge for a cookie?

_____ How much will you charge for a cake?

_____ How many people will come?

_____ How many people will sell the goods?

_____ How many hours will the bake sale last?

_____ How much money will the bake sale earn?

Car Wash

_____ How long will it take to wash one car?

_____ How much will you charge for washing each car?

_____ How many people will want their cars washed?

_____ How many people will wash each car?

_____ How many cars will you be able to wash during the day?

_____ How many hours will the car wash last?

_____ How much money will the car wash earn?

Dog Wash

_____ How long will it take to wash each dog?

_____ How much will you charge for washing one dog?

_____ How many people will want their dogs washed?

_____ How many people will be needed as washers?

_____ How many dogs will you be able to wash?

_____ How many hours will your dog wash last?

_____ How much money will the dog wash earn?

What other considerations, such as time, place, and advertising, will affect the success of your event? Compare your estimates with those of other groups.

Work together as a class to decide on the best activity or activities. Do you think your class could sponsor more than one event? Can you think of another event that might be more successful? Could you earn enough to take a class trip? How will you know?

Name

DIVIDING WITH REMAINDERS

CUT UPS

Cut out the shapes below. Then divide the shape into the given number of pieces. Cut only on the lines.

Into 2 equal pieces:

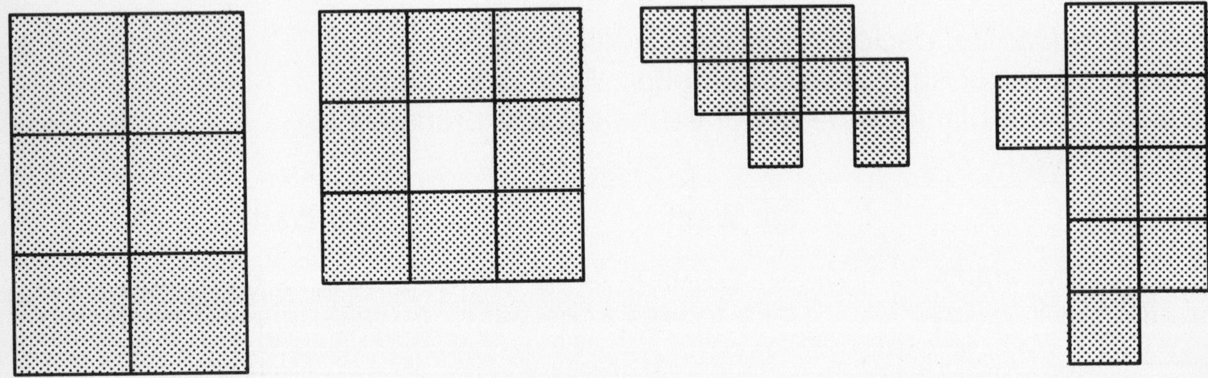

Into 3 equal pieces:

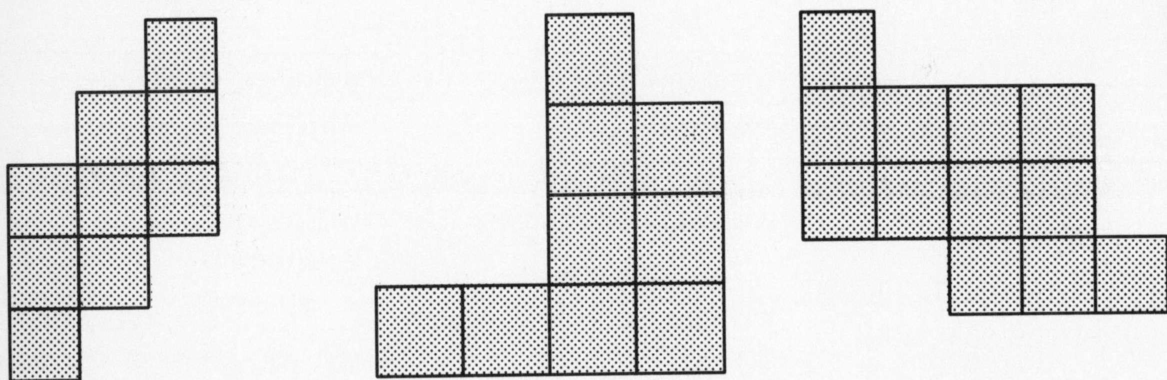

Into 4 equal pieces:

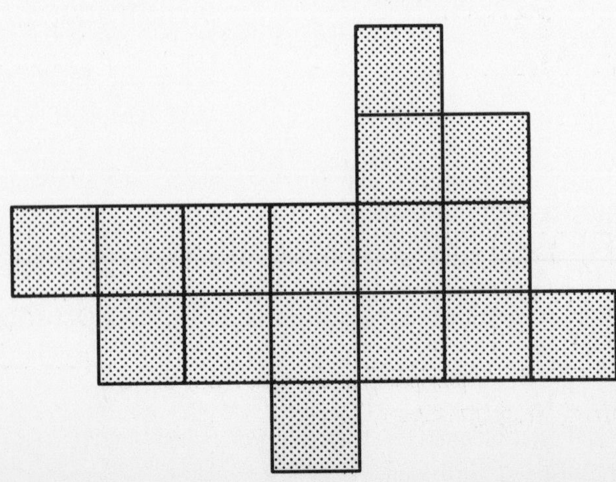

Name

MENTAL MATH: DIVIDING 10s AND 100s

WHAT'S LEFT?

Q: What kind of food reminds you of remainders?

Complete each division problem. Use the numbers at the bottom of the page. When you use a number, cross it out. Then cross out the letter underneath it. When you have finished, the remaining letters will spell out an answer to the riddle.

1. 5)36 = 7 R ____

2. 6)____ = 1 R4

3. ____)14 = 3 R2

4. 7)50 = ____ R1

5. ____)70 = 8 R6

6. 3)____ = 9 R0

7. 4)19 = 4 R ____

8. 7)55 = 7 R ____

9. 8)____ = 2 R6

10. 9)____ = 6 R8

11. 6)35 = ____ R5

12. ____)25 = 2 R7

4	24	62	3	11	29	9	7	19	5	14	10	25	8	22	15	27	20	1	17	6
A	L	T	O	E	F	S	I	T	V	O	R	V	I	U	E	C	R	I	S	G

Write the answer here:

____ ____ ____ ____ ____ ____ ____ ____ ____

Name

ESTIMATING QUOTIENTS

On Your Own Pair and Share In a Group

CHAIN REACTION

Circle the correct answer for the first exercise. Then use the remaining answers to write the next division fact. Repeat those steps until you have finished this page. Use mental math. The first two exercises have been done for you.

1. 900 ÷ 10 = 90

a. 100 (**b.**) 90 **c.** 20

2. 100 ÷ 20 = 5

(**a.**) 5 **b.** 10 **c.** 40

3. ______ ÷ ______ = ______

a. 400 **b.** 4 **c.** 4,000

4. ______ ÷ ______ = ______

a. 6,000 **b.** 20 **c.** 10

5. ______ ÷ ______ = ______

a. 900 **b.** 300 **c.** 3

6. ______ ÷ ______ = ______

a. 120 **b.** 30 **c.** 300

7. ______ ÷ ______ = ______

a. 4 **b.** 70 **c.** 5,600

8. ______ ÷ ______ = ______

a. 800 **b.** 80 **c.** 64,000

9. ______ ÷ ______ = ______

a. 8 **b.** 8,000 **c.** 80

10. ______ ÷ ______ = ______

a. 1,000 **b.** 50 **c.** 10,000

11. ______ ÷ ______ = ______

a. 2,000 **b.** 40 **c.** 200

12. ______ ÷ ______ = ______

a. 500 **b.** 3,500 **c.** 50

13. ______ ÷ ______ = ______

a. 70 **b.** 7 **c.** 49,000

14. ______ ÷ ______ = ______

a. 7 **b.** 70 **c.** 700

Name

PROBLEM SOLVING

On Your Own Pair and Share In a Group

DIVIDE AND COLOR

Estimate each quotient. Then follow this chart to color the picture.

If the quotient is...	Color that section
Less than 10	Red
Greater than 10 but less than 50	Dark blue
Greater than 50 but less than 600	Light blue
Greater than 600 but less than 1,500	Green
Greater than 1,500	Yellow

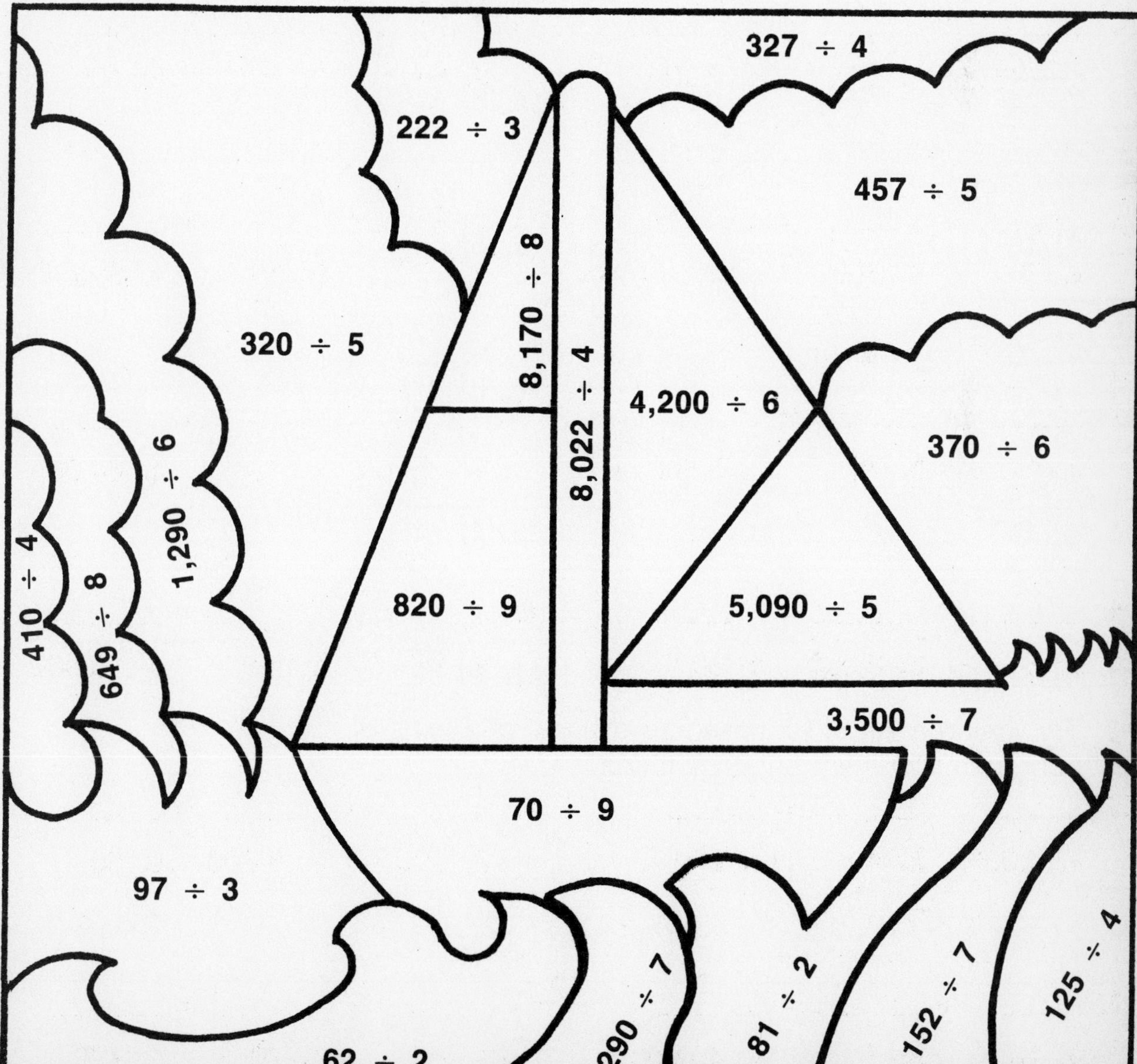

Macmillan/McGraw-Hill, MATHEMATICS IN ACTION
Grade 4, Chapter 7, Lesson 4, pages 264–265

Name

DIVIDING 2-DIGIT NUMBERS

On Your Own Pair and Share In a Group

RIGHTING WRONGS

None of the division problems below are correct! But you can fix them all by swapping numbers. You can exchange two divisors, two dividends, or two quotients. Circle the numbers you will change and draw a line connecting them. Make only one change in each problem. The first one is done for you.

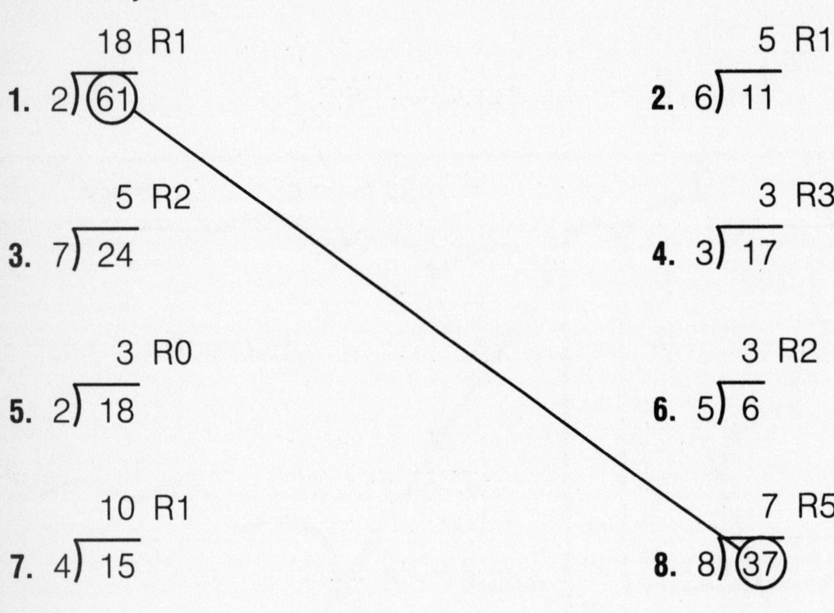

1. $\begin{array}{r} 18\ R1 \\ 2\overline{)61} \end{array}$

2. $\begin{array}{r} 5\ R1 \\ 6\overline{)11} \end{array}$

3. $\begin{array}{r} 5\ R2 \\ 7\overline{)24} \end{array}$

4. $\begin{array}{r} 3\ R3 \\ 3\overline{)17} \end{array}$

5. $\begin{array}{r} 3\ R0 \\ 2\overline{)18} \end{array}$

6. $\begin{array}{r} 3\ R2 \\ 5\overline{)6} \end{array}$

7. $\begin{array}{r} 10\ R1 \\ 4\overline{)15} \end{array}$

8. $\begin{array}{r} 7\ R5 \\ 8\overline{)37} \end{array}$

9. $\begin{array}{r} 1\ R1 \\ 4\overline{)14} \end{array}$

10. $\begin{array}{r} 3\ R3 \\ 4\overline{)41} \end{array}$

11. $\begin{array}{r} 8\ R5 \\ 6\overline{)77} \end{array}$

12. $\begin{array}{r} 13\ R4 \\ 9\overline{)82} \end{array}$

13. Try writing a set of six mixed-up division problems of your own. Try them out on a friend.

Name

ENRICHMENT-69

DIVIDING 3-DIGIT NUMBERS

On Your Own   Pair and Share   In a Group

MISSING ELEMENTS

Can you find all of the possible sets of divisors and dividends for each quotient and remainder?

The first four exercises tell you how many sets you need to find. In the last four, you have to decide how many sets you can find. (Do not use 1 as a divisor). Work with a partner to solve the problems.

1. 124
[?]) [?][?][?]

_____ ÷ _____

_____ ÷ _____

2. 101 R 5
[?]) [?][?][?]

_____ ÷ _____

_____ ÷ _____

_____ ÷ _____

_____ ÷ _____

3. 305
[?]) [?][?][?]

_____ ÷ _____

_____ ÷ _____

4. 244 R 2
[?]) [?][?][?]

_____ ÷ _____

_____ ÷ _____

5. 277 R 1
[?]) [?][?][?]

_____

6. 122 R 3
[?]) [?][?][?]

_____

7. 289 R 2
[?]) [?][?][?]

_____

_____

_____

8. 107 R 2
[?]) [?][?][?]

_____

_____

_____

Name

MORE DIVIDING 3-DIGIT NUMBERS

DIVIDED ATTENTIONS

Complete each division problem using the digits in the box to the right.

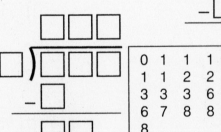

1.

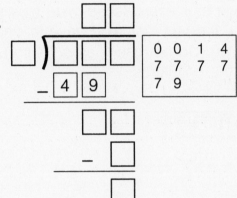

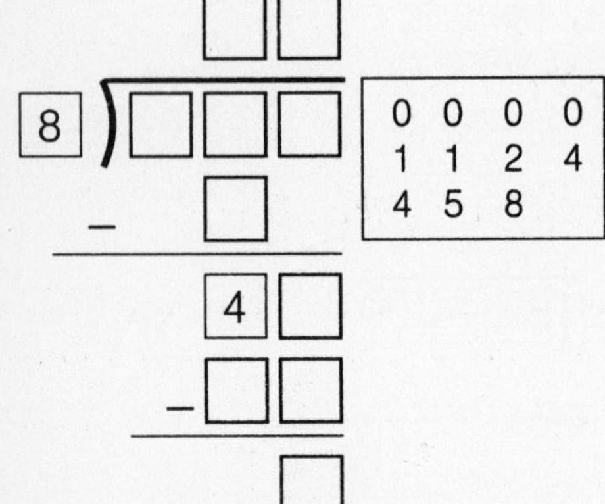

2.

Divisor: □; quotient: □□; dividend: □□□; subtract 4 9; □□; subtract □; remainder □

Digits: 0 0 1 4 / 7 7 7 7 / 7 9

3.

Divisor: □; quotient: 3 □□; dividend: □□□; subtract □; □□; subtract □; □□; subtract 9; remainder □

Digits: 0 0 0 3 / 3 3 3 9 / 9 9 9 9 / 9 9 9

4.

Divisor: □; quotient: □□□; dividend: □□□; subtract □; □□; subtract □□; 3 0; subtract □□; remainder □

Digits: 0 0 0 1 / 1 1 3 3 / 5 5 5 6 / 6 8 8

5.

Divisor: □; quotient: □□□; dividend: □□□; subtract □; □□; subtract □□; □□; subtract □□; remainder □

Digits: 0 1 1 1 / 1 1 2 2 / 3 3 3 6 / 6 7 8 8 / 8

Name

ZEROS IN THE QUOTIENT

On Your Own | Pair and Share | In a Group

EDWARDS' LETTERS

Each digit has been replaced with a specific letter in the problem below. For example, every 1 might be replaced with a V. Can you find out what digit each letter stands for? When you do, write each division problem. Then use the letter values you've found to answer the riddle at the bottom of the page.

Q: Why did the man name two of his children Edward? (*Hint:* T = 5)

1. T) TOE = RES
2. B) BTO = REA
3. W) OEW = WER
4. W) WEW = RER
5. N) NEE = REE
6. D) DOA = RED
7. O) SWS = WED
8. N) NEN = RER
9. W) BEB = NEN

A: ___ ___ ___ ___ ___ ___ ___ ___ ___

5 2 4 0 7 8 9 1 0

___ ___ ___ ___ ___ ___ ___ ___ ___ ___

6 0 5 5 0 1 3 4 3 0

Macmillan/McGraw-Hill, MATHEMATICS IN ACTION
Grade 4, Chapter 7, Lesson 10, pages 276-277

Name

DIVIDING MONEY

BAND AID

Jill's band, Sound-Off, is choosing among the three concert halls described below:

Memorial Auditorium	Sound Stage	New Variety Theater
600 seats	630 seats	532 seats
24 rows	30 rows	28 rows
Rental fee:	Rental fee:	Rental fee:
$525/night	$577/night	$418/night

Jill makes several calculations to compare each space. Use a calculator to help you. Round your answers. Then discuss your answers in a group.

1. There are an equal number of seats in every row. How many seats are in each row?

Memorial Auditorium ______

Sound Stage ______

New Variety Theater ______

2. Jill wants to sell at least $2,000 worth of tickets. Assume that she can sell out any of the theaters. What is the lowest price she can charge for tickets?

Memorial Auditorium ______

Sound Stage ______

New Variety Theater ______

3. What is Jill's cost per seat for renting each hall?

Memorial Auditorium _____ Sound Stage _____ New Variety Theater _____

4. Suppose that Jill decides to charge $4 for each ticket. How much will she take in if she sells all of the tickets? How much will she earn (have left)?

	Take In	Earn
Memorial Auditorium	________	________
Sound Stage	________	________
New Variety Theater	________	________

5. Which space do you think Jill should rent? Why?

____

____

____

Name

PROBLEM SOLVING

On Your Own Pair and Share In a Group

MATT'S LOST HIS MARBLES!

Matt has an ENORMOUS marble collection. He keeps it in an old bathtub he found in a junkyard. The tub holds 100,555 marbles!

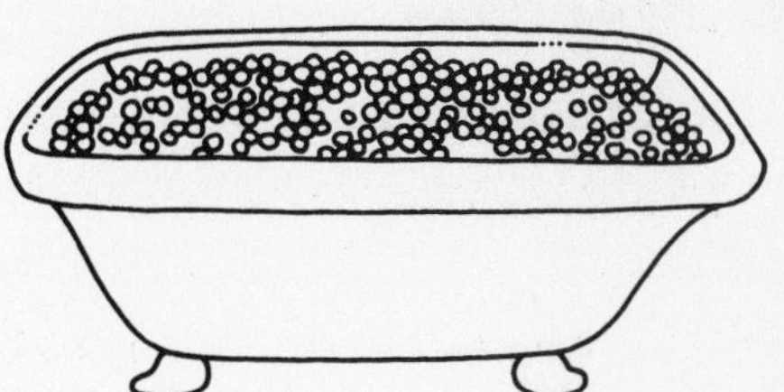

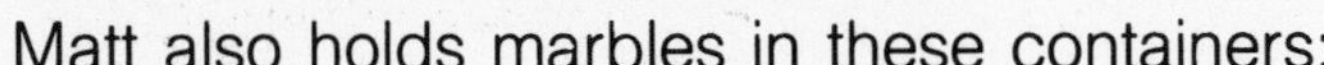

Matt also holds marbles in these containers:

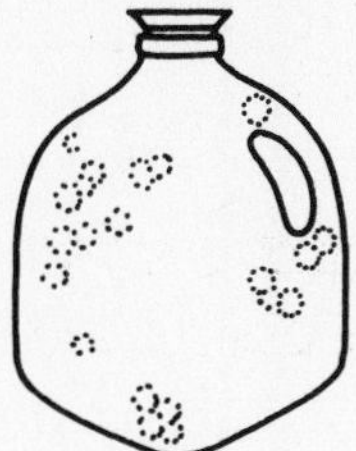

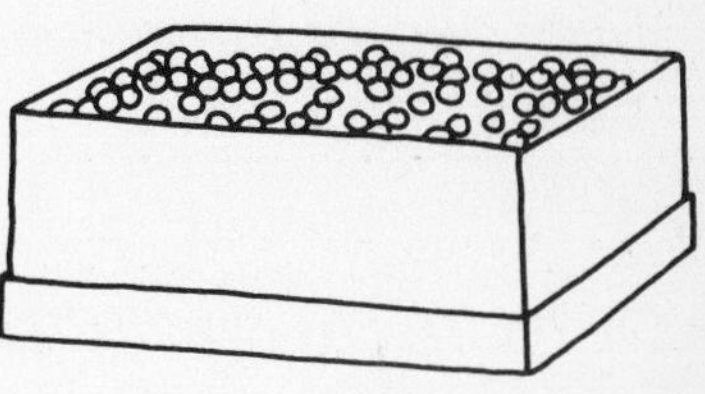

__________ marbles __________ marbles __________ marbles

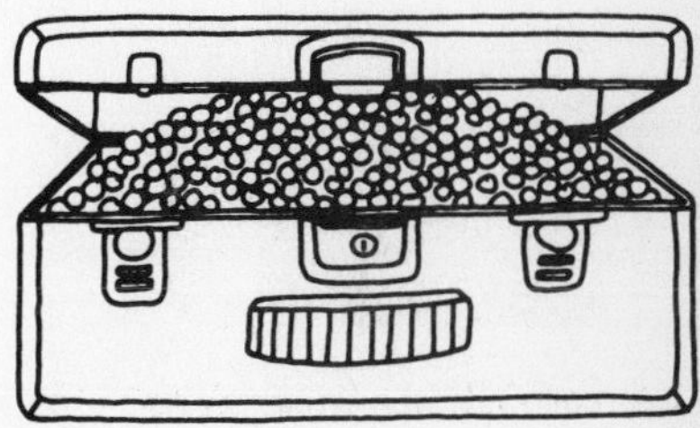

__________ marbles __________ marbles __________ marbles

Work with a partner. Using the clues below, can you find out how many marbles each container holds? A calculator will help!

- Matt fills the bucket 47 times with marbles from the bathtub, and there are 1,338 left over.
- He fills the jug twice with the marbles in one bucket, and there are 111 marbles left over.
- If the jug could hold 2 more marbles, Matt could fill the vase 6 times with the marbles in the jug.
- Matt uses 6 suitcases, 4 shoeboxes, and 45 glasses to fill the bathtub completely.
- The shoebox holds 389 more marbles than the bucket.
- Matt fills the vase with 4 glasses of marbles, but needs 11 more marbles to fill the vase all the way.

Name

MORE MEDIAN, RANGE, AND AVERAGE

On Your Own Pair and Share In a Group

ABOUT AVERAGES

Solve the problems. You may want to have a calculator handy.

1. Ms. Daley dropped the test papers from two of her classes after she had scored them. These are the scores:

70	70	70	72	73	74	75	80
81	82	87	91	91	92	92	96

- Each class has the same number of students.
- The test scores for Class 1 had a range of 70 to 96 and an average of 83.
- The test scores for Class 2 had a range of 70 to 91 and an average of 79.

Can you find which scores were in each class?

Class 1: ______________________

____

Class 2: ______________________

____

2. Use the numbers in this box:

$12.00	$12.25	$12.50	$12.75
$13.00	$13.50	$13.55	$13.75
$14.00	$14.50		

Form two sets.

- Each set has 5 numbers.
- Set 1 has a range of $12.00 to $13.50.
  It has a median of $12.75.
- Set 2 has a range of $12.50 to $14.50.
  It has a median of $13.75.

Find each set and its average.

Set 1: ______________________

____

Average: ______________________

Set 2: ______________________

____

Average: ______________________

3. Think about the counting numbers 1 to 20.

1 2 3 4 5 6 7 8 9 10 11 12 13 14 15 16 17 18 19 20

What is the average of the first 5 numbers? _____

The median? _____

Name

LINES, LINE SEGMENTS, AND RAYS

On Your Own · Pair and Share · In a Group

PICTURE THIS

Draw these lines, line segments, and rays to complete this picture.

Lines	Line Segments		Rays	
ST	*AB*	*OQ*	*DE*	*DJ*
YZ	*BC*	*UV*	*DF*	*DK*
	AC	*RP*	*DG*	*DL*
	CT	*OP*	*DH*	*DM*
	SB	*VW*	*DI*	*DN*
	XW	*UX*		

A E F
N G
D
M H
L I
B C K J
U V
X W O P
S Q R T
Y Z

Name

ANGLES

On Your Own   Pair and Share   In a Group

THREE-IN-ONE

The shape below contains answers to three different riddles! Sort the angles into the groups listed below. Then rearrange the letters in each group to answer each riddle.

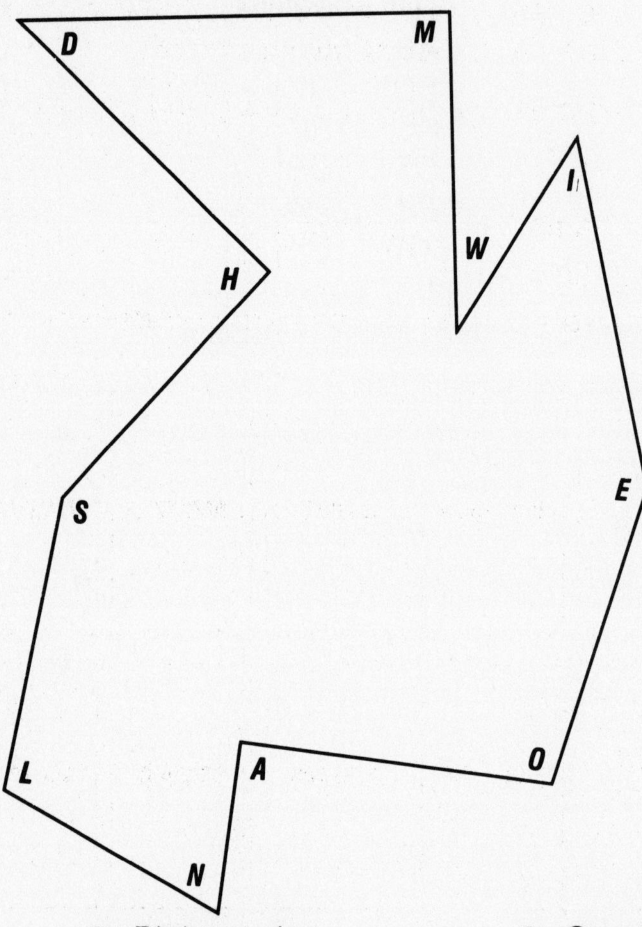

1. Less than a right angle:

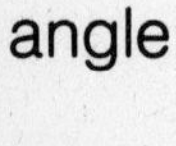

______

______

______

______

Q: What can be felt but never seen?

A: ___ ___ ___ ___

2. Right angle:

______

______

______

Q: What kind of food overacts?

A: ___ ___ ___

3. Greater than a right angle:

______

______

______

______

Q: What kind of fish can you find on your shoe?

A: ___ ___ ___ ___

Name

PLANE FIGURES

On Your Own Pair and Share In a Group

SHAPE UP!

Play this game with a partner. Cut out all of the cards and turn them upside down. On your turn, turn over two cards. If the cards match, take them and place them in your pile. Then pick two more cards. If the cards do not match, your turn is over. Turn the cards upside down.

The player with the most cards at the end of the game is the winner.

Two cards match if:

- They show the same type of shape.
- They show the same word.
- They show a word and a shape that are correctly matched.

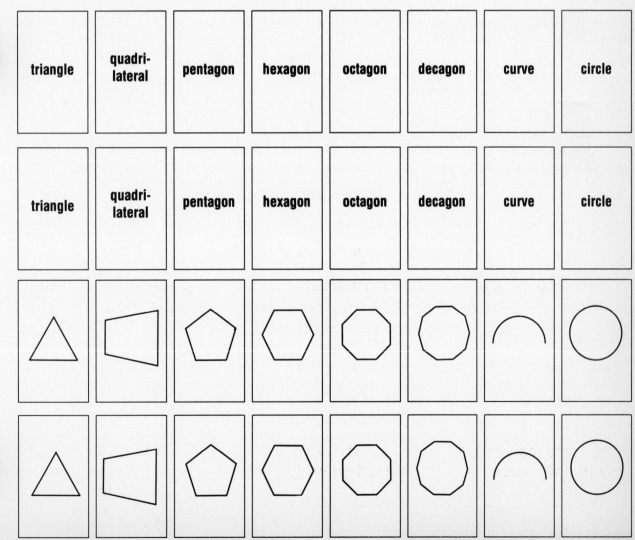

triangle	quadri-lateral	pentagon	hexagon	octagon	decagon	curve	circle
triangle	quadri-lateral	pentagon	hexagon	octagon	decagon	curve	circle

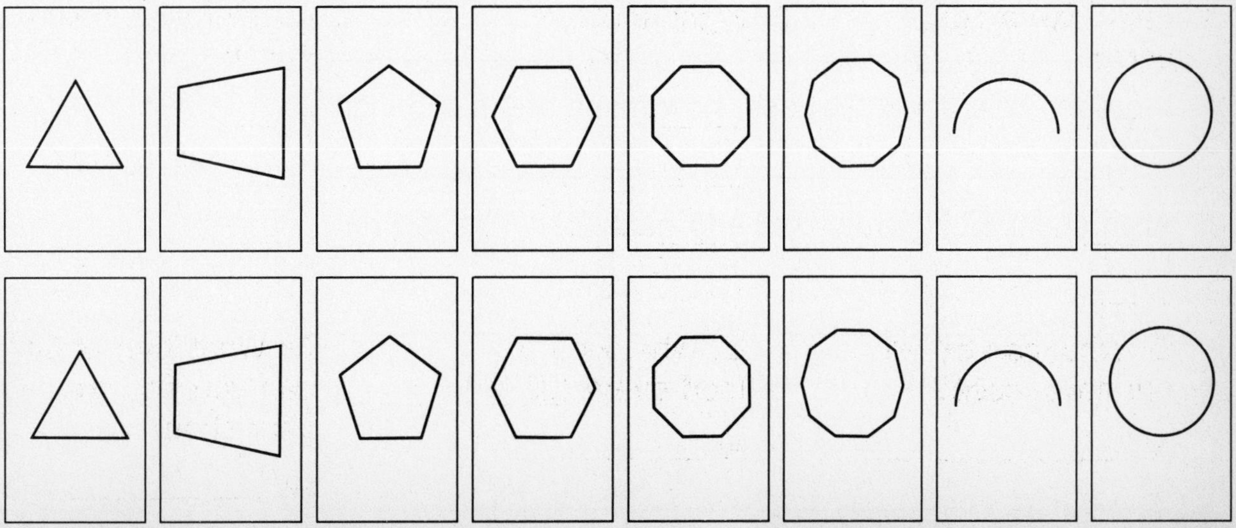

Name

PROBLEM SOLVING

On Your Own Pair and Share In a Group

BUNCHES and BAGS

This is Frieda's Fruit Store. Use information in the drawing to help you answer the questions below.

1. How much does each pound of pears cost?

____

2. Are apples or pears more expensive per pound?

____

3. If there are five bananas in a bunch, how much does each banana cost?

____

4. If grapes cost about 2¢ each, how many are in a bunch?

____

5. Allen spent $2.70 on apples and bananas. What did he buy?

____

6. Edna spent $3.00. What might she have bought?

____

____

Name

PROBLEM SOLVING

ARTFUL ROGER

Roger and his friends worked on their art projects together. Use the clues and the chart to help you find out which materials each friend used. Put a ✓ for yes and an X for no.

- Roger and the person who made a clay sculpture are best friends.
- Tina did not use clay or paint.
- The photographer took a photo of Ed and Cleo.
- In the background of the photo, you can see Tina using her crayons.
- Ed painted a picture of his goldfish.

	Crayons	Paint	Photographs	Clay
Roger				
Tina				
Ed				
Cleo				

After making their artworks, the friends had a contest to see who could clean up the fastest.

- Roger was faster than Tina.
- Cleo was slower than Tina, but faster than Ed.

Can you find the order of the four friends? Put a ✓ for yes and an X for no.

	First (fastest)	Second	Third	Fourth (slowest)
Roger				
Tina				
Ed				
Cleo				

Name

SLIDES, FLIPS, AND TURNS

On Your Own Pair and Share In a Group

SHAPE TWISTS

Work with a group of friends. Use the shapes and cards below to create puzzles. Cut out the four shapes and three cards. Turn the cards upside down.

Choose one shape. On another sheet of paper, trace the shape. Then pick one of the cards. Follow the instructions on the card. Return the card and pick again. After you have picked four cards, pass your artwork to your friends. See if they can guess what cards you picked to create it.

Can you guess what cards were picked to draw these pictures?

1.   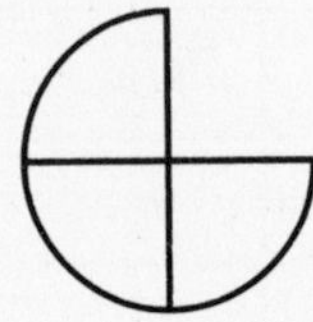

____

2. 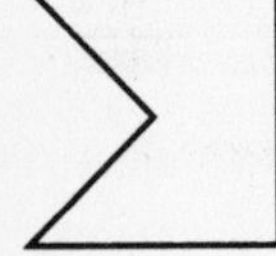 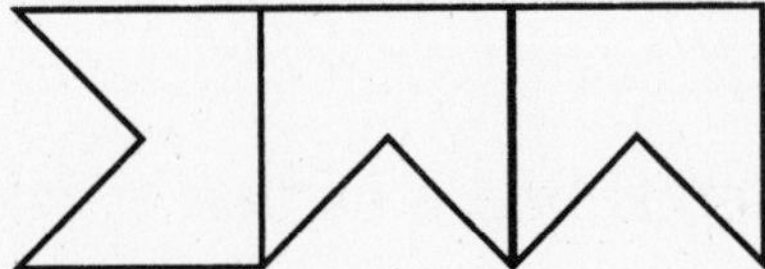 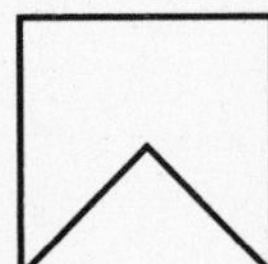

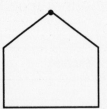

____

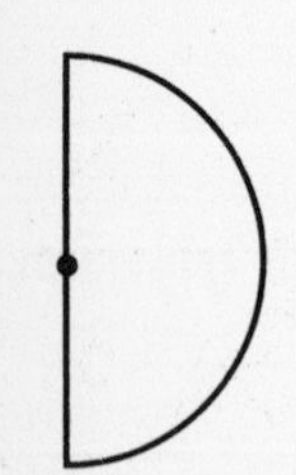 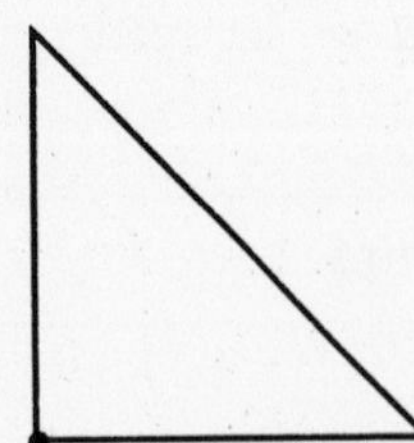  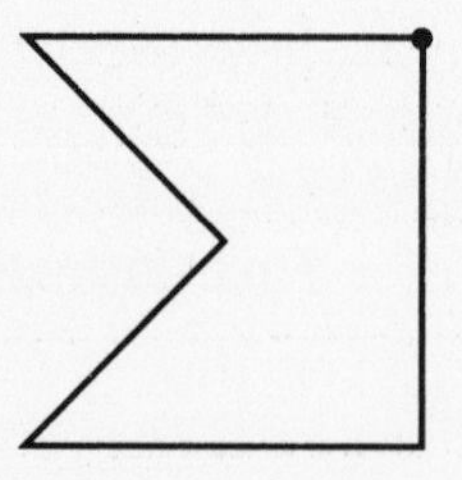

Slide
Slide your shape one inch to the right and trace it again.

Flip
Flip your shape over to the right and trace it again.

Turn
Turn your shape around the point shown and trace it again.

ENRICHMENT-81

Name

CONGRUENCE AND SIMILARITY

On Your Own Pair and Share In a Group

MATCHWORKS

Each of the drawings below contains similar and congruent shapes. Can you find them all?

1. Look at this drawing. Each shape in the drawing can be named with one or more letters. For example, Shape A is the square in the upper left corner. Shape AB is the rectangle along the top.

Can you complete these sentences to show which shapes match?
Shape A is similar to Shape ABCD.
Shape C is congruent to Shape ____.

Shape AC is congruent to Shape ____.

2. Now look at this drawing and complete the sentences:

Shape EF is similar to Shapes

____ and ____.
Shape F is congruent to Shapes

____ and ____.

Shape I is __________ to Shape GH.

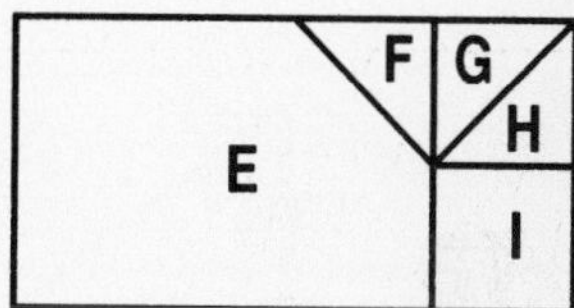

3. Now look at this drawing. How many sets of congruent or similar shapes can you find? Describe each pair or set.

____

____

____

____

____

____

____

____

____

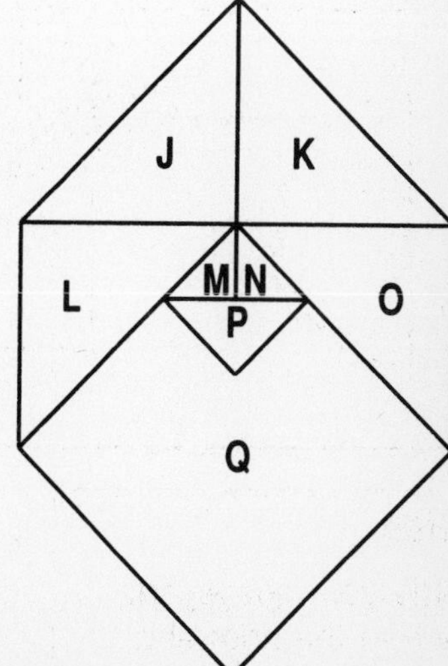

Name

LINE OF SYMMETRY

On Your Own Pair and Share In a Group

ANOTHER SIDE OF SYMMETRY

Complete this page to find a pattern. For each shape, draw every possible line of symmetry. Write the number of lines in the chart.

Shape	Number of lines of symmetry
triangle	3
square	4
pentagon	5
hexagon	6
octagon	8
decagon	10

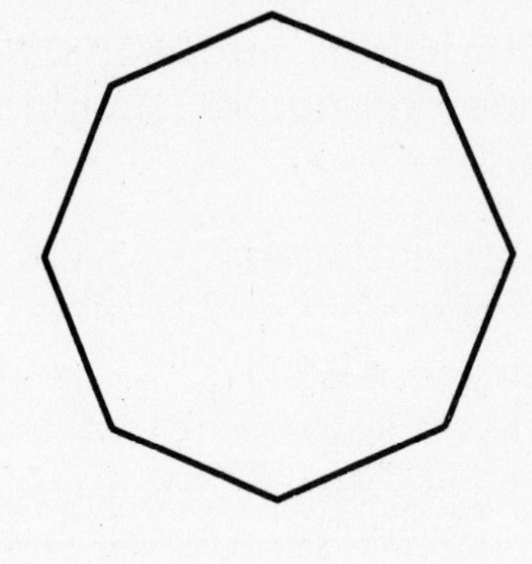

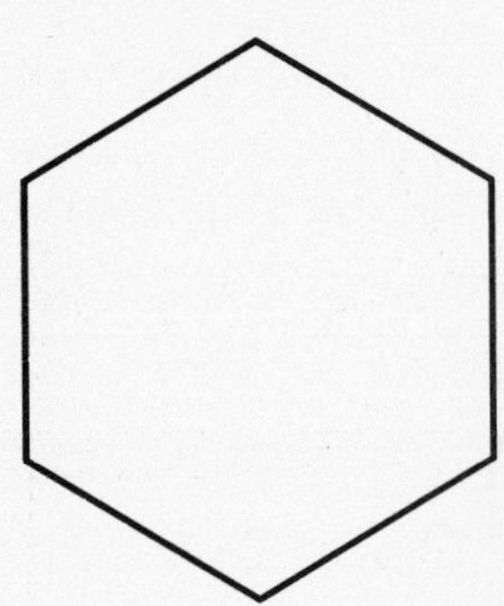

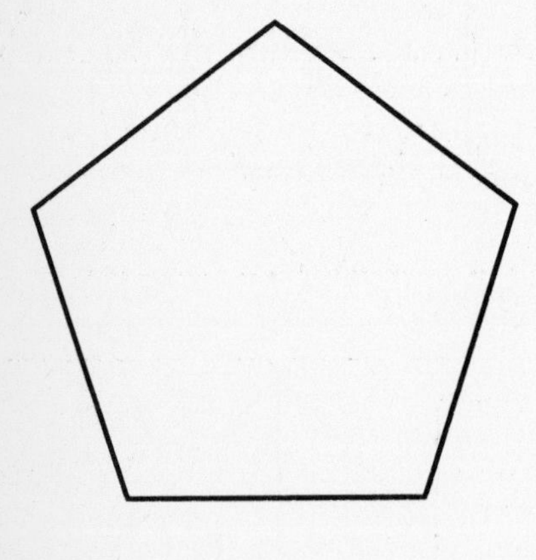

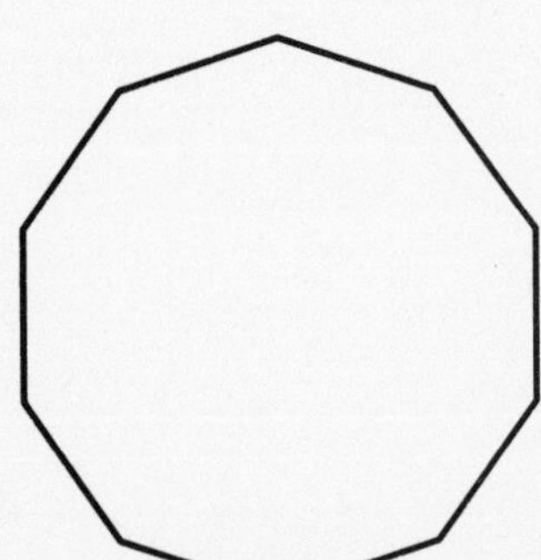

Describe the pattern you found for these shapes.

____

____

Name

SPACE FIGURES

On Your Own Pair and Share In a Group

NOW IN 3-D

Work on this activity with a group. Each set of shapes could be cut out and formed into a space figure. Can you see which figure each set would form? Write the name of the space figure below each set.

1.

2.

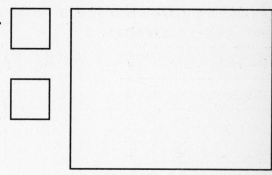

3.

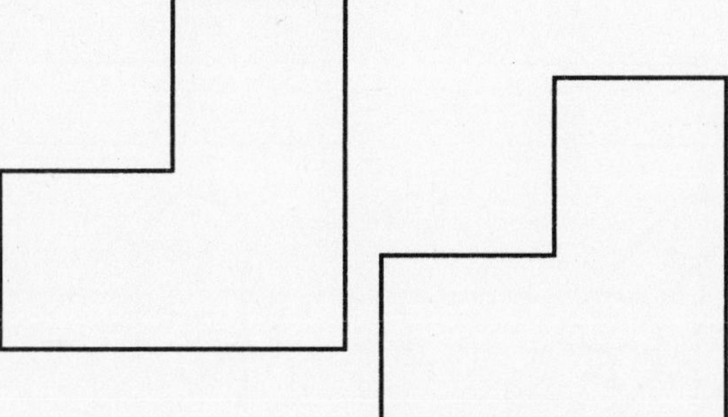

4.

5.

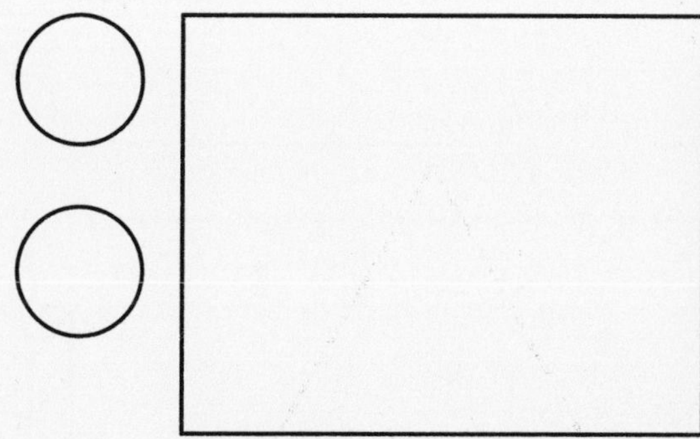

6. Now work with your group to make a set of space shapes using these patterns as guides. Make your shapes larger than the patterns so that they are easier to cut out and fold. Use tape to hold your shapes together.

Name

VOLUME

On Your Own Pair and Share In a Group

AROUND THE BLOCK

Imagine that each of the shapes below is made of blocks. What is the volume of each shape in cubic blocks? How much would each shape cost to build if blocks cost 25¢ each? How many sides would you have to paint to completely paint each shape? Write your answers in the lines below each shape.

1.

2.

3.

4.

5.

6.

7.

8.

Name ____________________

THE MEANING OF FRACTIONS

On Your Own | Pair and Share | In a Group

FLAG FRACTIONS

1. Color each country's flag below. Use these colors:

B – blue G – green Y – yellow W – white
R – red K – black O – orange

B
W
B

ARGENTINA

R
W
R

AUSTRIA

G W G

NIGERIA

W
R

POLAND

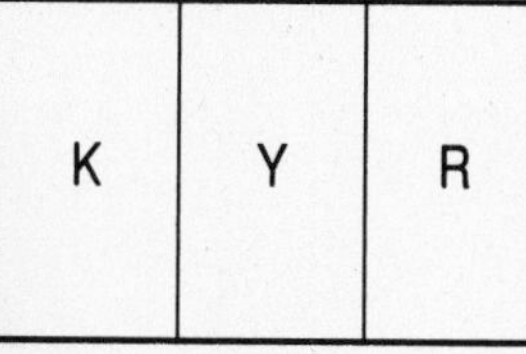

BELGIUM

G
W
B

SIERRA LEONE

R W R

PERU

K
Y
R
K
Y
R

UGANDA

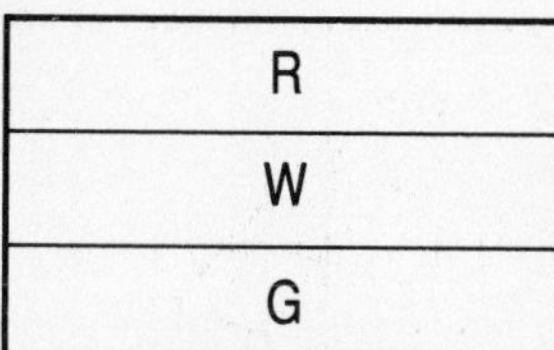

HUNGARY

O W G

IVORY COAST

G W R

ITALY

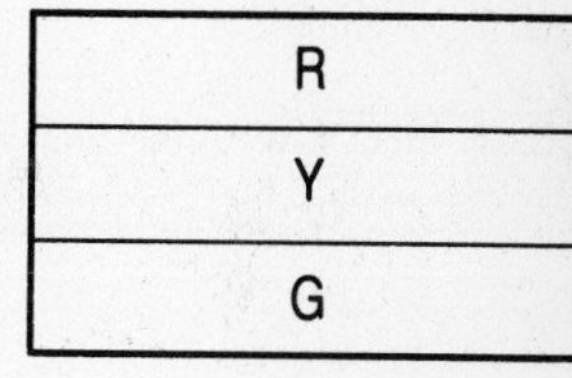

BOLIVIA

Use the flags to answer each question.

2. What fraction of Belgium's flag is yellow? ____________________

3. Name another country whose flag has the same part of red as Peru.

____

4. What fraction of Nigeria's flag is green? ____________________

5. Which country's flag has the greatest part of white? ____________________

6. Name another country whose flag has the same part of green as Italy.

____

7. What part of Uganda's flag is yellow? ____________________

8. Look at a world map or a globe. Find each country whose flag is shown above.

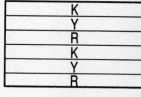

Name

PARTS OF A WHOLE

HOW DOES YOUR GARDEN GROW?

Sal is going to plant a vegetable garden this year.
These are the vegetables he wants to plant:

Peas	Tomatoes
Carrots	Corn
Lettuce	Broccoli
	Cabbage

This is what he has decided.

- The tomatoes and the lettuce will each take up an equal amount of space in the garden.
- The lettuce needs twice as much space as the cabbage.
- The broccoli needs only half as much space as the lettuce.
- The peas and the carrots will each get as much space in the garden as the broccoli.
- The corn needs as much space as the peas and carrots combined.

Help Sal design his garden. Use the grid below.
Show how much space each vegetable should get.

SAL'S VEGETABLE GARDEN

Name

PARTS OF A SET

AT THE BORDER

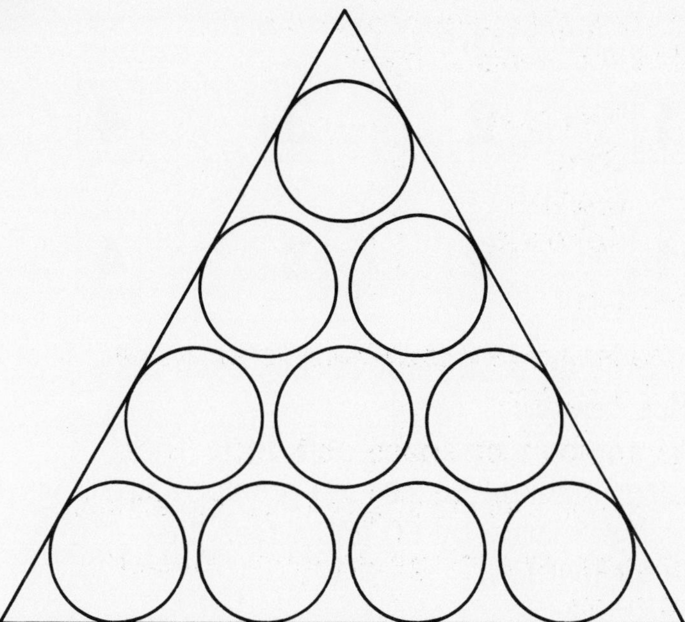

1. Some of the circles touch the border at exactly two points. Draw stripes on these circles.
2. Some of the circles touch the border at exactly one point. Draw dots on these circles.
3. Draw stars on any circle that does not touch the border at all.
4. What fraction of the circles have stripes? __________
5. What fraction of the circles have dots? __________
6. What fraction of the circles have stars? __________
7. What fraction of the circles touch the border? __________
8. What fraction of the circles do not touch the border? __________
9. What fraction of the circles touch only one other circle? __________

Name

FINDING THE FRACTION OF A NUMBER

On Your Own   Pair and Share   In a Group

FRACTION GAME

Here is a game for two or more players.

0	1	2	3	4	5
0	1	2	3	4	5

- Make two decks of cards as shown above. Mix each deck and put the deck face down.
- The first player picks the top card from each deck. The player uses the cards to make a fraction no greater than 1.
- The player multiplies the fraction by 60 and writes the answer as the score for that turn.

> For example, if you pick **2** and **4**
> you would find $\frac{2}{4}$ of 60 = 30
>
> Your score = 30

- Each card is replaced in the deck it came from and the decks are mixed again.
- Players take turns picking cards and adding to their scores.
- If a player picks 0, the player's score is 0 for that turn. If a player picks 0–0, the cards are replaced, and the player picks again.
- The first player whose score totals 100 or more is the winner.

Variations

- Try to score a different total.
- Change the rules for what happens when a player picks 0 or 0–0.
- Play the game using a calculator. Find fractions of 120.

Name

PROBLEM SOLVING

On Your Own Pair and Share In a Group

LARRY, CAREY, AND HARRY

Solve each problem by using the clues.

1. Larry, Carey and Harry went out for lunch. Each friend ordered a salad: the choices were egg, tuna, and chicken.

- Carey won't eat egg.
- Larry never orders tuna.
- Harry only likes chicken.
- Each friend ate something different.

What did each friend order for lunch?

Larry ordered ________

Carey ordered ________

Harry ordered ________

2. Larry, Carey, and Harry live in the same apartment building as Barry and Mary.

- Carey's apartment is on a higher floor than Mary's, but it is lower than Larry's apartment.
- Barry's apartment is between Larry's and Carey's.
- The only friend who lives on a lower floor than Harry is Mary.

List the names of the friends in the chart at the right.

	HIGHEST
	LOWEST

Name

FINDING EQUIVALENT FRACTIONS

On Your Own | Pair and Share | In a Group

CONCENTRATE ON FRACTIONS

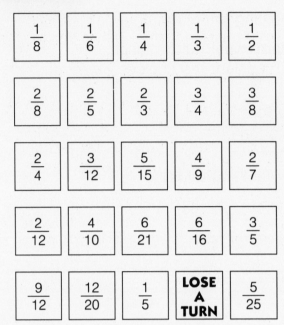

$\frac{1}{8}$	$\frac{1}{6}$	$\frac{1}{4}$	$\frac{1}{3}$	$\frac{1}{2}$
$\frac{2}{8}$	$\frac{2}{5}$	$\frac{2}{3}$	$\frac{3}{4}$	$\frac{3}{8}$
$\frac{2}{4}$	$\frac{3}{12}$	$\frac{5}{15}$	$\frac{4}{9}$	$\frac{2}{7}$
$\frac{2}{12}$	$\frac{4}{10}$	$\frac{6}{21}$	$\frac{6}{16}$	$\frac{3}{5}$
$\frac{9}{12}$	$\frac{12}{20}$	$\frac{1}{5}$	LOSE A TURN	$\frac{5}{25}$

Here is a fraction game to play with a friend.

- Make a set of 25 cards as shown above. Shuffle the cards together and place them face down—5 in each row and 5 in each column.
- The first player turns over two cards. If the fractions are equivalent, the player keeps the cards and goes again.
- If the cards do not show equivalent fractions, the cards are turned face down again and the second player goes.
- If a player picks the LOSE A TURN card, the other player gets to take two turns. The LOSE A TURN card is replaced face down.
- The game continues until all cards except LOSE A TURN have been taken. The player with the most cards is the winner.

**You can make up your own set of equivalent fraction cards and play concentration with them.

Name

SIMPLIFYING FRACTIONS

On Your Own Pair and Share In a Group

AS SIMPLE AS POSSIBLE

My nickname is the Coyote State. People visit me to see Mount Rushmore, where the faces of Presidents Washington, Jefferson, Lincoln, and Theodore Roosevelt are carved. My state tree is the Black Hills spruce. What state am I?

To find out, complete the exercises below. In each exercise, three of the fractions have the simplest form shown at the right. Circle the fraction that does not belong. Then match each letter to its exercise number in the boxes below.

1.

$\frac{8}{12}$	$\frac{6}{8}$	$\frac{4}{6}$	$\frac{6}{9}$
C	U	R	E

$= \frac{2}{3}$

2.

$\frac{12}{16}$	$\frac{6}{8}$	$\frac{8}{10}$	$\frac{9}{12}$
R	I	D	E

$= \frac{3}{4}$

3.

$\frac{4}{20}$	$\frac{3}{24}$	$\frac{5}{40}$	$\frac{2}{16}$
S	O	F	T

$= \frac{1}{8}$

4.

$\frac{4}{16}$	$\frac{6}{15}$	$\frac{4}{10}$	$\frac{10}{25}$
H	A	N	D

$= \frac{2}{5}$

5.

$\frac{3}{18}$	$\frac{5}{30}$	$\frac{2}{12}$	$\frac{8}{24}$
B	A	N	K

$= \frac{1}{6}$

6.

$\frac{6}{14}$	$\frac{10}{20}$	$\frac{12}{24}$	$\frac{25}{50}$
T	E	A	R

$= \frac{1}{2}$

7.

$\frac{50}{80}$	$\frac{20}{32}$	$\frac{36}{48}$	$\frac{40}{64}$
L	E	A	P

$= \frac{5}{8}$

8.

$\frac{18}{42}$	$\frac{12}{21}$	$\frac{15}{35}$	$\frac{9}{21}$
C	O	Z	Y

$= \frac{3}{7}$

Answer:

___ ___ ___ ___ ___   ___ ___ ___ ___ ___ ___
3 8 1 6 4   2 7 5 8 6 7

Macmillan/McGraw-Hill, MATHEMATICS IN ACTION
Grade 4, Chapter 9, Lesson 8, pages 358-359

Name

WHOLE NUMBERS AND MIXED NUMBERS

On Your Own | Pair and Share | In a Group

FRACTION BINGO

Write each fraction as a mixed number or whole number. The fraction part of each mixed number should be in simplest form.

Then make BINGO on the gamecard below by drawing an X over each answer that appears on the card. (Some answers do not appear.)

1. $\frac{9}{4}$ ______
2. $\frac{7}{3}$ ______
3. $\frac{8}{5}$ ______
4. $\frac{9}{6}$ ______
5. $\frac{11}{2}$ ______
6. $\frac{15}{5}$ ______
7. $\frac{12}{7}$ ______
8. $\frac{14}{4}$ ______
9. $\frac{12}{9}$ ______
10. $\frac{10}{6}$ ______
11. $\frac{13}{8}$ ______
12. $\frac{15}{6}$ ______
13. $\frac{20}{10}$ ______
14. $\frac{22}{7}$ ______
15. $\frac{12}{10}$ ______
16. $\frac{18}{3}$ ______
17. $\frac{17}{8}$ ______
18. $\frac{16}{4}$ ______
19. $\frac{44}{16}$ ______
20. $\frac{13}{3}$ ______

B	I	N	G	O
$4\frac{1}{2}$	$1\frac{1}{8}$	$2\frac{1}{4}$	6	3
$3\frac{1}{7}$	$2\frac{1}{3}$	$1\frac{2}{3}$	$4\frac{3}{4}$	$1\frac{5}{8}$
$3\frac{1}{2}$	5	**FREE SPACE**	$1\frac{3}{5}$	4
$1\frac{4}{5}$	$2\frac{3}{4}$	$2\frac{1}{2}$	$2\frac{5}{6}$	$1\frac{1}{5}$
$1\frac{1}{3}$	$5\frac{1}{2}$	7	$2\frac{1}{8}$	$4\frac{1}{3}$

Name

COMPARING FRACTIONS AND MIXED NUMBERS

On Your Own   Pair and Share   In a Group

POINT THE WAY

Draw arrows in order from the least to the greatest fraction or mixed number in each box. The first problem is started for you.

1. $\frac{7}{8}$ ← $\frac{5}{8}$, $1\frac{1}{8}$, $\frac{8}{8}$

2. $\frac{1}{6}$, $\frac{1}{2}$, $\frac{1}{3}$, $\frac{1}{4}$

3. $\frac{2}{5}$, $\frac{2}{10}$, $\frac{2}{3}$, $\frac{2}{8}$

4.  $1\frac{7}{8}$, $1\frac{3}{4}$, $1\frac{1}{2}$, $1\frac{5}{6}$

5.  $\frac{9}{15}$, $\frac{7}{10}$, $\frac{4}{5}$, $1\frac{1}{10}$

6. $2\frac{3}{4}$, $2\frac{1}{3}$, $2\frac{3}{8}$, $2\frac{3}{12}$

7.  $\frac{2}{3}$, $\frac{3}{4}$, $\frac{5}{6}$, $\frac{3}{5}$

8. $1\frac{3}{8}$, $1\frac{1}{5}$, $2\frac{1}{10}$, $\frac{15}{16}$

9.  $3\frac{1}{2}$, $3\frac{5}{8}$, $3\frac{2}{3}$, $3\frac{5}{6}$

Name

MEASURING LENGTH: CUSTOMARY UNITS

On Your Own   Pair and Share   In a Group

EXPERIMENT TO ESTIMATE

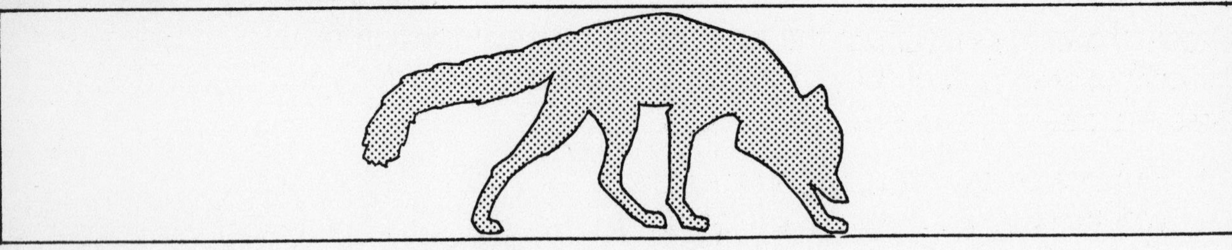

1. What part of the picture do you think is shaded? Write your guess as a fraction.

____

Now use this method to find an estimate.

2. Close your eyes. Put your pencil down on the picture and make a dot.
3. Repeat 49 times.
4. Count the number of times you made a dot in the shaded part. Write your answer here.

____

5. Write a fraction as an estimate of the shaded part. Use your answer to question 4 as the numerator. What number will you use as the denominator?

____

Fraction $\frac{\square}{\square}$

6. Compare the fraction you found by experimenting with the guess you wrote for question 1. Was your guess close? Explain?

____

____

7. To repeat the experiment, trace the picture. Try it again yourself or ask a friend to try. Compare the results of your experiments.
8. Draw a picture of your own. Use the same method to estimate the part that is shaded.

Name

ESTIMATING LENGTH: CUSTOMARY UNITS

On Your Own   Pair and Share   In a Group

MEASUREMENT OLYMPICS

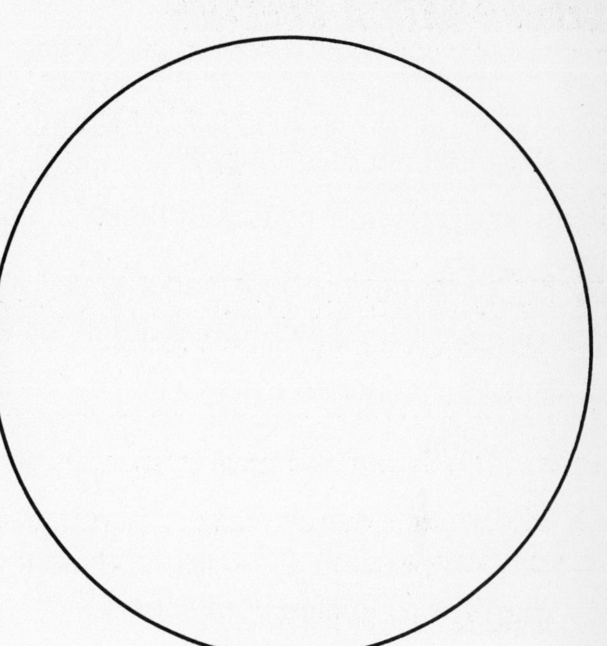

Trace the circle at the right on a piece of cardboard and cut it out. You will toss the cardboard circle like a frisbee.

1. First, estimate how many inches you think you can throw the circle. Record your estimate.

   ______________________ inches

2. Choose a starting place. Throw the circle three times. Measure the distance each time to the nearest inch. Record the distances on a scorecard like the one shown below.

3. Compute your score for each throw. Find the difference between the estimate and the actual measurement. (Subtract the smaller number from the larger.)

	Distance	**Score = Difference between estimate and distance**
First Throw		
Second Throw		
Third Throw		

4. What is your best (lowest) score? ______________

5. Try this activity with teams of 3.

The team score is the sum of each team player's best (lowest) score:

______________ + ______________ + ______________ = ______________
Player A's Best   Player B's Best   Player C's Best   Team Score

See which team gets the gold medal.

Name ______________________________________

PROBLEM SOLVING

On Your Own   Pair and Share   In a Group

ANSWER WITH A QUESTION

These problems already have answers. Use the information given and logical thinking to write a question that fits each answer.

Compare your questions with those of some friends.

1. Karen is making bookmarks to sell at the school fair. She uses $\frac{1}{3}$ of a 12-inch piece of felt for each bookmark.

   Answer: 4 inches

   Question: ______________________________________

   ____

2. Karen's house is $2\frac{3}{4}$ miles from school. Her friend Joe's house is $2\frac{1}{2}$ miles from school.

   Answer: Karen

   Question: ______________________________________

   ____

3. Karen is 48 inches tall. Karen's little brother Nick is one-half as tall as she is.

   Answer: 24 inches

   Question: ______________________________________

   ____

4. A display table at the fair is 4 feet long. Each table is covered with a cloth that is twice as long as the table.

   Answer: 8 feet long

   Question: ______________________________________

   ____

5. Sara has a piece of ribbon that is 60 inches long. She will use two-thirds of the ribbon to make bows.

   Answer: 20 inches

   Question: ______________________________________

   ____

Name

FINDING SUMS

TINA'S TOYSHOP

This drawing shows some of the toys that Tina sells at her shop. Look at the picture. Then answer the questions below. Write your answers in simplest form.

1. What fraction of the balls are striped? ____________
2. What fraction of the cars have stars? ____________
3. What fraction of all of the toys are dotted? ____________
4. What fraction of the toy soldiers and the dolls are

   striped? __________ are dotted? ____________ have stars? __________

Write each fraction described. Then circle the answer that describes the greater fraction.

5. **a.** the fraction of dolls that have stripes

   ____

   b. the fraction of dolls and balls that have stripes

   ____

6. **a.** the fraction of all toys that have stars

   ____

   b. the fraction of dolls and cars that do not have stars

   ____

7. **a.** the fraction of dolls that do not have stripes

   ____

   b. the fraction of toy soldiers and cars that have dots

   ____

Macmillan/McGraw-Hill, MATHEMATICS IN ACTION
Grade 4, Chapter 10, Lesson 2, pages 388–389

Name

FINDING GREATER SUMS

On Your Own Pair and Share In a Group

FRACTIONS IN ACTION

Each problem below uses this fraction pattern:

$\frac{\square}{\square} + \frac{\square}{\square}$

Write your answers in the last column. The first problem in each table is done for you.

	Arrange these digits:	To get a sum of:	Your answer:
1.	3 4 5 5	$1\frac{2}{5}$	$\frac{4}{5} + \frac{3}{5}$
2.	2 7 7 8	$1\frac{3}{7}$	
3.	2 3 4 8	1	
4.	2 3 4 6	$1\frac{2}{3}$	
5.	2 3 4 6	$1\frac{1}{3}$	
6.	3 4 8 8	$1\frac{3}{4}$	

	Arrange these digits:	To get two sums of:	Your answer:
7.	2 2 3 3 3 4 4 5	$1\frac{2}{3}$ and $1\frac{3}{4}$	$\frac{2}{3} + \frac{3}{3}$ $\frac{2}{4} + \frac{5}{4}$
8.	3 4 5 6 6 6 8 8	$1\frac{1}{6}$ and $1\frac{3}{8}$	
9.	2 5 5 5 6 7 7 7	$1\frac{4}{5}$ and $1\frac{4}{7}$	

Name

Problem Solving

On Your Own   Pair and Share   In a Group

STRATEGY GRAB BAG

Welcome to Strategy! You and your partner can win the game by answering all of the questions below. You can use any strategy you want to find your answers. If one strategy doesn't work, just try another. The first pair to answer all the questions correctly wins!

Here are some strategies you can use:

- Find a pattern
- Draw a picture
- Guess and test
- Solve a similar problem

1. There is a staircase with 18 steps. You walk halfway up the steps, then down 2 steps, then up 4 steps, then down 7 steps, and then halfway up the remaining steps. What step do you finish on? (1 is the first step, 18 is the last.)

____

2. You are watching Marvin the Magician pull rabbits from a hat. First he pulls 2 rabbits, then he pulls 6 rabbits. Next he pulls 18 rabbits, and then 54 rabbits! How many rabbits do you think he will pull out of the hat next time? Why?

____

____

3. You take a trip to a city 240 miles away. You drive half of the distance in the morning. Then you drive half of the remaining distance before stopping for lunch. Then you drive half of the remaining distance before your car gets a flat tire. How far are you from the city?

____

4. You are building a playhouse. Plastic bricks cost 27¢ each; wood bricks cost 74¢ each, and stone bricks cost $1.44 each. You can use any combination of the bricks to build the playhouse. Can you find a way to spend exactly $100 on bricks for your playhouse?

____

____

____

____

Name

FINDING DIFFERENCES

On Your Own Pair and Share In a Group

FUNNY FRACTIONS

Each subtraction problem has been broken into three parts. Draw lines showing how to connect the problems. The answer to each numbered problem has a letter. Place these letters in the blanks below. Is there something funny about your answer?

1. $\frac{5}{7}$ −	$\frac{1}{2}$ =	$\frac{1}{6}$	H
2. $\frac{11}{12}$ −	$\frac{5}{6}$ =	$\frac{1}{2}$	R
3. $\frac{6}{8}$ −	$\frac{3}{4}$ =	$\frac{3}{7}$	L
4. $\frac{3}{5}$ −	$\frac{1}{8}$ =	$\frac{4}{7}$	T
5. 1 −	$\frac{2}{5}$ =	$\frac{7}{12}$	A
6. $\frac{6}{7}$ −	$\frac{3}{7}$ =	$\frac{3}{8}$	U
7. $\frac{10}{12}$ −	$\frac{3}{8}$ =	$\frac{1}{5}$	G
8. $\frac{5}{8}$ −	$\frac{1}{3}$ =	$\frac{1}{3}$	A
9. $\frac{4}{5}$ −	$\frac{2}{7}$ =	$\frac{1}{12}$	E
10. $\frac{5}{6}$ −	$\frac{1}{5}$ =	$\frac{3}{5}$	I

Where do circus clowns eat?

In the ____ ____ ____ ____ ____ -A- ____ ____ ____ ____ ____!
1 2 3 4 5 6 7 8 9 10

Name

PROBLEM SOLVING

On Your Own Pair and Share In a Group

HOUSE NUMBER PROJECT

You and a group of students are trying to raise money by building house number boards. You can buy metal numbers at the local hardware store and glue them onto a wooden board.

Work together with your group to plan how you will complete this project.

The wooden board you are going to use costs 5¢ per square inch. The numbers are sold in three different sizes and prices. Here are examples for the number 8.

Which size do you think would be best? Measure the one you choose to the nearest $\frac{1}{8}$ inch.

After you have chosen a size, consider the following:

- How much space will you allow for each number?
- Will every number take the same amount of space?
- How much wood will you allow for a border?

1. Work together to make a model of one of the products you will try to sell. You might use stencils to make sure that your numbers are neatly done. Draw your house number on the back of this worksheet.
2. Look at the digits in your house number and the spaces between them. What size board will you need? Draw a board around your numbers.
3. How much did the materials (numbers and board) for your project cost? Use a calculator to help you.

   ____

   ____

4. How much should you charge for your completed house number board if you want to make a profit of $2.00 for your classroom? ______________________________

Name

PERIMETER AND AREA

On Your Own Pair and Share In a Group

FENCE ME IN

Imagine that your class has been given an 18 foot by 18 foot garden. How will you arrange the garden areas? Work with a group to decide how you will place the fences and the path.

Here are some things to consider:

- You want to plant both vegetables and flowers. You will use a fence to separate the flowers from the vegetables.
- The vegetables need at least twice as much space as the flowers.
- You want to place a fence completely around each garden area.
- You want one path 3 feet wide through your garden.

1. What other factors do you need to consider? ____________

____

2. After you have designed the shape of your garden and its path and fences, draw them on the grid below. Label the vegetable section V and the flower section F.

3. Find the perimeter and area of each garden section.

____

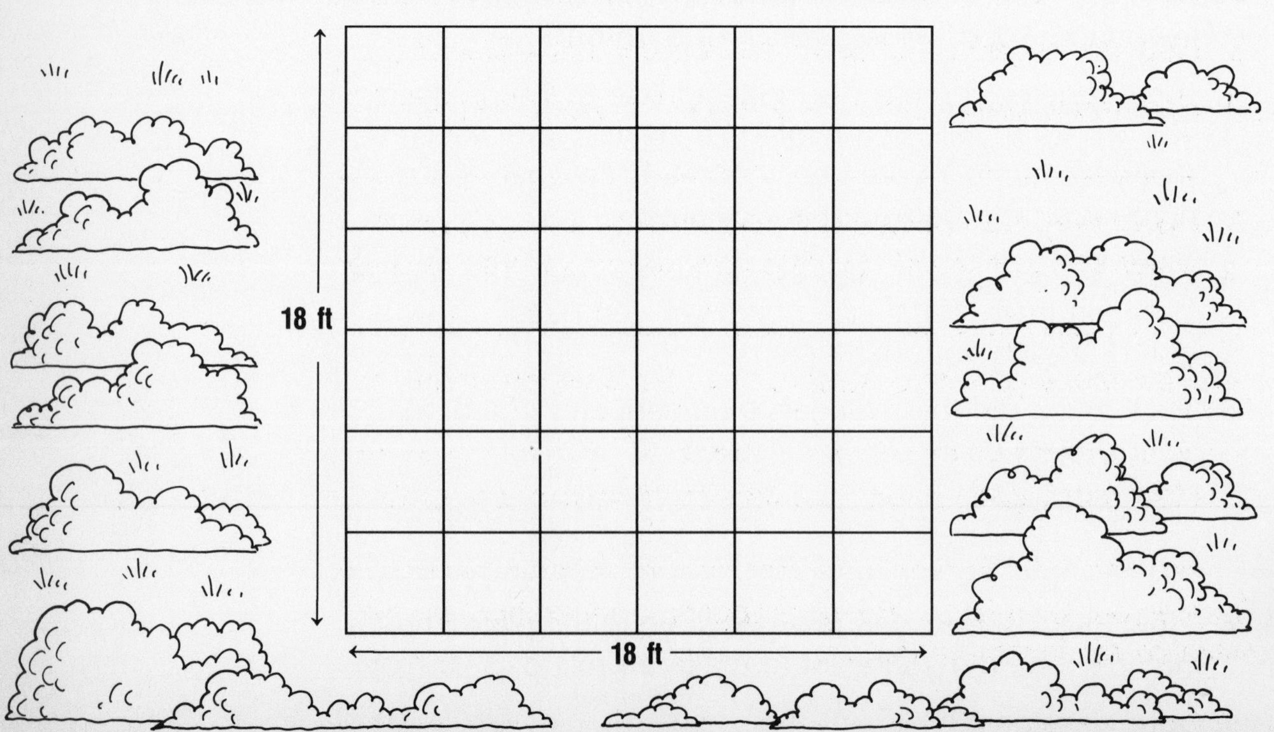

Name

ENRICHMENT-103

CAPACITY

On Your Own   Pair and Share   In a Group

FILL 'ER UP

First complete this set of comparisons.

There are 2 cups in a pint.

There are 2 pints in a quart.
There are _____ cups in a quart.

There are 4 quarts in a gallon.
There are _____ pints in a gallon.
There are _____ cups in a gallon.

Next, work with several friends to find a reasonable estimate for each problem. Use the answers above to help you estimate.

1. How many cups would it take to fill a bucket?

____

2. How many gallons would it take to fill a fish tank? ______
3. How many quarts would it take to fill a bathtub? ________
4. How many pints would it take to fill an egg carton with water? _______________________________________
5. How many pints of water can you drink at one time. ____
6. How many gallons of water do you drink in a week? ____
7. How many quarts would it take to fill a waste basket?

____

8. How many people would it take to drink 100 gallons of water in one minute? Explain how you found your answer.

____

9. How many gallons of water are in a swimming pool?

____

10. How many gallons would it take to fill your classroom?

____

Create your own list of "filling" problems. Have others try to estimate reasonable answers.

____

Name

WEIGHT

FISH SCALES

Put the fish in order from lightest to heaviest. Number them 1 (for lightest) to 14 (for heaviest). Write the letter of each fish in the numbered space in the cartoon below. The letters will complete the "fishy" discussion.

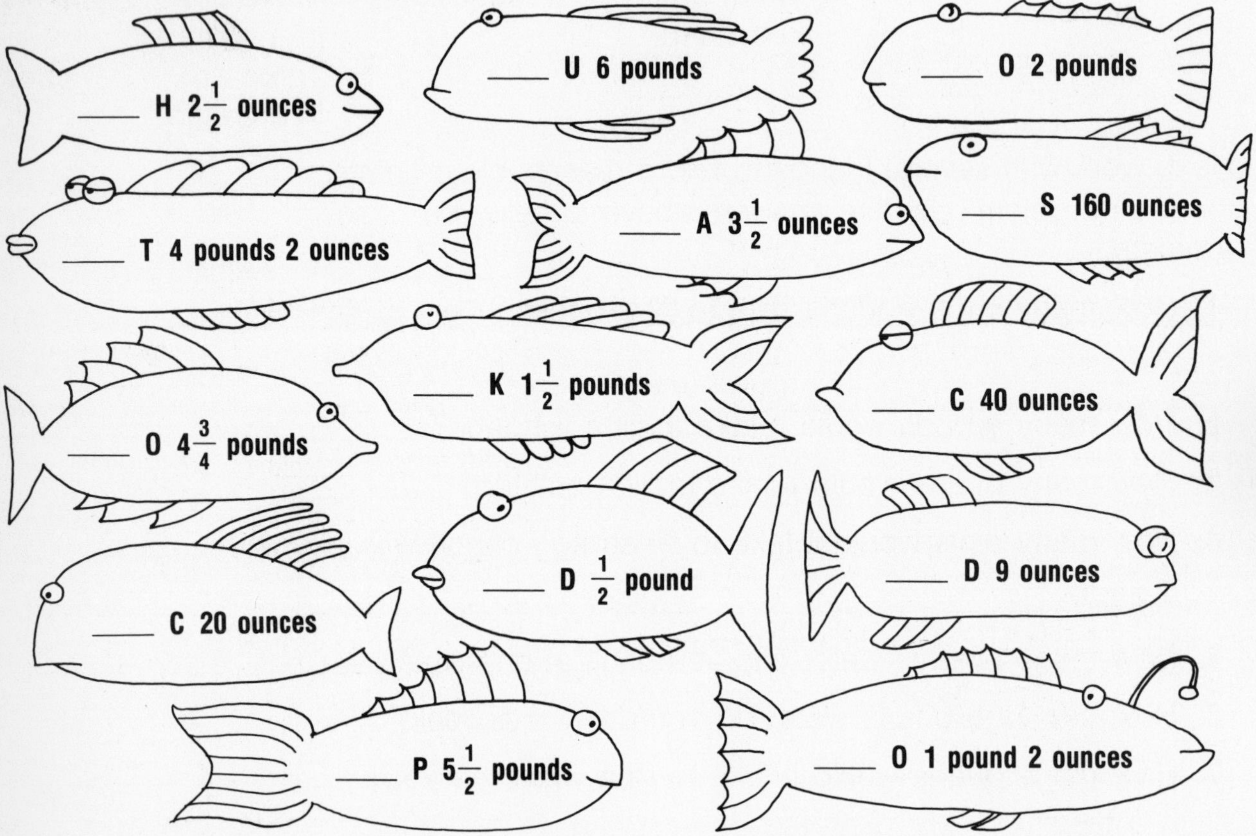

____ H $2\frac{1}{2}$ ounces

____ U 6 pounds

____ O 2 pounds

____ T 4 pounds 2 ounces

____ A $3\frac{1}{2}$ ounces

____ S 160 ounces

____ K $1\frac{1}{2}$ pounds

____ C 40 ounces

____ O $4\frac{3}{4}$ pounds

____ D $\frac{1}{2}$ pound

____ D 9 ounces

____ C 20 ounces

____ P $5\frac{1}{2}$ pounds

____ O 1 pound 2 ounces

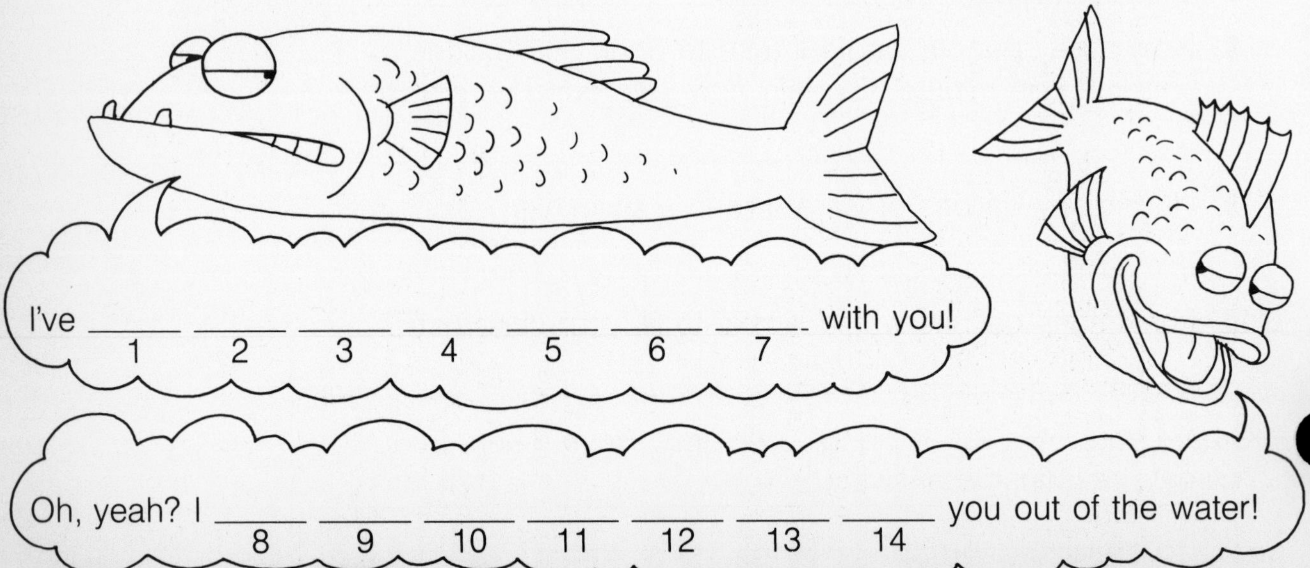

I've ____ ____ ____ ____ ____ ____ ____ with you!
1 2 3 4 5 6 7

Oh, yeah? I ____ ____ ____ ____ ____ ____ ____ you out of the water!
8 9 10 11 12 13 14

Name

Temperature

On Your Own | Pair and Share | In a Group

TEMPERATURE'S RISING

Each of the pictures below suggests a temperature range. On the thermometer next to each picture, draw a band to show a range of possible temperatures. Use an arrow to show temperatures that might be higher (↑) or lower (↓) than those given on the thermometer. Here is an example.

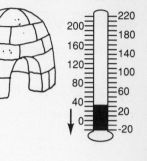

Compare your answers with those of other students. Explain why you think each range is reasonable.

1. 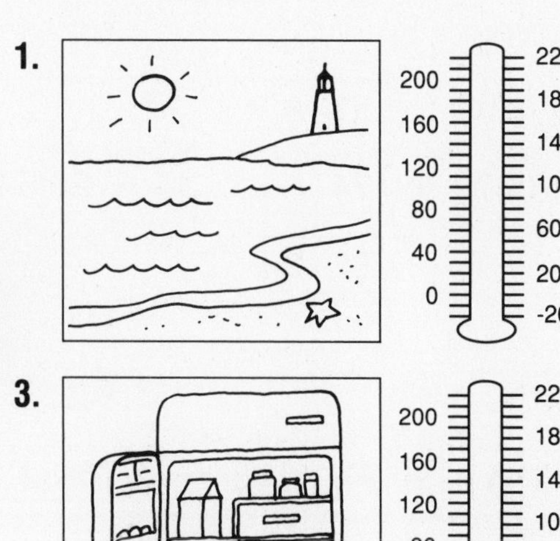

2. 

3. 

4. 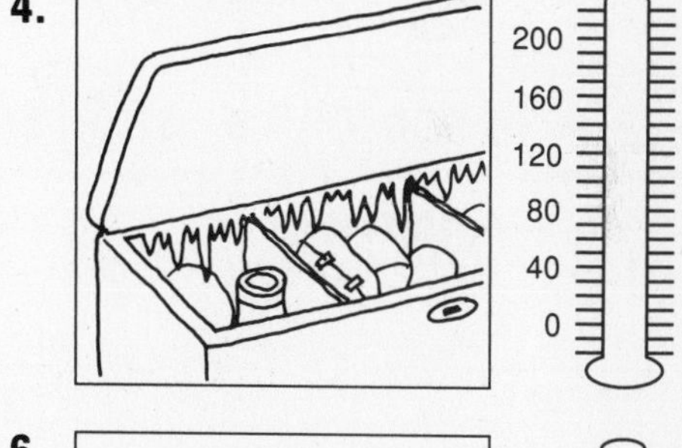

5. 

6. 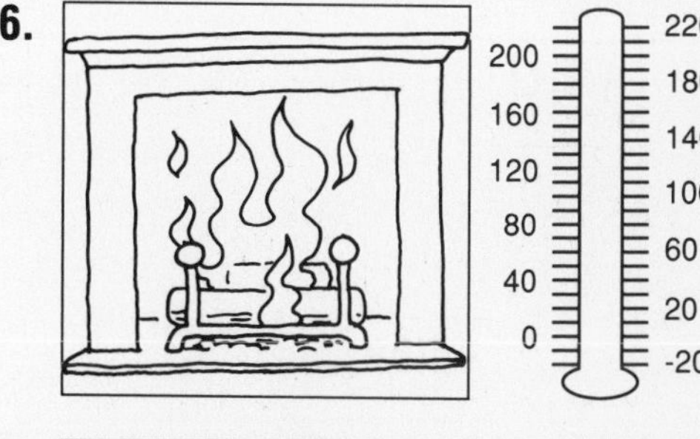

7. 

8. 

Name

TENTHS AND HUNDREDTHS

On Your Own | Pair and Share | In a Group

SQUARE OFF

Use estimation to choose the box that correctly completes each fact. Circle the correct boxes. Then write the letter in the circled box in the riddle answer below.

1. 45 × [23 T / 65 R / 87 Y] = 3,915
2. 66 × [18 M / 29 O / 41 P] = 1,914
3. 31 × [77 U / 87 S / 97 E] = 2,387
4. [92 R / 61 O / 34 C] × 53 = 1,802
5. [14 D / 28 N / 53 A] × 19 = 1,007
6. [51 A / 74 N / 92 D] × 36 = 2,664
7. 23 × 72 = [726 I / 1,656 C / 4,980 K]
8. 61 × 55 = [3,355 O / 4,735 A / 8,665 R]
9. 21 × 88 = [1,848 U / 2,768 L / 5,018 Y]
10. 82 × [71 N / 84 O / 98 T] = 5,822
11. 64 × [32 I / 48 T / 57 S] = 3,072
12. 27 × [63 S / 71 O / 85 P] = 1,917
13. 14 × 92 = [1,288 N / 2,188 E / 3,218 T]
14. 38 × 39 = [1,056 A / 1,482 M / 1,927 N]
15. 88 × 65 = [3,720 D / 4,720 R / 5,720 E]

What did the calculator say to the student?

__ __ __   __ __ __   __ __ __ __ __   __ __   __ __!

1 2 3   4 5 6   7 8 9 10 11   12 13   14 15

Name

Comparing and Ordering Decimals

On Your Own Pair and Share In a Group

MORE NUMBER JUMBLES

Use the digits in the boxes to complete each exercise. Use a calculator to help.

1. 0 2 5 9 ☐☐ × ☐☐ = 4,680
2. 0 1 7 8 ☐☐ × ☐☐ = 5,680
3. 0 3 6 7 ☐☐ × ☐☐ = 4,410
4. 0 2 4 5 ☐☐ × ☐☐ = 2,100
5. 0 3 8 9 ☐☐ × ☐☐ = 2,670
6. 0 4 7 9 ☐☐ × ☐☐ = 3,880
7. 0 2 5 6 ☐☐ × ☐☐ = 3,120
8. 0 6 7 8 ☐☐ × ☐☐ = 6,080
9. 0 1 1 2 2 ☐☐ × ☐☐☐ = 2,240
10. 0 1 5 5 5 ☐☐ × ☐☐☐ = 27,550
11. 0 0 7 7 7 ☐☐ × ☐☐☐ = 53,900
12. 0 4 4 6 6 ☐☐ × ☐☐☐ = 25,840

Name

PROBLEM SOLVING

On Your Own Pair and Share In a Group

TRAIN OF THOUGHT

You and several friends have decided to enter a racetrack contest. The prize goes to the most interesting track for model race cars. The drawings show the sizes you can purchase. You have $15 to spend. How many of each piece of track will you purchase? Write your answer in the blank beneath each piece. Write the total cost of your track in the box at the bottom of the page. What will your train track look like? Work with your group to make a drawing of your final pattern.

Straight pieces:

3 inches: 55¢ each

6 inches: 85¢ each

12 inches: $1.50 each

Curves:

half curve: $1.10

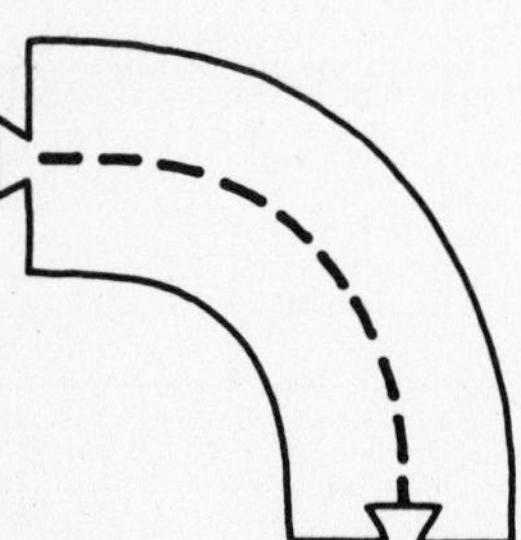

full curve: $2.15

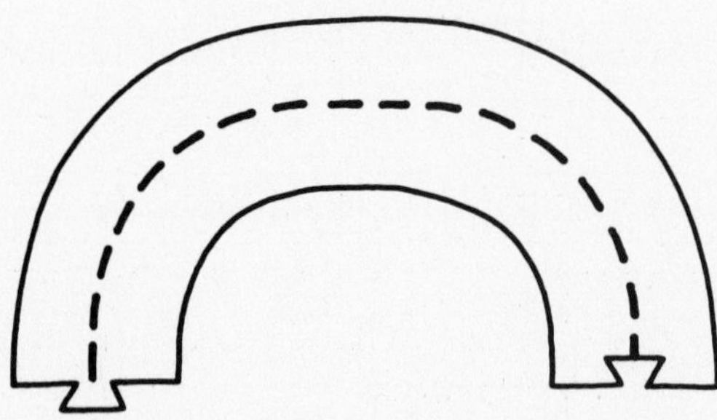

Special shapes:

loop: $3.25

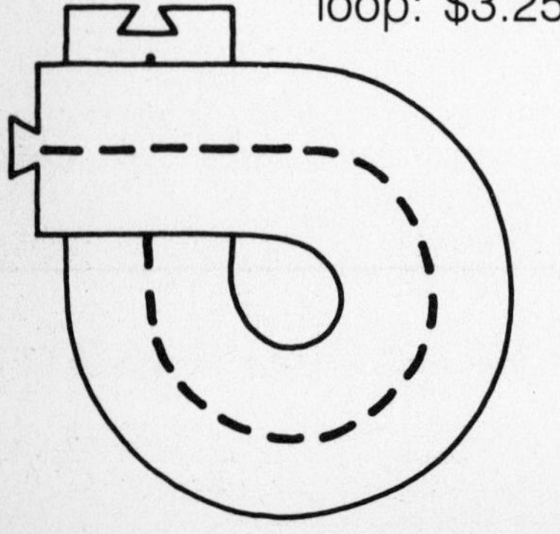

zig-zag, 12 inches: $2.95

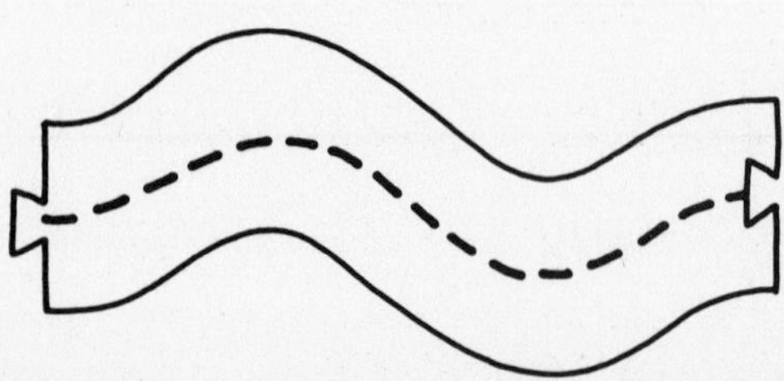

Total cost of our track: $

Name

ESTIMATING DECIMAL SUMS AND DIFFERENCES

On Your Own Pair and Share In a Group

FOUR SCORE

Play this game with a partner.

Part One

Player 1 picks any number in a circle below and writes it in the first box for that round. Player 1 then crosses out the circle. Player 2 picks any number that is not crossed out. Players take turns until each has chosen four numbers. Use estimation to try to pick four numbers that will have a sum close to 15.

Part Two

Players use a calculator to add their numbers. They also find the difference between their sum and 15. The player closest to 15 wins that round. Players go on to the next round.

Round		Numbers				Sum	How close to 15?
1	Player 1						
	Player 2						
2	Player 1						
	Player 2						
3	Player 1						
	Player 2						
4	Player 1						
	Player 2						
5	Player 1						
	Player 2						

4.31 3.38 5.67 1.02 3.56 6.89 8.72 3.54 4.98 2.20

3.10 2.22 7.98 1.15 3.75 3.87 4.96 5.52 4.12 2.78

1.12 8.79 1.82 2.78 4.10 5.22 3.28 4.99 5.14 3.85

3.33 4.44 2.67 3.39 4.29 6.82 7.72 7.21 2.09 0.77

Name

ENRICHMENT-110

ADDING DECIMALS

On Your Own Pair and Share In a Group

IT'S A FACT

Work with a partner. Each set of numbers can be used to make addition facts. Each number in a set should be used exactly once. Can you find all the facts? The first fact has been done for you. When you are finished, use a calculator to check your work.

~~8.21~~	5.74	13.73
7.78	2.28	~~4.75~~
5.50	7.99	~~12.96~~

4.75 + 8.21 = 12.96
_____ + _____ = _____
_____ + _____ = _____

3.54	1.11	2.21
5.75	14.43	8.55
5.88	8.71	9.82

_____ + _____ = _____
_____ + _____ = _____
_____ + _____ = _____

3.68	6.66	9.98
5.01	8.11	0.89
2.22	8.69	15.85
9.09	4.44	7.74

_____ + _____ = _____
_____ + _____ = _____
_____ + _____ = _____
_____ + _____ = _____

The next set is tricky, so be careful.

7.07	8.66	18.40
8.48	8.08	4.24
1.01	3.58	5.25
13.35	9.74	4.24
6.11	9.77	11.36

_____ + _____ = _____
_____ + _____ = _____
_____ + _____ = _____
_____ + _____ = _____
_____ + _____ = _____

Name

SUBTRACTING DECIMALS

On Your Own Pair and Share In a Group

DIFFERENT TRIANGLES

Work with a partner or small group to solve these puzzles. The numbers in the top row of each triangle tell you how to complete the triangle. Each circle shows the difference between the two numbers directly above it. Look at the first triangle. The difference between 5.43 and 2.21 is 3.22.

Can you finish every triangle? Sometimes there is more than one way. Compare your work with another group. Did you get the same numbers?

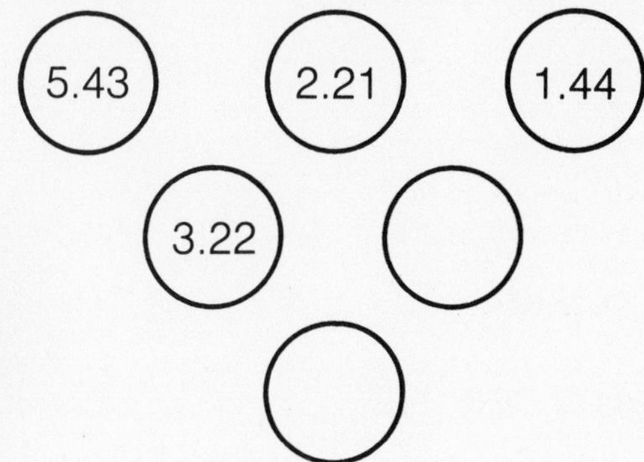

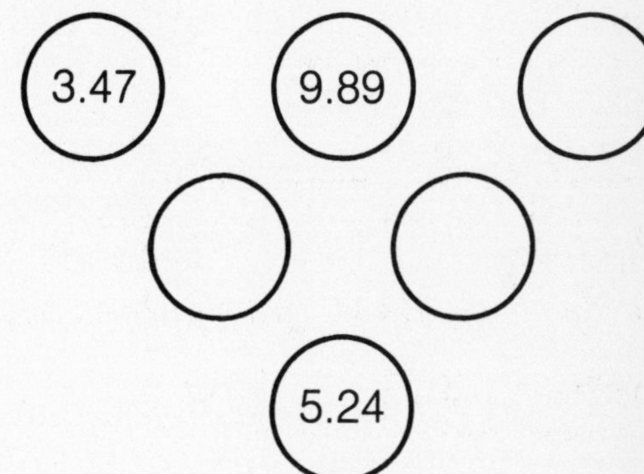

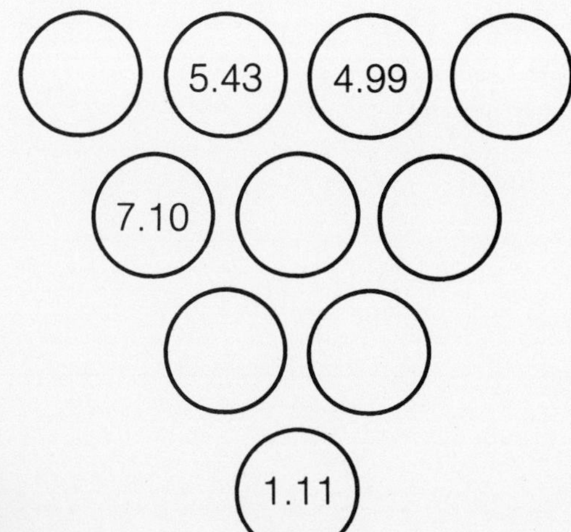

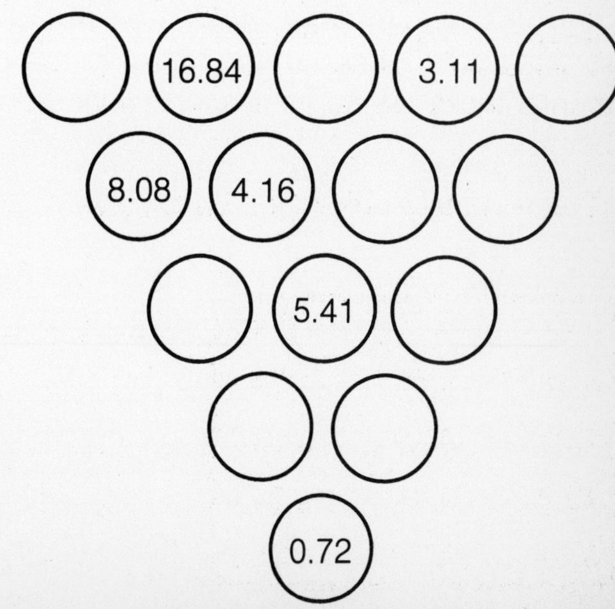

Name ______________________________

Problem Solving

On Your Own Pair and Share In a Group

WHAT TIME IS IT?

Do you know how long a minute is? Try this experiment with a partner to find out.

You will need a watch or a clock with a second hand.

For the first experiment, you will try to guess when ten seconds have passed. First close your eyes. Your partner will tell you when to start by saying "Go." When you think ten seconds have passed, say "Stop." Your partner will tell you and write down how much time actually passed. After you have tried three times, switch roles with your partner.

Goal: Ten Seconds
First Try: ____________ seconds
Second Try: ____________ seconds
Third Try: ____________ seconds
Did your guesses grow more accurate or less accurate?

Next, find out how close you can come to estimating one minute. Try this experiment twice.

Goal: One Minute
First Try: ____________ seconds
Second Try: ____________ seconds

How close did you get? Did you guess too short or too long a time? Compare your results with the rest of your class. Did students who guessed very close to the correct time use any mental tricks? Write your conclusions about this experiment below.

____

____

____

____

____

____

____

____

Name

PROBABILITY

CLEO'S CLUTTERED CLOSET

This is Cleo's closet. Look carefully at the picture. Then answer the questions below.

Cleo's closet contains:
4 shirts
3 pairs of pants
5 hats
1 scarf
2 purses
3 pairs of shoes

Cleo dresses in a hurry. She usually picks clothes from her closet without looking.

1. Cleo picks a shirt. What are the chances she will pick the white shirt? __________

2. Next she picks a pair of pants. What are the chances that she will pick the black pants? __________

3. If she picks a hat, what are the chances she will pick the flowered one? __________

4. What are the chances that she will pick the black purse? __________

5. If Cleo picks two shoes from her closet, what are the chances that she will get a matching pair? __________

6. Now suppose that Cleo picks a shirt and a pair of pants. What are the chances that they will match? (*Hint:* draw a tree diagram to help you.) __________

7. Now suppose that Cleo picks a shirt, a pair of pants, and a hat. What are the chances that all three items will match? __________

Name

PREDICTION

On Your Own Pair and Share In a Group

TAILSPIN

Play this game with a partner. You will need three coins and two markers to play.

Each player places a marker on START. When it is your turn, guess what your toss will be, and then toss the three coins. Move your marker the number of spaces shown below. If your guess was correct, double the number of spaces your marker moves. The first player to reach FINISH wins. Can you find a way to improve your chances of winning?

If you toss . . .	**move . . .**
3 heads	3 spaces forward
2 heads and 1 tail	2 spaces forward
1 head and 2 tails	1 space forward
3 tails	1 space backward

Note: If you ever fall off the gameboard, go back to START.

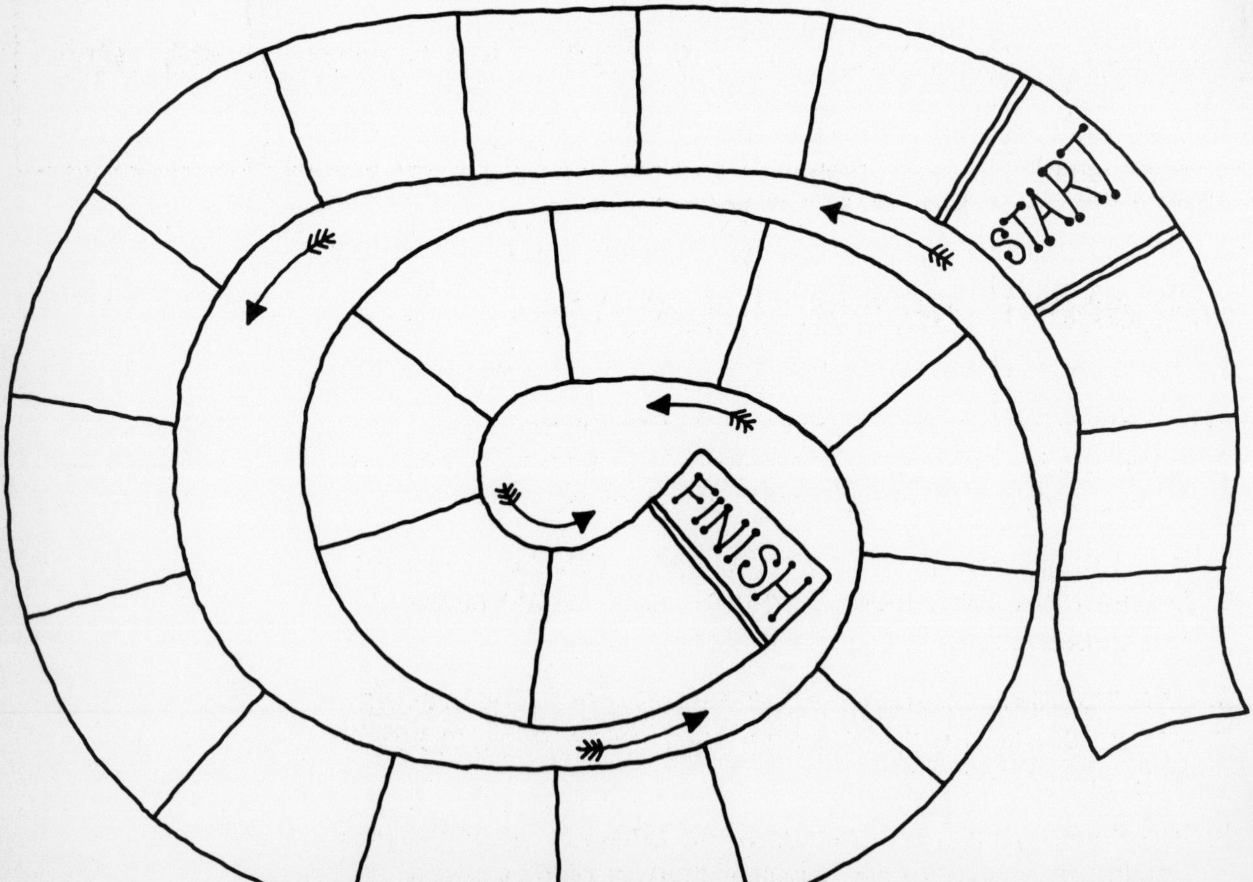

START

FINISH

Name

MENTAL MATH: MULTIPLY 10s; 100s; 1,000s

MULTIPLICATION RACE

A. This is a game for 2 or more players.

30	40	50	60	70
80	300	400	500	600
700	800	2,400	16,000	25,000
42,000	56,000	180,000		

1. Each player cuts out a set of 18 cards with the numbers shown above. All players start at the same time.
2. Each player works as quickly as he or she can to make 6 correct multiplication sentences using all the cards in the deck exactly once.
3. The first player to finish is the winner. The other players should check the multiplication sentences to make sure they are correct.

B. Work with your friends to create a different set of playing cards. Then exchange cards with another group. Try playing each other's games.

Name

ESTIMATING PRODUCTS

On Your Own Pair and Share In a Group

FAMILY AFFAIR

What did the baby volcano say to its mother?

To find the answer, complete each multiplication.
Write the letter for each product in the spaces below.

20 × 36 Y _______	47 × 30 T _______	60 × 25 O _______	20 × 74 S _______
65 × 70 L _______	56 × 40 D _______	22 × 30 I _______	18 × 80 L _______
112 × 40 A _______	70 × 210 M _______	160 × 30 L _______	20 × 433 E _______
50 × 139 A _______	30 × 462 O _______	40 × 236 V _______	60 × 385 U _______

Answer:

_____ _____   _____ _____ _____   _____ _____ _____ _____ _____
2,240 1,500   720 13,860 23,100   1,480 1,410 660 4,800 1,440

_____ _____ _____ _____   _____ _____ ?
4,550 6,950 9,440 4,480   14,700 8,660

Name

MULTIPLYING BY MULTIPLES OF TEN

TARGET PRACTICE

Work with a partner. Decide which two numbers on each target have a product closest to the given score. Ring the numbers you choose.

1\.

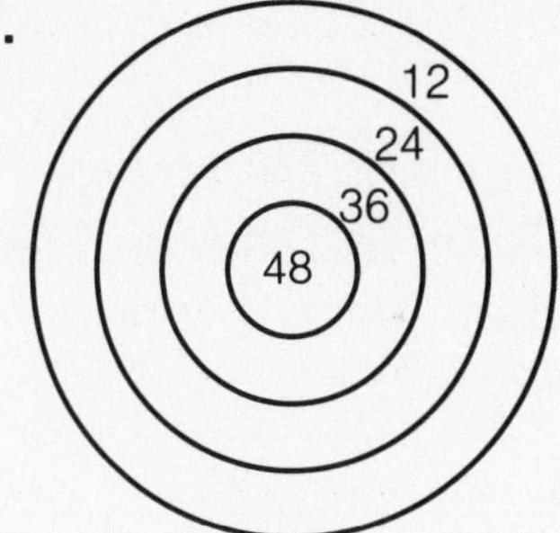

Score 600

2\.

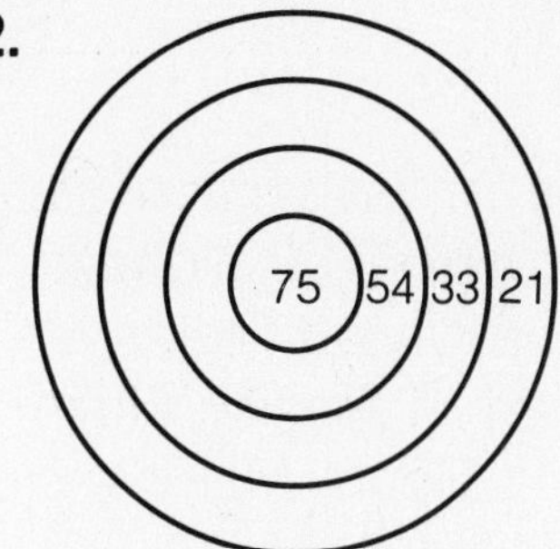

Score 2,500

3\.

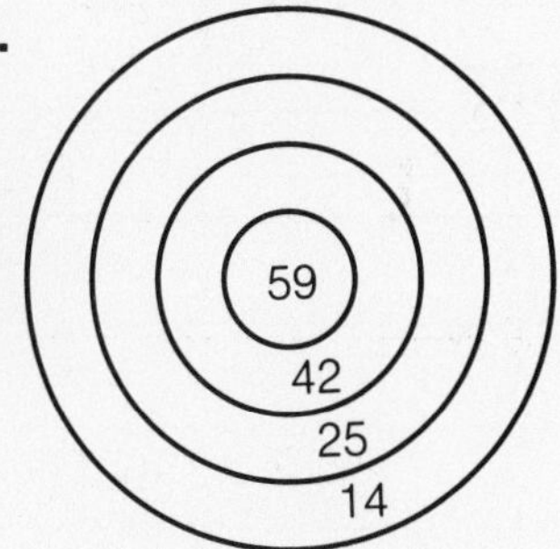

Score 1,000

4\.

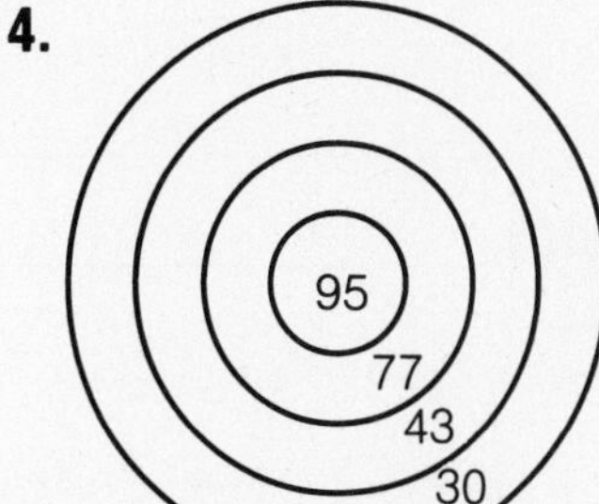

Score 3,200

5\.

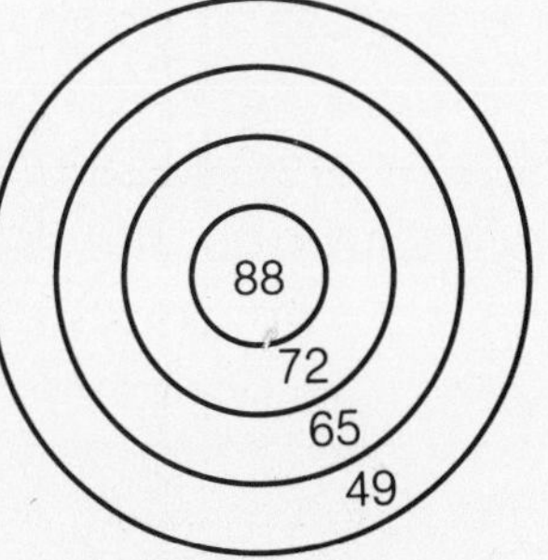

Score 6,300

6\.

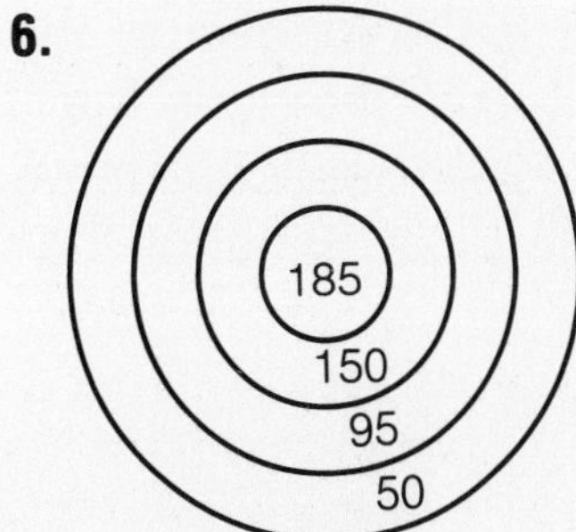

Score 20,000

7\.

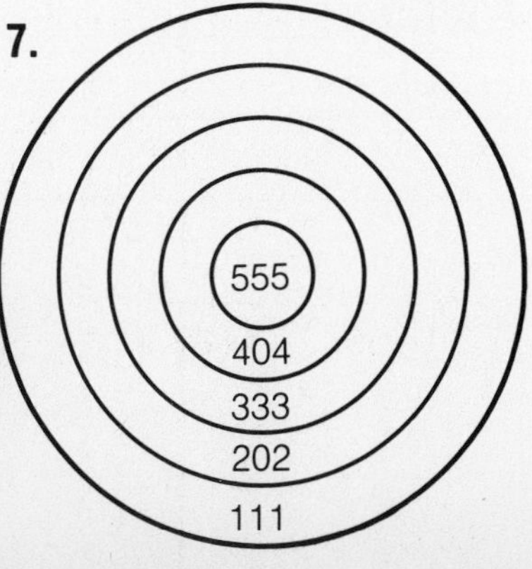

Score 40,000

8\.

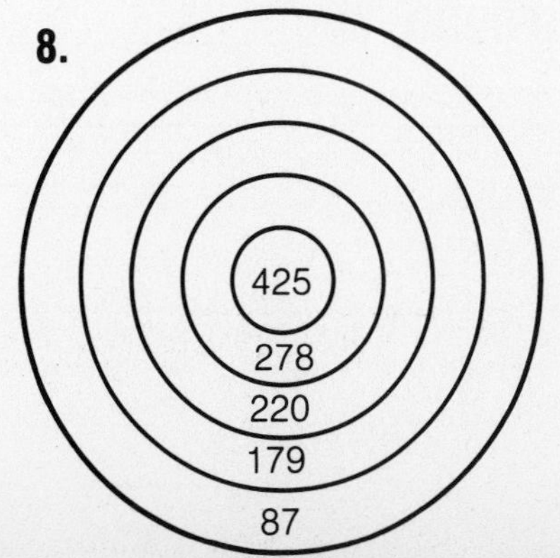

Score 24,000

Macmillan/McGraw-Hill, MATHEMATICS IN ACTION
Grade 4, Chapter 12, Lesson 3, pages 478-479

Name

PROBLEM SOLVING

On Your Own | Pair and Share | In a Group

YOU FIND OUT

Each problem below is missing a fact needed to solve it. Work with a partner to decide what fact is missing. Then use a reference book to find the fact. Solve the problem using the fact you found.

1. Mount Rainier in Washington State is 14,410 feet high. The highest mountain in the United States is Mount McKinley in Alaska. How much higher is Mount McKinley than Mount Rainier?

   MISSING FACT ____________________

   FACT YOU FOUND ____________________

   ANSWER ____________________

2. The Snake River is in Wyoming. The Wabash River in Ohio is 529 miles long. Which river is longer? How much longer?

   MISSING FACT ____________________

   FACT YOU FOUND ____________________

   ANSWER ____________________

3. Lake Superior is the longest of the Great Lakes. Lake Ontario is the shortest. It is 193 miles long. How much longer is Lake Superior than Lake Ontario?

   MISSING FACT ____________________

   FACT YOU FOUND ____________________

   ANSWER ____________________

4. Illinois became a state in 1818. Nebraska became a state many years later. How many years after Illinois did Nebraska become a state?

   MISSING FACT ____________________

   FACT YOU FOUND ____________________

   ANSWER ____________________

Name

MULTIPLYING 2-DIGIT NUMBERS

On Your Own Pair and Share In a Group

CLIMB THE LADDER

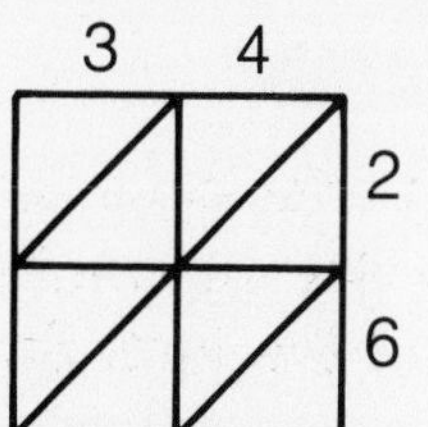

This is an old way of multiplying. You use a square like the one shown at the right.

Suppose you want to find the product of 34 × 26.

Write the first factor (34) across the top and the second factor (26) down the right side.

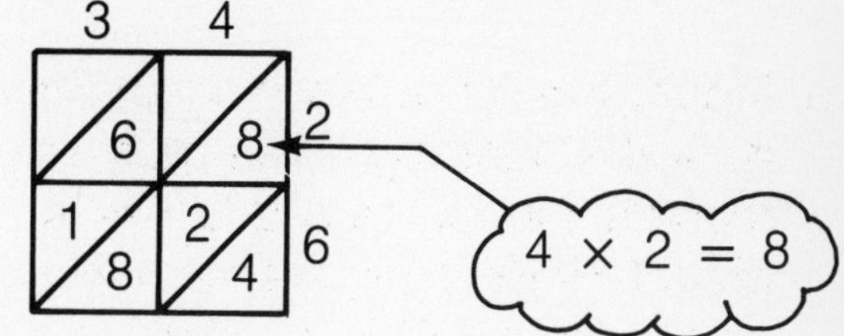

Fill in the spaces by multiplying each digit of one factor by each digit of the other factor.

Add along the diagonals, starting at the lower right corner. Regroup if necessary.

The product is 884.

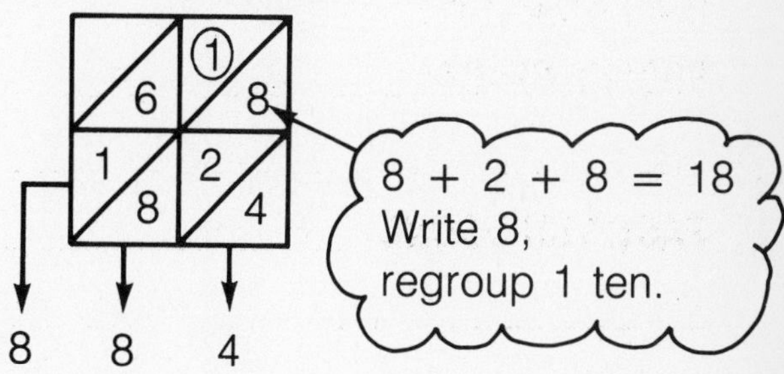

Find each product using the method above. Check each answer using regular multiplication.

1. 19 × 35

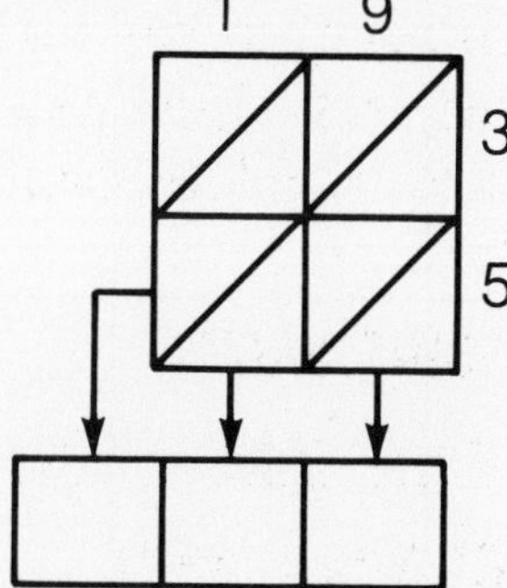

2. 27 × 38

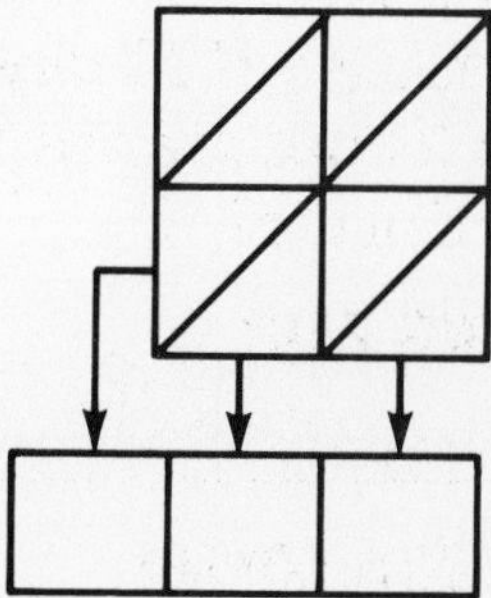

3. 42 × 53

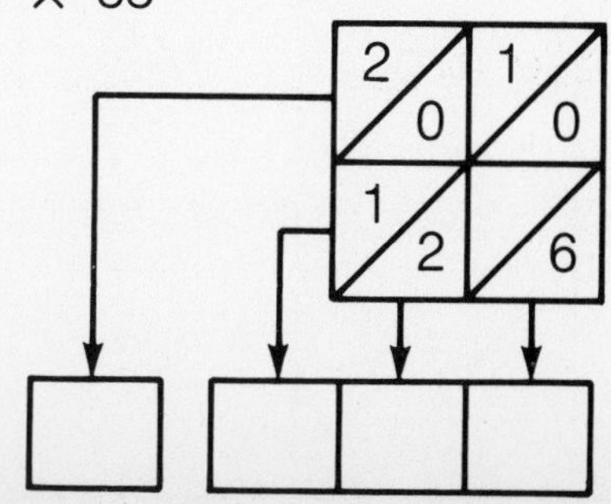

4. 39 × 64

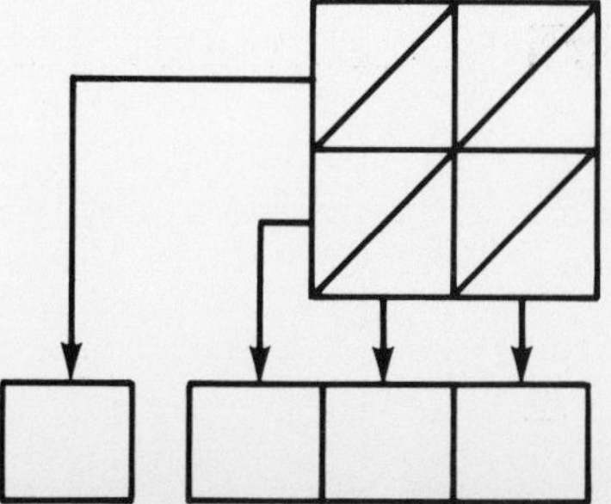

MACMILLAN/McGRAW-HILL

Name

MORE MULTIPLYING 2-DIGIT NUMBERS

A-MAZING MULTIPLICATION

Find a path through the maze. Multiply each factor in the bowl by each factor on the spoon. Cross out each product that you find. Then draw a path through the crossed-out boxes to get from START to FINISH.

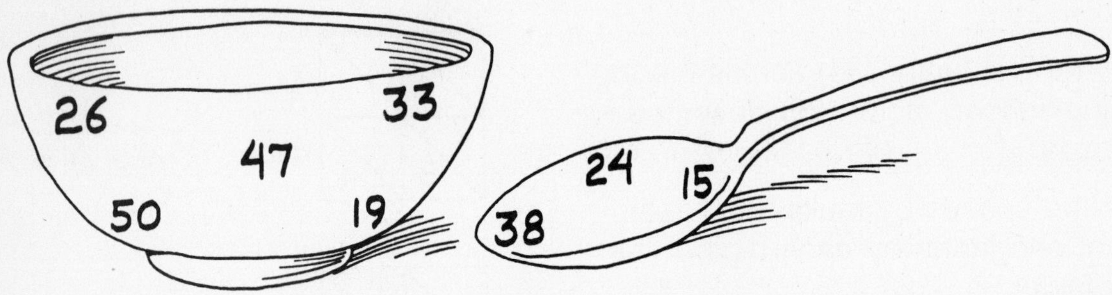

FINISH

1,355	2,400	1,233	456	390	705
1,880	1,456	943	750	1,254	1,298
824	285	1,786	624	722	1,156
1,050	792	1,900	348	742	1,078
595	1,300	988	782	970	595
1,200	495	1,128	1,558	651	280

START

Name

MULTIPLYING 3-DIGIT NUMBERS

On Your Own Pair and Share In a Group

WAGES AND HOURS

Here is a game for 2 to 4 players.

- Make the two spinners shown below. (You can cut them out and glue them on cardboard. Use a paper clip for each pointer.)
- Each player takes a turn spinning both spinners. The player then multiplies the hourly wage by the number of hours to find the total earnings for that turn.
- The other players check the multiplication to be sure it is correct. (Calculators may be used only for checking.) A player who multiplies incorrectly receives no earnings for that turn.
- The players record the amounts they earn for each turn on individual score sheets.
- After 5 rounds of play, each player calculates his or her total earnings for the game. (Calculators may be used.) The player who has earned the most money is the winner.

Here is part of a score sheet for a player named Laurie.

Player: Laurie		
Hours	Hourly Wage	Earnings
12 25	\$2.60 \$1.75	12 × \$2.60 = \$31.20 25 × \$1.75 = \$43.75

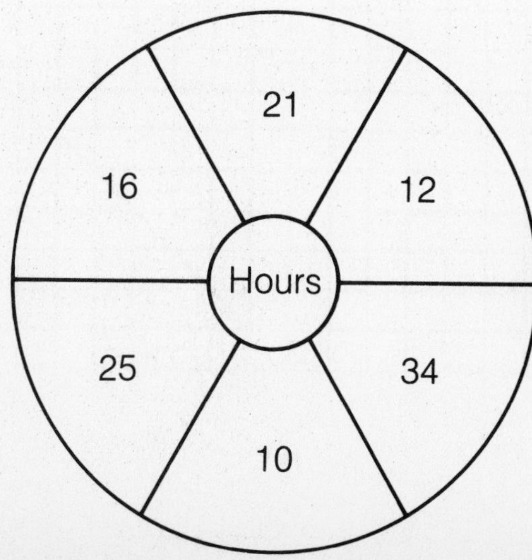

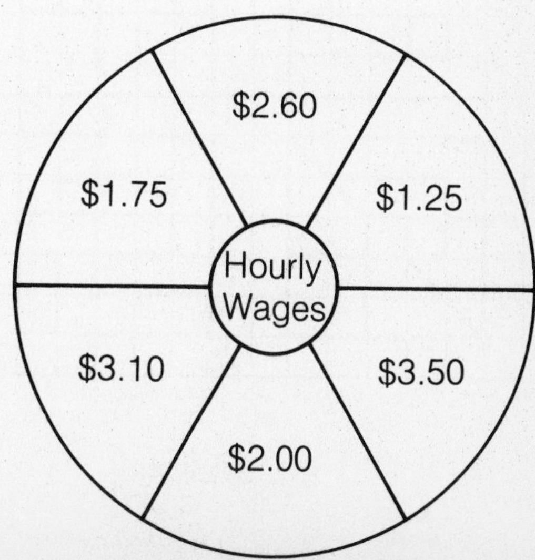

Name

MENTAL MATH: DIVIDE 10s; 100s; 1,000s

LOOK BOTH WAYS

1. Ring two that are exactly alike and in the same position.

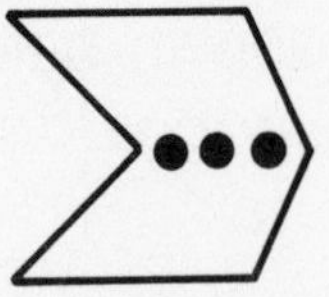
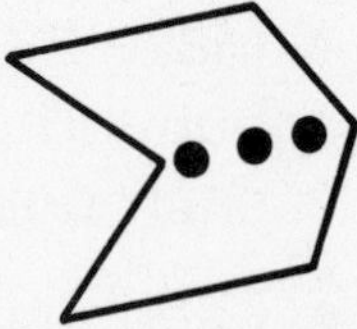

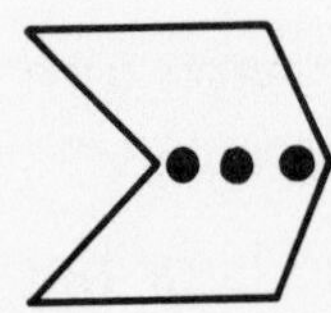
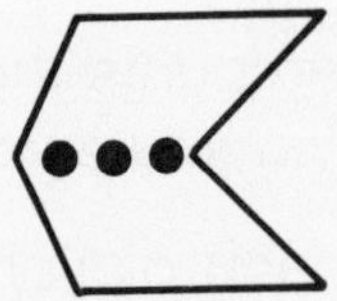

2. Ring the puzzles that do *not* have two or more pieces that are the same. The pieces may be in different positions.

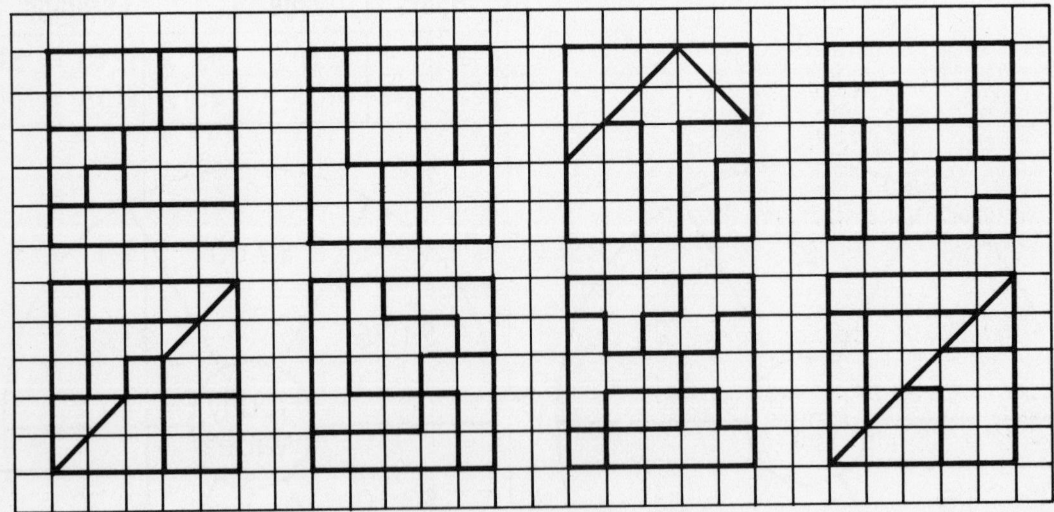

MACMILLAN/McGRAW-HILL

Name

DIVIDING BY MULTIPLES OF TEN

On Your Own   Pair and Share   In a Group

MODERN MACHINERY

A. The machines below have been given the following instructions:

	Example
INPUT A NUMBER	INPUT 65
DIVIDE BY 20	65 ÷ 20 = 3 R5
MULTIPLY THE REMAINDER BY 40	5 × 40 = 200
DIVIDE BY 10	200 ÷ 10 = 20
OUTPUT THE RESULT	OUTPUT 20

Give the output for each machine.

1. 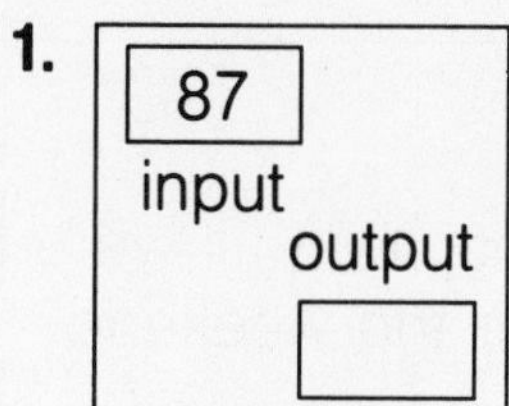

2. 146 input output

3. 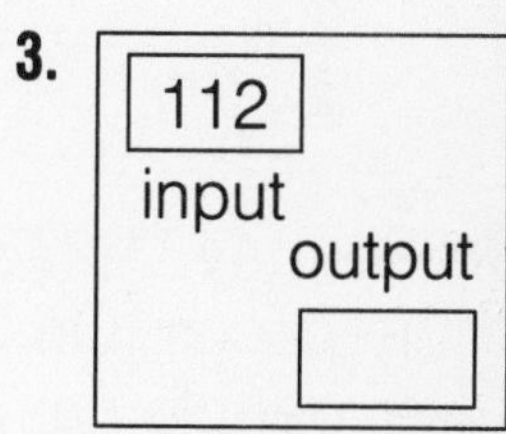

4. 188 input output

5. 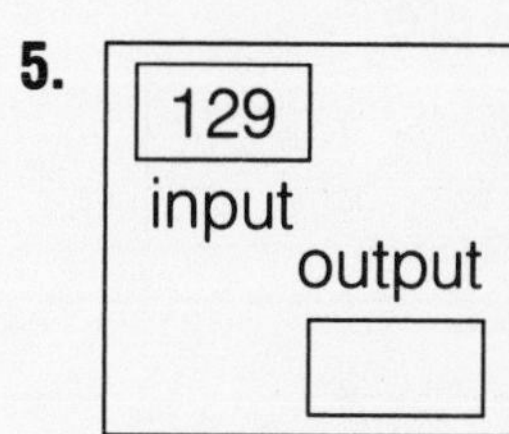

6. 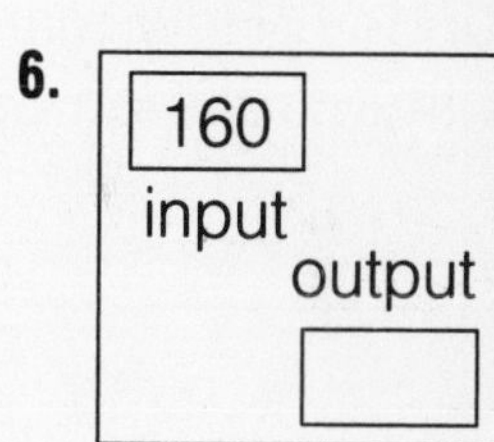

B. The machines were given new instructions.

INPUT A NUMBER
DIVIDE BY 30
MULTIPLY THE REMAINDER
BY 50
DIVIDE BY 100
OUTPUT THE RESULT

Ring the machines that are not working properly.
Write the correct output.

7. 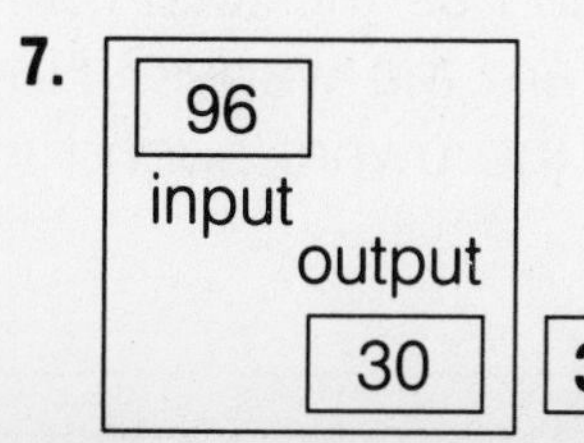

8. 158 input output 4

9. 2 244 input output 0

Name

PROBLEM SOLVING

On Your Own Pair and Share In a Group

DON'T DELAY, RELAY

In each set, use your answer from Problem A to solve Problem B.

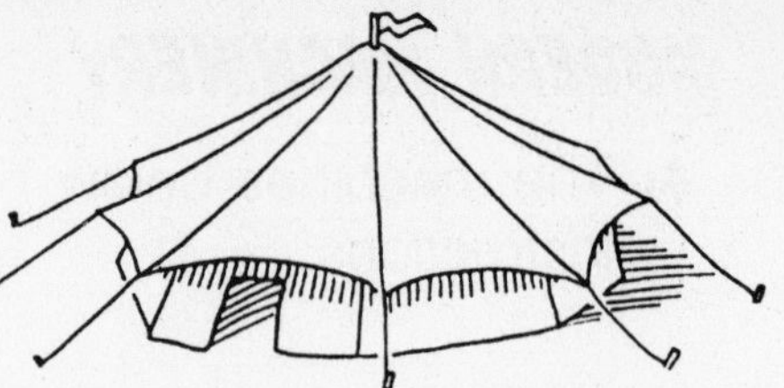

Set 1

A. Last year, a ticket to the circus cost \$4.75. This year, a ticket costs \$.75 more. How much does a ticket cost this year?

____

B. Neil bought 7 tickets to the circus this year. How much money did he spend for tickets?

____

Set 2

A. On Sunday, 1,238 people came to the circus. On Saturday, 166 fewer people came than on Sunday. How many people were at the circus on Saturday?

____

B. How many people in all were at the circus over the weekend?

____

Set 3

A. There are 32 rows of seats in the circus tent. Each row has 26 seats. How many seats are in the tent?

____

B. A circus program is placed on each seat in the tent. There are 80 programs in a bundle. How many bundles will have to be opened?

____

Set 4

A. The circus is in town for 28 days. The circus owner pays \$195 a day to rent the circus grounds. How much rent will the owner pay in all?

____

B. The performers' total wages are twice as much as the total rent. How much are the wages? How much does the owner spend in all?

____

Name

ENRICHMENT-2

THOUSANDS

On Your Own · Pair and Share · In a Group

THE GREATEST GAME

Form two teams. Cut out the markers at the bottom of this page, turn them face down, and mix them up. To play, one person in each team turns one marker over. Another person writes that digit in any one of the boxes for Round 1. Repeat this step using the remaining markers until you have completed the number. Together, look at the digits your team picked and write the greatest possible number you can make using these digits. Turn the markers face down and repeat the process for rounds 2, 3, and 4.

Score 3 points if your team's picked number in each round is the greatest possible number.
Score 1 point if your team's picked number is the second greatest possible number. Count the points to find your total score. **Answers will vary**

Team	Round	Number Picked	Greatest Possible Number	Score
1	1	☐ ☐ ☐ ☐		
	2	☐ ☐ ☐ ☐		
	3	☐ ☐ ☐ ☐		
	4	☐ ☐ ☐ ☐		
			Total	

Team	Round	Number Picked	Greatest Possible Number	Score
2	1	☐ ☐ ☐ ☐		
	2	☐ ☐ ☐ ☐		
	3	☐ ☐ ☐ ☐		
	4	☐ ☐ ☐ ☐		
			Total	

1 2 3 4 5 6 7 8 9

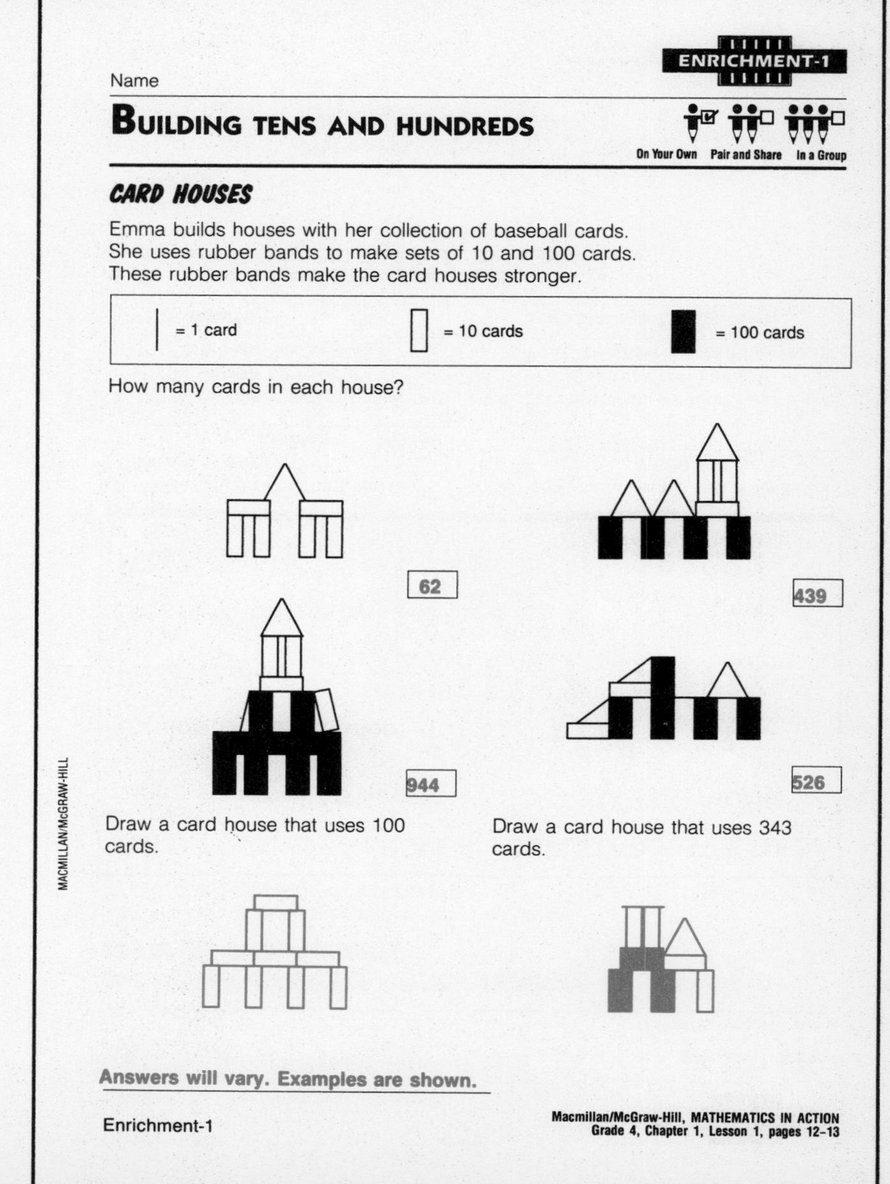

Name

ENRICHMENT-1

BUILDING TENS AND HUNDREDS

On Your Own · Pair and Share · In a Group

CARD HOUSES

Emma builds houses with her collection of baseball cards.
She uses rubber bands to make sets of 10 and 100 cards.
These rubber bands make the card houses stronger.

= 1 card   = 10 cards   = 100 cards

How many cards in each house?

62

439

944

526

Draw a card house that uses 100 cards.

Draw a card house that uses 343 cards.

Answers will vary. Examples are shown.

ENRICHMENT-4

Name

Problem Solving

On Your Own · Pair and Share · In a Group

SPELLING BY NUMBERS

The words in the list are hidden horizontally, vertically, or diagonally in the puzzle below. But they aren't spelled the same way. Part of each word has been replaced with a number that sounds the same. For example, TUESDAY appears in the puzzle as 2SDAY. Write the new spelling of each word with your partner and circle it in the puzzle. The first one has been done for you.

canine	CA9	once	1CE
cartoon	CAR2N	slate	SL8
classics	CLA6	stewed	S2D
donate	DON8	straight	STR8
everyone	EVERY1	stupid	S2PID
force	4CE	tender	10DER
forgotten	4GO10	Tuesday	2SDAY
fork	4K	tutu	22
great	GR8	weighty	W80
inflate	INFL8	wonderful	1DERFUL

```
2 S D A Y 2 N 1 C A 9
W N S O 4 K S L A D E
P D 2 2 U G A 4 R O V
D 4 P 4 S 6 O 8 2 N E
6 T I C T W S 1 N 8 R
1 O D E R W L 7 O R Y
C 4 G R 8 2 8 S 2 D 1
E I N F L 8 1 O 4 C 2
2 S D 1 D E R F U L 8
```

MACMILLAN/McGRAW-HILL

ENRICHMENT-3

Name

Millions

On Your Own · Pair and Share · In a Group

ONE PICTURE IS WORTH A HUNDRED THOUSAND WORDS (OR EVEN A MILLION!)

Robby is preparing a social studies report on Europe. He draws a chart to compare populations.

POPULATION OF EUROPE'S FOUR LARGEST CITIES

(large figure) = 1 million people (small figure) = 100,000 people

London, United Kingdom

Paris, France

Essen, W. Germany

Milan, Italy

1. Which city on the chart has the largest population? **London**

2. How many people live in Essen? **7,600,000**

3. Do more than 9 million people live in Paris? How can you tell? **No. There are fewer than 9 large figures.**

4. Do more than 4 million people live in Milan? How can you tell? **Yes. There are 6 small figures in addition to 4 large ones.**

5. Manchester is Europe's 5th largest city. It has a population of 4,100,000. How would Robby show this on his chart? **4 large figures, one small one**

MACMILLAN/McGRAW-HILL

MACMILLAN/McGRAW-HILL

Name

ENRICHMENT-6

MAKING CHANGE

On Your Own Pair and Share In a Group

TAKE-AWAY

Each player starts with 2 quarters, 2 dimes, 2 nickels, and 2 pennies.

Part 1

Players take turns placing one coin in each box until all boxes are filled. Then you flip a coin to see who begins Part Two.

Part 2

Players take turns removing coins. Each turn, you can remove only one type of coin. You can remove coins from any one row or column on the board.

For example, you might remove 2 nickels from the top row. Or you might remove 3 pennies from the right column. You can always remove at least one coin.

The player with the greatest amount of money at the end of the game is the winner.

Answer these questions after you have played the game several times.

1. Which coins are usually taken away first? last?
   Why? **Quarters; pennies; the most valuable coins are taken first.**
2. Why is it important to play carefully in Part One of this game? **Players need to be careful about placing similar coins in rows or columns.**
3. Can you think of any strategies that help you win? **Answers will vary. Usually take higher value coins before lower. Place coins so that matching coins are not next to each other.**

Name

ENRICHMENT-5

COUNTING MONEY

On Your Own Pair and Share In a Group

JAN, STAN, FRAN, AND WILBUR

Jan, Stan, Fran, and Wilbur each have the same amount of money. Work with your group to find out which coins each person has.

I have 9 coins.
I have 5 coins.
I have 3 coins.
I have only 1 coin and it's not a silver dollar.
JAN
STAN
FRAN
WILBUR

Jan has: **4 nickels**, **5 pennies**

Stan has: **5 nickels**

Fran has: **2 dimes**, **1 nickel**

Wilbur has: **1 quarter**

Jan, Stan, Fran, and Wilbur each have a different coin.

My coin is worth two of Fran's.
My coin is worth more than anyone else's coin.
If I had 4 more of my coins, I'd have as much as Stan.
And if I had 4 more of *my* coins, I'd have as much as Fran.
JAN
STAN
FRAN
WILBUR

I have **10** ¢. I have **25** ¢. I have **5** ¢. I have **1** ¢.

WILBUR
Would you rather have a quart of pennies or a pint of quarters? Why?

A pint of quarters would be worth more.

ENRICHMENT-8

Name

ROUNDING NUMBERS

On Your Own Pair and Share In a Group

A SHOCKING SITUATION

The numbers at the left have been rounded. You are given the place to which each number was rounded. Find the original number in the list at the right. Write the letter of the original number next to the rounded number. When you are done, you will have the answer to the riddle.

What did they call Adam after he put his finger in an electric socket?

T	1,900 (nearest 10)
H	$25.50 (nearest $.10)
E	2,000 (nearest 1,000)
T	$15.00 (nearest $1.00)
O	$14.40 (nearest $.10)
A	40 (nearest 10)
S	768,200 (nearest 100)
T	400 (nearest 100)
O	620 (nearest 10)
F	2,300,200 (nearest 100)
T	2,700 (nearest 10)
H	500 (nearest 10)
E	3,400 (nearest 100)
T	$12.00 (nearest $1.00)
O	$14.00 (nearest $.10)
W	3,000 (nearest 1,000)
N	56,000 (nearest 1,000)

T. $14.70
O. $14.42
T. 1,897
O. 616
T. $12.35
T. 2,707
I. $26.50
H. $24.46
H. 2,720
T. 377
I. 629
A. 37
G. $12.90
A. $14.21
R. 768,290
E. 3,372
H. 498
E. 2,438
N. 2,300,121
W. 2,600
S. 768,220
N. 55,800
O. $13.96
Y. 56,800
F. 2,300,243

Macmillan/McGraw-Hill, MATHEMATICS IN ACTION
Grade 4, Chapter 1, Lesson 10, pages 30-31

ENRICHMENT-7

Name

COMPARING AND ORDERING NUMBERS

On Your Own Pair and Share In a Group

THE SCALE OF THINGS

Look at the value that each letter represents. Order the letters from least to greatest values in the boxes below.

I	H	E	J	C	K	F	D	B	G	A

A. Distance from Earth to Saturn: 887,140,000 miles

B. Number of words in the Encyclopedia Britannica: 44,000,000 words

C. Diameter of Jupiter: 88,846 miles

D. Highest price paid for a diamond: 4,580,000 dollars

E. Weight of the largest ice cream sundae: 33,616 pounds

F. Area of the United States: 3,540,939 square miles

G. Average number of people in the United States watching TV during prime time: 94,900,000 people

H. Greatest speed of the fastest airplane: 2,193 mph

I. Greatest speed of the fastest animal (the peregrine falcon): 217 mph

J. Largest number of pieces in a jigsaw puzzle: 61,752 pieces

K. Amount of food eaten by a wild elephant in one year: 255,500 pounds

Circle the most reasonable value for each. Then use your answers to order the letters from least to greatest values in the boxes below.

L	N	M

L. Length in miles of the Mississippi River

3   (3,880)   3,880,000

M. Words in the English language

(600,000)   600   6,000

N. Number of books in a bookstore

100   (10,000)   1,000,000

Macmillan/McGraw-Hill, MATHEMATICS IN ACTION
Grade 4, Chapter 1, Lesson 9, pages 28-29

Name

ENRICHMENT-10

USING TABLES

On Your Own | Pair and Share | In a Group

SCRAMBLED EGGS (AND OTHER THINGS, TOO)

Julio makes banana bread and granola for charity bake sales. He uses the amounts shown in these tables.

Banana Bread			
Batches	Eggs	Flour	Bananas
1	2	1c	3

Granola					
Batches	Oats	Raisins	Bran	Nuts	Apricots
1	4c	2c	2c	1c	1c

He often makes several batches, so he made two charts showing the amounts to use for 1 to 6 batches. Unfortunately, he accidently cut up his charts instead of cutting the bread. Can you and your partner match the pieces at the bottom of this page with their correct position in Julio's charts? (*Hint:* You can cut out the pieces and try rearranging them in the spaces.)

Batches	Eggs	Flour	Bananas
E		B	
L		I	
D		O	

Batches	Oats	Raisins	Bran	Nuts	Apricots
J		K		H	
A		C		M	
G		N		F	

3	12c
4	16c

A

1c	3
2c	6

B

6c	6c
8c	8c

C

5	10
6	12

D

1	2
2	4

E

5c	5c
6c	6c

F

5	20c
6	24c

G

1c	1c
2c	2c

H

3c	9
4c	12

I

1	4c
2	8c

J

2c	2c
4c	4c

K

3	6
4	8

L

3c	3c
4c	4c

M

10c	10c
12c	12c

N

5c	15
6c	18

O

Macmillan/McGraw-Hill, MATHEMATICS IN ACTION
Grade 4, Chapter 1, Lesson 12, pages 34-35

Name

ENRICHMENT-9

PROBLEM SOLVING

On Your Own | Pair and Share | In a Group

IT'S ALL RELATIVE

Match each item on the left with its correct quantity or best estimate on the right. You don't have to know the answers—just use your common sense. Decide which item in each set is smallest or largest. That will help you choose the correct answers.

A 1. The weight of a one-day-old kitten — **A.** 3 ½ oz
C 2. The weight of a one-day-old whale — **B.** 150 lb
B 3. The weight of a one-day-old giraffe — **C.** 4,000 lb

F 4. Approximate number of leaves on a tree — **D.** 1,000
D 5. Approximate number of pages in a dictionary — **E.** 2,500
E 6. Approximate number of letters on a book page — **F.** 100,000

I 7. Number of days a 70-year-old has been alive — **G.** 240
H 8. Average number of heartbeats in an hour — **H.** 3,900
G 9. Average hours spent sleeping in one month — **I.** 25,000

K 10. Length of the world's longest river — **J.** 5½ miles
L 11. Distance around the equator — **K.** 4,180 miles
J 12. Height of the world's tallest mountain — **L.** 7,927 miles

O 13. Number of ants in an ant colony — **M.** 100
P 14. Number of grains of sugar in a sugar bowl — **N.** 4,000
N 15. Hours of sunlight in one year — **O.** 10,000
M 16. Number of rainy days in one year — **P.** 100,000

Q 17. Number of people at a concert — **Q.** 2,000
S 18. Population of Canada — **R.** 600,000
T 19. Number of women in the world — **S.** 25,900,000
R 20. Number of doctors in the United States — **T.** 2,500,000,000

Macmillan/McGraw-Hill, MATHEMATICS IN ACTION
Grade 4, Chapter 1, Lesson 11, pages 32-33

ENRICHMENT-12

Name

FACT FAMILIES

On Your Own | Pair and Share | In a Group

MORRA

Morra is an ancient counting game. There is one way to play. The two players face each other. At a given signal, each player holds up 0 to 5 fingers and says a number between 0 and 10. A player scores one point for correctly stating the sum of both players' fingers. Write each player's score in the boxes.

Seven / Nine — 1 | 0

Two / Six — 1 | 0

Nine / Three — 0 | 0

There is another way to play Morra. Players score one point if they say the sum of the numbers and one point if they say the difference between the numbers. Fill in the correct score in each box.

Two / Six — 1 | 1

Eight / Four — 0 | 1

Eight / Zero — 0 | 1

Fill in the words so that the scores are correct.

7 or 1 / 0, 2, 3, 4, 5, 6, 8 or 9 — 1 | 0

0 or 8 / 0 or 8 — 1 | 1

0, 1, 2, 4, 5, 6, 8, or 9 / 7 or 3 — 0 | 1

Can you describe how a player could score two points in one turn? **Both players hold no fingers and a player says "zero," or one player holds no fingers and a player says the number of fingers on the other hand.**

Now try playing Morra with a friend!

Macmillan/McGraw-Hill, MATHEMATICS IN ACTION
Grade 4, Chapter 2, Lesson 2, pages 54-55

ENRICHMENT-11

Name

MEANING OF ADDITION AND SUBTRACTION

On Your Own | Pair and Share | In a Group

PATHEMATICS

Follow the path of correct number sentences through this maze. You can enter a box more than once.

Start

7

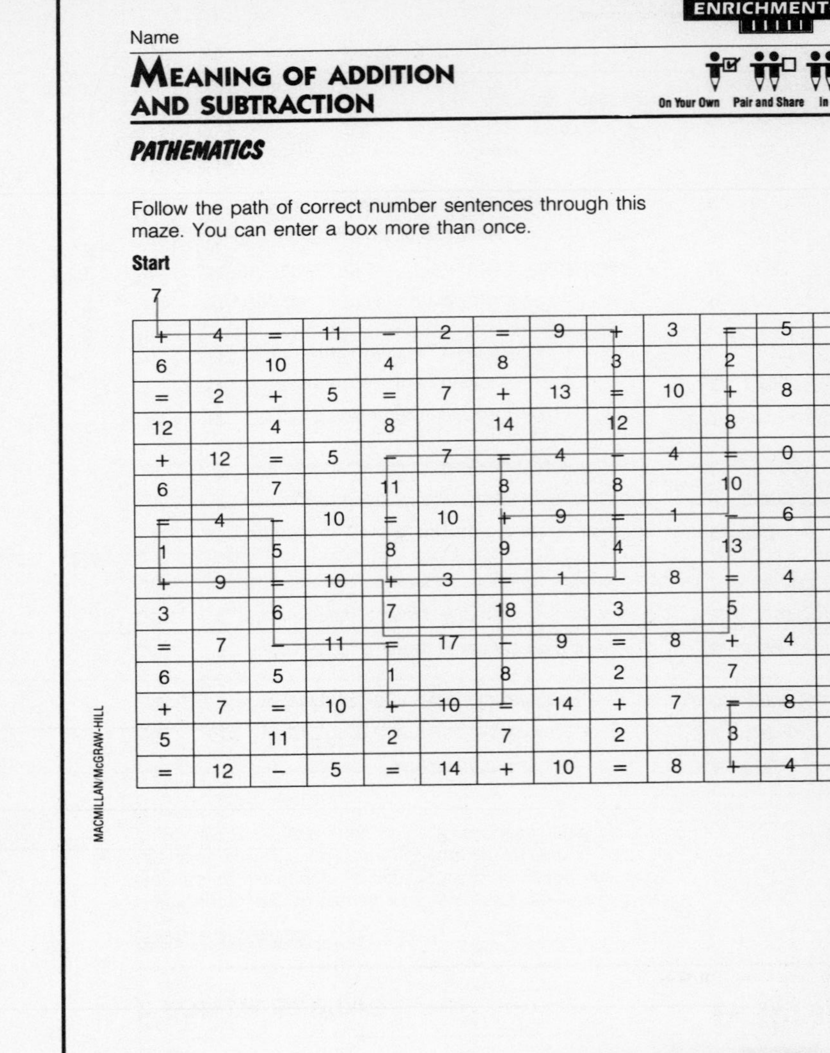

+	4	=	11	−	2	=	9	+	3	=	5	−
6		10		4		8		3		2		7
=	2	+	5	=	7	+	13	=	10	+	8	=
12		4		8		14		12		8		7
+	12	=	5	−	7	=	4	−	4	=	0	+
6		7		11		8		8		10		1
=	4	−	10	=	10	+	9	=	1	−	6	=
1		5		8		9		4		13		7
+	9	=	10	+	3	=	1	−	8	=	4	+
3		6		7		18		3		5		4
=	7	−	11	=	17	−	9	=	8	+	4	=
6		5		1		8		2		7		11
+	7	=	10	+	10	=	14	+	7	=	8	−
5		11		2		7		2		3		5
=	12	−	5	=	14	+	10	=	8	+	4	=

7

End

Macmillan/McGraw-Hill, MATHEMATICS IN ACTION
Grade 4, Chapter 2, Lesson 1, pages 52-53

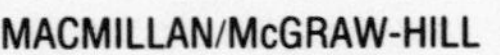

Name

ENRICHMENT-14

MENTAL MATH: SUBTRACTION FACTS

On Your Own · Pair and Share · In a Group

COUNTDOWN

Complete this exercise with a classmate. Take turns filling in the blank with the correct answer.

9 − 8 + 7 − 6 + 5 − 4 + 3 − 2 + 1 = 5

Write a + or a − sign in each blank so that the answers shown are correct. You may use a calculator to help you.
Answers may vary. Possible answers are given.

9 + 8 − 7 + 6 − 5 + 4 − 3 + 2 − 1 = 13

9 + 8 − 7 − 6 + 5 − 4 − 3 − 2 + 1 = 1

9 − 8 + 7 + 6 − 5 + 4 − 3 − 2 − 1 = 7

9 + 8 − 7 + 6 − 5 − 4 − 3 − 2 + 1 = 3

What is the greatest sum you can get using 3 − signs?

9 + 8 + 7 + 6 + 5 + 4 − 3 − 2 − 1 = 33

What is the greatest sum you can get using 4 − signs?

9 + 8 + 7 + 6 + 5 − 4 − 3 − 2 − 1 = 25

What is the lowest sum you can get using 4 + signs?

9 − 8 + 7 − 6 + 5 − 4 − 3 + 2 + 1 = 3

Macmillan/McGraw-Hill, MATHEMATICS IN ACTION
Grade 4, Chapter 2, Lesson 4, pages 58–59

Name

ENRICHMENT-13

MENTAL MATH: ADDITION FACTS

On Your Own · Pair and Share · In a Group

IT ALL ADDS UP

Use this code for the digits 0–9.

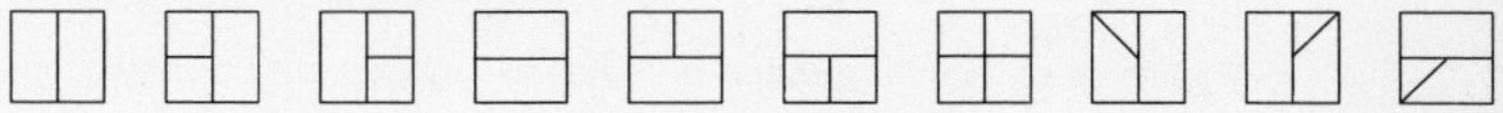

0 1 2 3 4 5 6 7 8 9

Use two boxes for a 2-digit number. For example:

16

Find each sum. Write the answer in code.

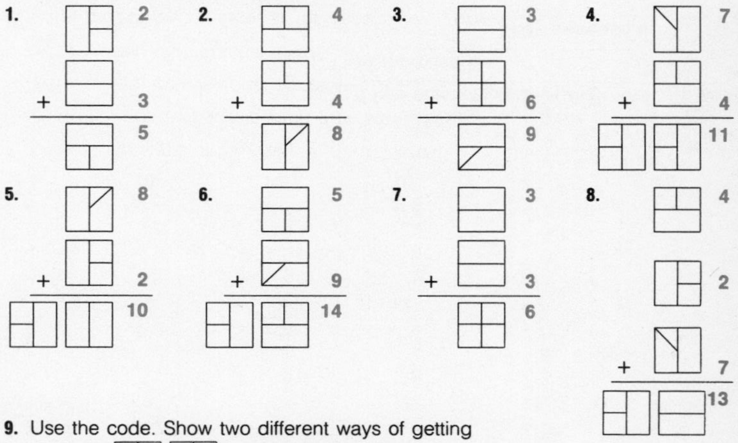

1. 2 + 3 = 5

2. 4 + 4 = 8

3. 3 + 6 = 9

4. 7 + 4 = 11

5. 8 + 2 = 10

6. 5 + 9 = 14

7. 3 + 3 = 6

8. 4 + 2 + 7 = 13

9. Use the code. Show two different ways of getting the sum.  **Answers will vary**

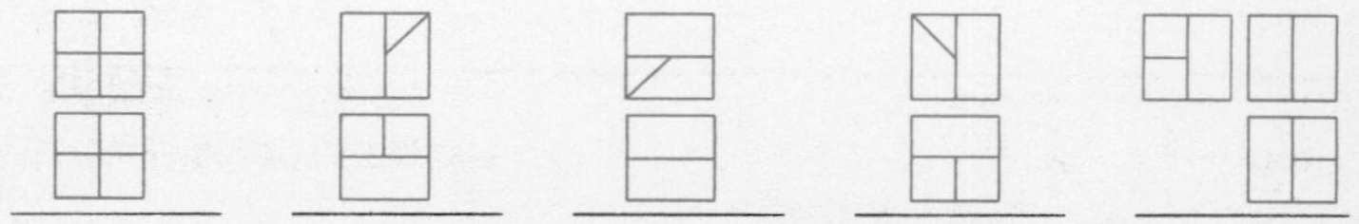

Macmillan/McGraw-Hill, MATHEMATICS IN ACTION
Grade 4, Chapter 2, Lesson 3, pages 56–57

ENRICHMENT-16

Name

PROBLEM SOLVING

On Your Own · Pair and Share · In a Group

EASIER THAN MEETS THE EYE

These two problems have one thing in common. They seem more difficult than they really are! Just think carefully before you answer, and you'll quickly find the solutions.

The Bus Route

You are the driver of a public bus. There are 9 people on your bus. At the first stop, Zach and Zelda get off; Bob, Brenda, and Billy get on. At the next stop, Alma and Anthony get on and Kyle and Keith get off. Hal, Hank, Hannah, and Henry get off at the next stop. A group of 12 gets on at the stop after that, while Alma and Anthony get off. Mark and Melba get on the bus two stops later, but Timothy, Tara, Talbot, and Tillie leave the bus. At the next-to-last stop, Paula, Peter, Phil, and Paulo leave through the side door. Martin and Martha leave with the rest of the riders at the last stop.

What is the name of the bus driver? (Student's Name— "you")

DIVIDING EVENLY

These figures have each been divided into four equal parts.

Can you divide this shape into five equal parts?

ENRICHMENT-15

Name

MENTAL MATH: THREE OR MORE ADDENDS

On Your Own · Pair and Share · In a Group

ALL IN A ROW

Fill in the sums for the problems below.

0 + 1 = 1; 1 + 2 = 3; 2 + 3 = 5; 3 + 4 = 7; 4 + 5 = 9; 5 + 6 = 11

0 + 1 + 2 = 3; 1 + 2 + 3 = 6; 2 + 3 + 4 = 9; 3 + 4 + 5 = 12; 4 + 5 + 6 = 15; 5 + 6 + 7 = 18

0 + 1 + 2 + 3 = 6; 1 + 2 + 3 + 4 = 10; 2 + 3 + 4 + 5 = 14; 3 + 4 + 5 + 6 = 18; 4 + 5 + 6 + 7 = 22; 5 + 6 + 7 + 8 = 26

1. Look at the sums of the first row of problems.
   How may addends are in each problem? 2
   What pattern do the addends follow? They are consecutive numbers.
   What pattern do the sums follow? They increase by 2.
2. What pattern do the sums of the second row follow? They increase by 3.
3. Based on the pattern you found in question 2, find these sums:
   6 + 7 + 8 = 21   7 + 8 + 9 = 24   8 + 9 + 10 = 27
4. What pattern do the sums of the third row follow? They increase by 4.
5. Based on the pattern you found in question 4, find these sums:
   6 + 7 + 8 + 9 = 30   7 + 8 + 9 + 10 = 34
6. Can you guess what pattern the sums of these problems will follow?
   0 + 1 + 2 + 3 + 4 = 10   The pattern is: The sums increase by 5.
   1 + 2 + 3 + 4 + 5 = 15
   2 + 3 + 4 + 5 + 6 = 20
   3 + 4 + 5 + 6 + 7 = 25

Name

ENRICHMENT-18

ESTIMATING LENGTH: METRIC UNITS

On Your Own   Pair and Share   In a Group

NATURE'S LITTLE SECRET

Circle the best estimate for each length. Then find the number next to the correct answer in the drawing below and color in that area. When you are done, you will find the answer to the riddle below.

A.	The height of a tree	**1.** 60 cm	**2.** 60 m (circled)	**3.** 60 km
B.	The length of an alligator	**4.** 130 dm (circled)	**5.** 130 m	**6.** 130 km
C.	The height of an acorn	**7.** 2 cm (circled)	**8.** 2 dm	**9.** 2 m
D.	The length of a forest	**10.** 50 cm	**11.** 50 dm	**12.** 50 km (circled)
E.	The height of a bear	**13.** 250 cm (circled)	**14.** 250 dm	**15.** 250 m
F.	The distance a leaf falls	**16.** 8 cm	**17.** 8 m (circled)	**18.** 8 km
G.	The distance across a lake	**19.** 20 cm	**20.** 20 dm	**21.** 20 km (circled)
H.	The length of a rattlesnake	**22.** 4 cm	**23.** 4 m (circled)	**24.** 4 km
I.	The height of a rose bush	**25.** 5 dm (circled)	**26.** 50 cm	**27.** 500 dm
J.	The length of a centipede	**28.** 4 cm (circled)	**29.** 40 cm	**30.** 400 cm

What kind of room is impossible to enter?

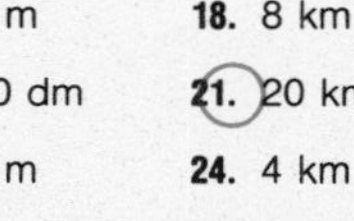

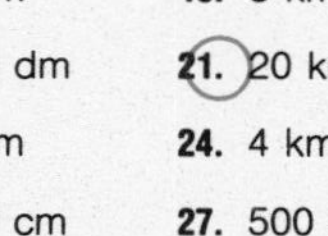

Macmillan/McGraw-Hill, MATHEMATICS IN ACTION
Grade 4, Chapter 2, Lesson 9, pages 68–69

Name

ENRICHMENT-17

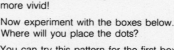

MEASURING LENGTH: METRIC UNITS

On Your Own   Pair and Share   In a Group

ART FROM MEASUREMENT

You can create beautiful designs with a ruler! Experimenting with measurements can produce amazing results.

Measure the box below. What is the length of each side? 6 cm

On the top line, draw dots 2 cm from each corner.
On the side lines, draw dots 2 cm from each corner.
Draw a dot in the middle of the bottom line.
Now connect every dot to every other dot on the box.
You can color the design to make it more vivid!

Now experiment with the boxes below. Where will you place the dots?

You can try this pattern for the first box, or invent your own: On the top and bottom lines, draw 4 dots spaced equally apart. On each side line, draw 2 dots spaced equally apart. Then connect all the dots.

Below each drawing, explain how you created it. Tell how you placed each dot.

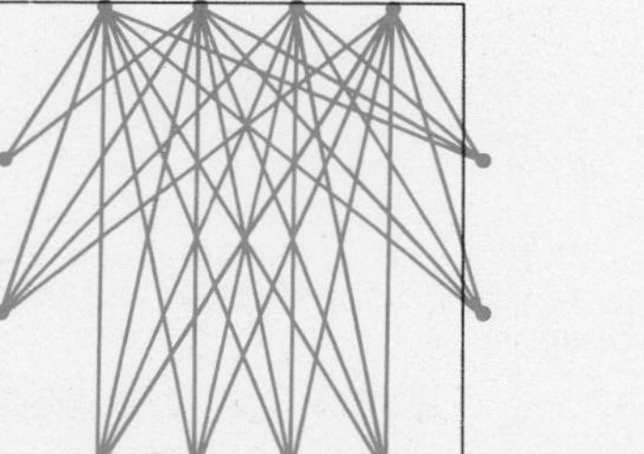

Answers will vary. This pattern follows the example.

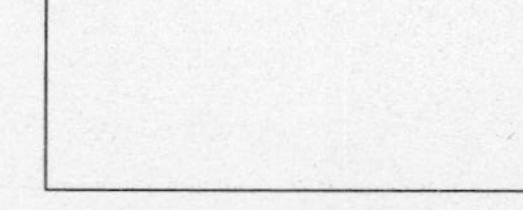

Answers will vary.

Macmillan/McGraw-Hill, MATHEMATICS IN ACTION
Grade 4, Chapter 2, Lesson 8, pages 66–67

ENRICHMENT-20

Name

Making Bar Graphs

On Your Own · Pair and Share · In a Group

AND THE SURVEY SAYS...

Stacy polled her fellow students about their favorite sports. The bar graph below shows the results of her poll.

1. Which sport was most popular in Stacy's class? **baseball**
2. Which two sports did the same number of people vote for? **basketball and swimming**
3. How many more people voted for football than soccer? **5**

STUDENT'S FAVORITE SPORTS

No. of Students: 0, 5, 10

Baseball · Basketball · Football · Soccer · Swimming

Now conduct your own poll. Ask your fellow students about one of these topics, or choose one or your own:

favorite sport · favorite TV show · favorite movie · favorite food · favorite animal

To conduct your own poll, make a chart and keep track of everyone's answer on a separate sheet of paper. Label each heading. For example, if you are asking people about their favorite animal, the first might be labeled "cat." Then, each time someone answers "cat," put a mark in that box.

Now make a bar graph showing the information in your poll. Remember to label and draw each bar carefully.

No. of Students: 0, 5, 10, 15, 20

Macmillan/McGraw-Hill, MATHEMATICS IN ACTION
Grade 4, Chapter 2, Lesson 11, pages 72-73

ENRICHMENT-19

Name

Problem Solving

On Your Own · Pair and Share · In a Group

FORM ONE LINE, PLEASE

Can you draw each of these designs using only one line? Each member of your group can try. Do not lift your pen from the paper or go over a part more than once. But be warned! One of these problems is impossible! Which one? Circle it when you find it.

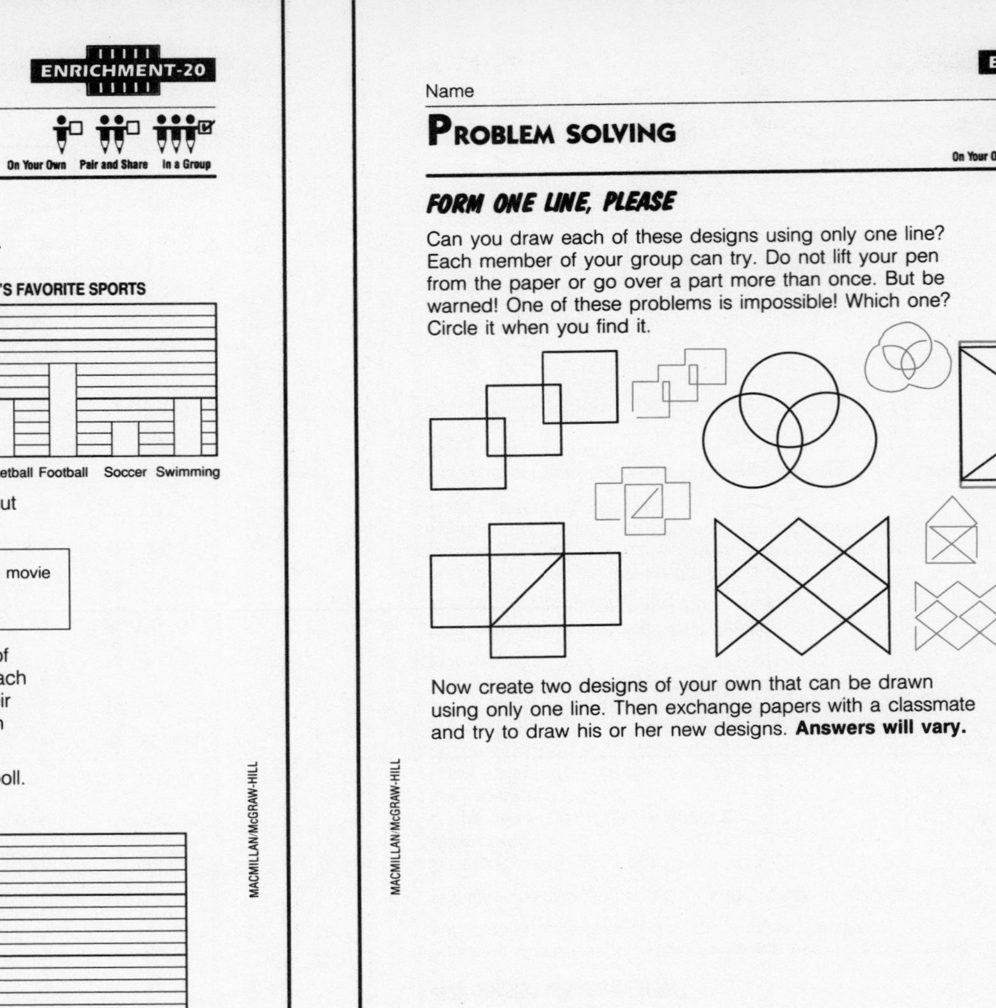

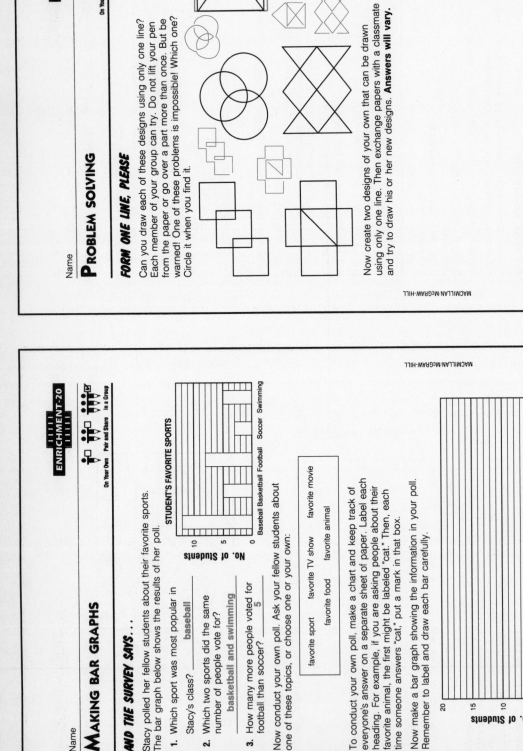

Now create two designs of your own that can be drawn using only one line. Then exchange papers with a classmate and try to draw his or her new designs. **Answers will vary.**

Macmillan/McGraw-Hill, MATHEMATICS IN ACTION
Grade 4, Chapter 2, Lesson 10, pages 70-71

ENRICHMENT-22

Name

ESTIMATING SUMS BY ROUNDING

On Your Own | Pair and Share | In a Group

THE CAT'S MEOW

Estimate each sum by rounding. Then find the letter that goes with each answer. Fill in the blanks to answer this riddle:

"What is a cat's favorite breakfast food?"

1. 420 + 380 + 187 → 1,000
2. $7.35 + 1.18 + 3.75 → $12.00
3. $8.89 + 3.98 + 2.66 → $16.00
4. 81 + 407 + 15 → 500
5. $10.66 + 4.23 + 16.44 → $30.00
6. 485 + 243 + 68 → 800
7. $2.75 + 4.45 + 5.48 → $12.00
8. $7.72 + 6.72 + 4.72 → $20.00
9. 355 + 432 + 189 + 74 → 1,100
10. $3.32 + 3.67 + 3.49 + 2.26 → $12.00
11. 76 + 59 + 188 + 92 → 500
12. $1.53 + 7.07 + 10.59 + 0.40 → $20.00

1,400	$30.00	500	$12.00	1,000	$11.00	1,100	800	$20.00	700	$16.00
A	C	E	I	M	N	P	R	S	T	C

The answer to the riddle is

M	I	C	E	C	R	I	S	P	I	E	S
1	2	3	4	5	6	7	8	9	10	11	12

ENRICHMENT-21

Name

MENTAL MATH: ADDING 10s; 100s; 1000s

On Your Own | Pair and Share | In a Group

WIPE OUT!

The object of this game is to wipe out every number on this list.

10	100	1,000	40	400	4,000	70	700	7,000
20	200	2,000	50	500	5,000	80	800	8,000
30	300	3,000	60	600	6,000	90	900	9,000

You wipe out a number by using it in an addition fact. For example, if you add 7,000 + 200 + 300, you wipe out those three numbers.

You can use up to four numbers in each addition fact.

The sum of your numbers must be less than 10,000.

1. Here is a set of sums that will wipe out the list. Can you find the addition facts that were used?

Sum	Addition Facts
9,990	9,000 + 900 + 90
9,880	8,000 + 1,000 + 800 + 80
7,780	7,000 + 700 + 70 + 10
6,760	6,000 + 600 + 100 + 60
5,570	5,000 + 500 + 50 + 20
5,230	3,000 + 2,000 + 200 + 30
4,740	4,000 + 400 + 300 + 40

2. Now create your own set of sums. Show your addition facts as well. Can you wipe out the set with seven sums that each total less than 10,000? (*Remember,* use no more than four numbers for each sum.)

Sum	Addition facts
____	Answers will vary.
____	____
____	____
____	____
____	____

ENRICHMENT-24

Name

Problem Solving

On Your Own | Pair and Share | In a Group

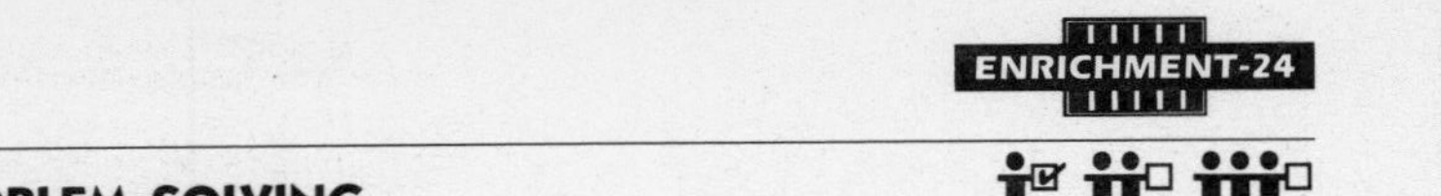

MATH WITHOUT MATH

You don't have to do any calculations on this worksheet! Just circle *every* answer that seems reasonable. Some questions have more than one possible answer that is reasonable. Circle all of them. Then shade or color the shapes that show your answers. You'll find a hidden picture.

1. Allen ran 1 mile on his way to school this morning. How long did it take him?

   15 seconds   15 minutes   15 hours

2. Allen delivers newspapers in the morning. His route takes about half an hour. How many papers does he deliver?

   3   25   35   350

3. When he got to school, Allen worked on addition problems. How many did he do in 20 minutes?

   10   20   200   2,000

4. At recess he cut out a paper airplane. How far did it fly?

   1 inch   2 yards   4 yards   4 miles

5. How tall is Allen?

   1 foot   4 feet   5 feet   15 feet

6. How much does Allen weigh?

   10 pounds   70 pounds   80 pounds   800 pounds

7. Allen has a snack of carrots when he comes home. How many does he eat?

   1   2   25   200

8. Allen gets a good night's sleep before going to school. How many hours does he sleep?

   4 hours   8 hours   9 hours   18 hours

9. Now shade or color your answers in the drawing. What kind of pet does Allen have?

Macmillan/McGraw-Hill, MATHEMATICS IN ACTION
Grade 4, Chapter 3, Lesson 4, pages 96-97

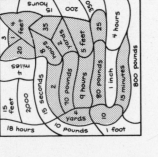

ENRICHMENT-23

Name

Front-End Estimation

On Your Own | Pair and Share | In a Group

GREAT ESTIMATIONS

1. Use front-end estimation with adjustment to find an estimated value for the three paths shown (—— , - - - - , and — - —). Write your estimates at the end of the paths. Then find a new path that follows these rules.

   The path begins at START.

   The path can go from one circle to any circle next to it.

   The path travels through 7 circles (including the START circle).

   The path ends at any circle on the outside.

2. Can you find the path with the highest possible total? Use front-end estimation with adjustment to help. Draw your path using a dashed line (-----).

START

$5.12 $4.07 $1.22 $9.78

$2.52 $6.80 $2.89 $1.14 $31 ?

$8.02 $4.25 $7.71 $3.52 $44

$6.89 $5.72 $8.18 $1.11

$31 ? $37 ?

Macmillan/McGraw-Hill, MATHEMATICS IN ACTION
Grade 4, Chapter 3, Lesson 3, pages 94-95

Name

ENRICHMENT-26

COLUMN ADDITION

On Your Own · Pair and Share · In a Group

SLOW-POKE JOE

"Joe is the slowest person I know. In fact, he's so slow that . . ."

To find out how slow Joe is, circle the sets of numbers that add up to the sums given. Each set will be together in a column.

When you have finished, write the letters in the numbered blanks. The first one has been done for you.

1. 2 numbers that add up to 187
2. 2 numbers that add up to 43
3. 3 numbers that add up to 323
4. 3 numbers that add up to 271
5. 3 numbers that add up to 181
6. 4 numbers that add up to 35
7. 4 numbers that add up to 204
8. 4 numbers that add up to 1,307

10	T (3)	205	L (14)	16	E (23)
20	H (12)	14	M (5)	111	R (17)
108	E (2)	360	V (25)	12	A (6)
109	A (15)	172	A (4)	7	M (16)
106	O (23)	15	N (19)	4	D (25)
50	C (7)	70	P (17)	12	A (11)
201	D (24)	77	H (10)	24	S (20)
318	H (1)	82	I (18)	19	T (9)
593	R (3)	22	E (17)	101	I (15)
295	D (13)	20	Y (14)	20	A (8)
101	C (22)	80	N (24)	42	C (14)
567	W (1)	92	E (21)	80	N (5)
390	O (6)	99	B (7)	62	N (12)

Joe is so slow that

H	E	R	A	N	A	B	A	T	H
1	2	3	4	5	6	7	8	9	10

A	N	D	C	A	M	E	I	N
11	12	13	14	15	16	17	18	19

S	E	C	O	N	D
20	21	22	23	24	25

Name

ENRICHMENT-25

ADDING WHOLE NUMBERS

On Your Own · Pair and Share · In a Group

CLUNK!

Play this game with another student. First cut out the circles and triangles on this page. Then turn them upside down.

At each turn, a player can take one triangle or two circles. Write down your scores. Keep a running total as you play. Take turns choosing shapes until they are all gone. The player with the highest total is the winner.

But watch out for the CLUNKS! If you pick one, you lose all the points you have gained so far!

Think about your strategy.

1. What is the most you can score in a single turn? 570
2. What is the least you can score in one turn? 210
3. How will your strategy change as pieces are taken? Answers will vary. Students may suggest that, after a while, the better scoring chance shifts from taking two circles to taking one triangle.

100	170	240	310	380	440
110	180	250	320	390	450
120	190	260	330	400	460
130	200	270	340	410	470
140	210	280	350	420	480
150	220	290	360	430	490
160	230	300	370	CLUNK!	CLUNK!
CLUNK!	CLUNK!	CLUNK!	CLUNK!		

ENRICHMENT-28

Name

ESTIMATING DIFFERENCES

On Your Own · Pair and Share · In a Group

ADDITIONAL SUBTRACTION

1. The arrow points to the number being subtracted. Estimate the difference between each pair of boxes connected by a horizontal, vertical, or diagonal line. Use rounding. Write your estimate on the line.

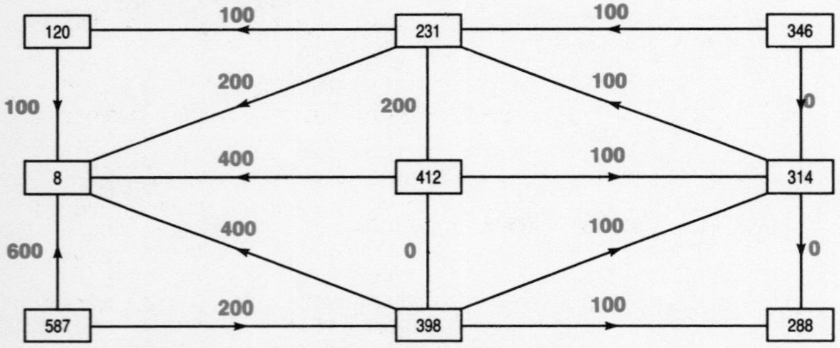

120 — 100 — 231 — 100 — 346

100 · 200 · 200 · 100 · 0

8 — 400 — 412 — 100 — 314

600 · 400 · 0 · 100 · 0

587 — 200 — 398 — 100 — 288

2. The numbers on the lines show the difference between each pair of boxes. The arrow points to the number being subtracted. Can you fill in every box in this puzzle? (*Hint:* Using addition may help.)

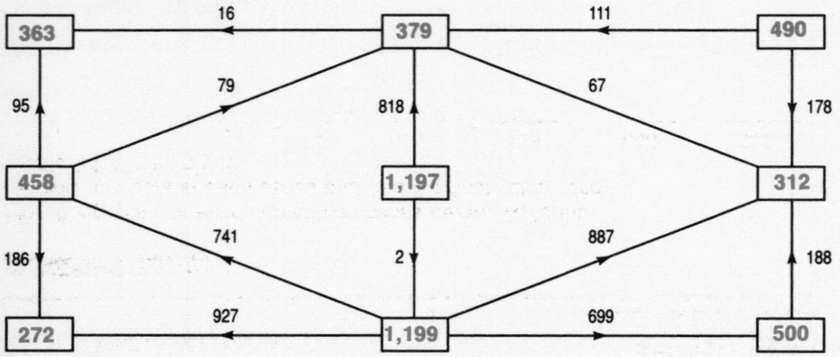

363 — 16 — 379 — 111 — 490

95 · 79 · 818 · 67 · 178

458 — 1,197 — 312

186 · 741 · 2 · 887 · 188

272 — 927 — 1,199 — 699 — 500

Macmillan/McGraw-Hill, MATHEMATICS IN ACTION
Grade 4, Chapter 3, Lesson 9, pages 106–107

ENRICHMENT-27

Name

MENTAL MATH: SUBTRACTING 10s; 100s; 1000s

On Your Own · Pair and Share · In a Group

JUST THE FACTS

Make subtraction facts by matching two numbers from the first two columns with a difference in the third column. Use each number in each group only once. Write the number sentence in the blank at the right. One has been done for you.

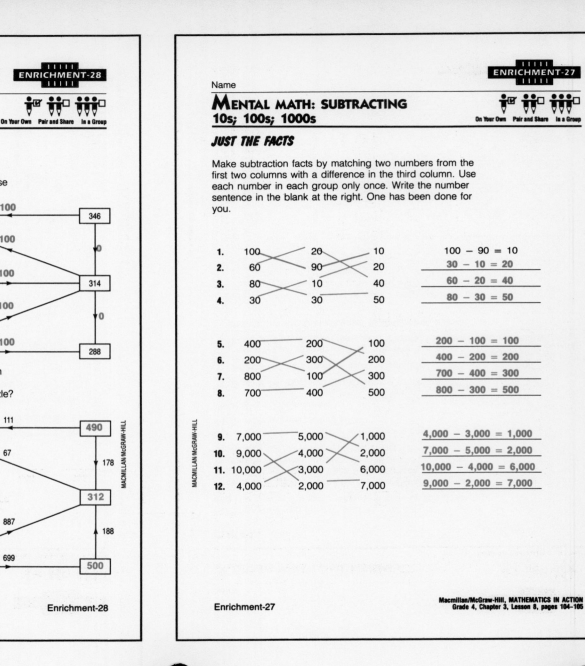

1.	100	20	10	100 − 90 = 10
2.	60	90	20	30 − 10 = 20
3.	80	10	40	60 − 20 = 40
4.	30	30	50	80 − 30 = 50
5.	400	200	100	200 − 100 = 100
6.	200	300	200	400 − 200 = 200
7.	800	100	300	700 − 400 = 300
8.	700	400	500	800 − 300 = 500
9.	7,000	5,000	1,000	4,000 − 3,000 = 1,000
10.	9,000	4,000	2,000	7,000 − 5,000 = 2,000
11.	10,000	3,000	6,000	10,000 − 4,000 = 6,000
12.	4,000	2,000	7,000	9,000 − 2,000 = 7,000

Macmillan/McGraw-Hill, MATHEMATICS IN ACTION
Grade 4, Chapter 3, Lesson 8, pages 104–105

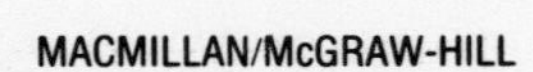

Name

ENRICHMENT-30

SUBTRACTING ACROSS ZEROS

On Your Own · Pair and Share · In a Group

NUMBER SHRINKING

Find the pattern of each subtraction series below. Write the missing numbers in each series and find the final value. Use a calculator to help you.

1. 10,000 − 999 − 888 − 777 − 666 − 555 − 444 − 333 − 222 − 111 = 5,005

2. 10,000 − 987 − 876 − 765 − 654 − 543 − 321 − 210 = 5,644

3. 10,000 − 919 − 818 − 717 − 616 − 515 − 414 − 313 − 212 − 111 = 5,365

4. 10,000 − 90 − 80 − 70 − 60 − 50 − 40 − 30 − 20 − 10 = 9,550

5. 100,000 − 9,955 − 8,844 − 7,733 − 6,622 − 5,511 − 4,400 = 56,935

6. 100,000 − 9,079 − 8,068 − 7,057 − 6,046 − 5,035 − 4,024 − 3,013 = 57,687

7. 100,000 − 1,213 − 2,324 − 3,435 − 4,546 − 5,657 − 6,768 − 7,879 = 68,178

8. 100,000 − 135 − 246 − 357 − 468 − 579 = 98,215

MACMILLAN/McGRAW-HILL

Name

ENRICHMENT-29

SUBTRACTING WHOLE NUMBERS

On Your Own · Pair and Share · In a Group

LESS AND LESS

Find the missing digits.

1. 3 2 1 − 8 7 = 2 3 4

2. 8 6 2 − 1 2 = 8 5 0

3. 5 1 5 − 9 2 = 4 2 3

4. 7 2 6 − 6 0 3 = 1 2 3

5. 3 1 2 − 2 7 7 = 3 5

6. 5 6 2 − 3 8 5 = 1 7 7

7. 2,1 6 5 − 7 2 = 2,0 9 3

8. 8,4 4 4 − 8 6 1 = 7,5 8 3

9. 7,2 6 8 − 3,5 2 2 = 3,7 4 6

10. Use the numbers in the box to complete the problems. Use each number only once.

363	458	519	882
403	476	584	954
409	478	867	987

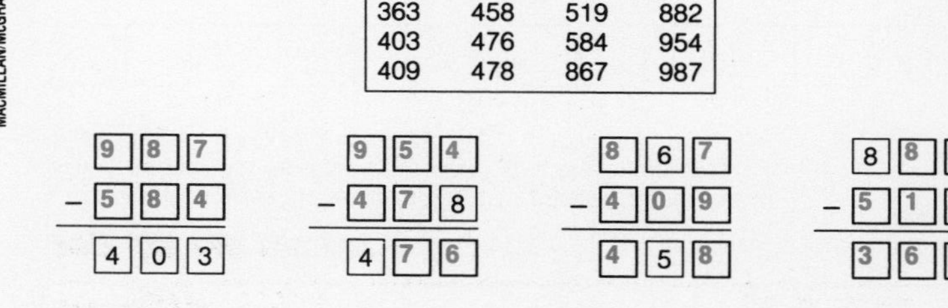

987 − 584 = 403

954 − 478 = 476

867 − 409 = 458

882 − 519 = 363

MACMILLAN/McGRAW-HILL

Name

FINDING PERIMETER

TWO BUGS TO BUG YOU

Play this game with a classmate.

Doug Bug and Barney Beetle both crawled from the rock to the flower. They crawled on the grid shown below. They never crawled on the same line twice and they never crossed each other's path.

Doug crawled 36 cm. Barney crawled 46 cm. Take turns measuring the lengths of the lines. Use your metric ruler to measure. Then draw the paths Doug and Barney might have taken. One player should use ▬ ▬ for Doug's path and the other player should use ▪▪▪▪▪ for Barney's path. Then compare each other's paths.

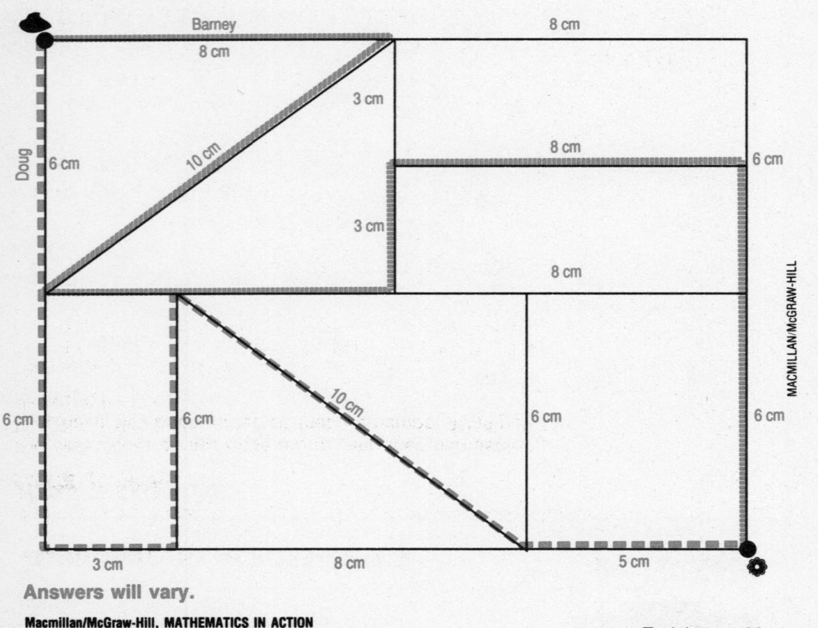

Answers will vary.

Macmillan/McGraw-Hill, MATHEMATICS IN ACTION
Grade 4, Chapter 3, Lesson 14, pages 116–117

ENRICHMENT-31

On Your Own · Pair and Share · In a Group

Name

PROBLEM SOLVING

HOW LOW CAN YOU GO?

Cut out the shapes at the bottom of this page. The numbers are in squares □, and the operation signs are in triangles △. Place the numbers and operation signs in this pattern.

□ □ △ □ □ △ □ □ △ □ □ △ □

1. What is the greatest value you can get?
   240: 96 + 85 + 74 − 13 − 2

2. What is the least value you can get?
   0: 18 + 24 + 57 − 96 − 3; other answers are possible.

Now place the shapes in any pattern to find new values. For example, you might find 321 + 7 − 8 + 904 − 56, which equals 1,168.

3. What is the greatest value you can get when you use all the numbers and operation signs? Write the pattern as a number sentence.
   98,769: 98,765 + 4 + 3 − 2 + 1 = 98,769

4. What is the least value you can get when you use all the numbers and operation signs? Write the pattern as a number sentence.
   0: 18 + 24 + 57 − 96 − 3 = 0; other arrangements equal to 0 are possible.

5. Form a pattern that uses every shape and that equals 100. Write the pattern as a number sentence.
   98 + 67 − 54 − 13 + 2 = 100; other arrangements equal to 100 are possible.

1	2	3	4	5	6	7	8	9	△+	△+	△-	△-

Macmillan/McGraw-Hill, MATHEMATICS IN ACTION
Grade 4, Chapter 3, Lesson 13, pages 114–115

Name

ENRICHMENT-34

TELLING TIME

On Your Own Pair and Share In a Group

CLOCK JUMBLES

The nine clocks on this page are missing their numbers. They have also been turned so that the number 12 is not always at the top.

The clocks show these times:

1:00	2:00	3:00	4:00	5:00	6:00
7:00	8:00	9:00	10:00	11:00	12:00

Try to match each of the times above with a clock below. Then mark a 12 on each clock to show which way is up!

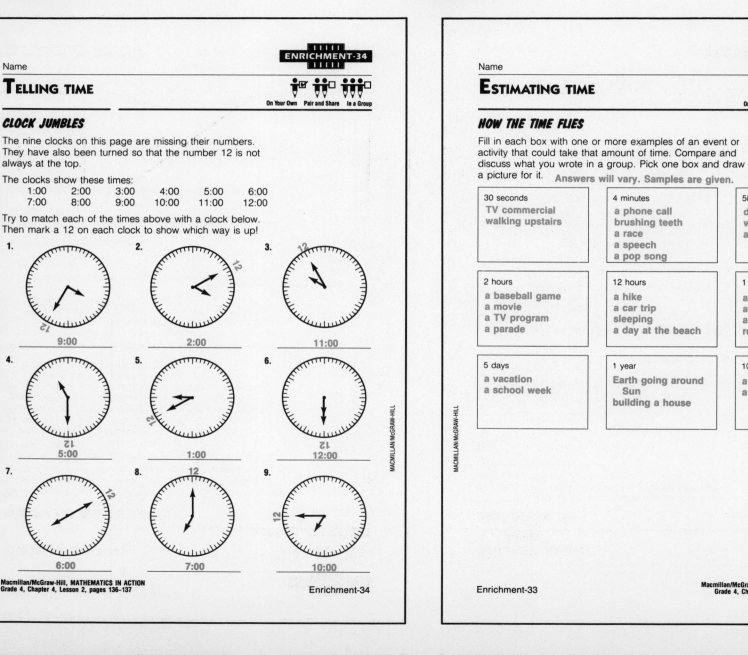

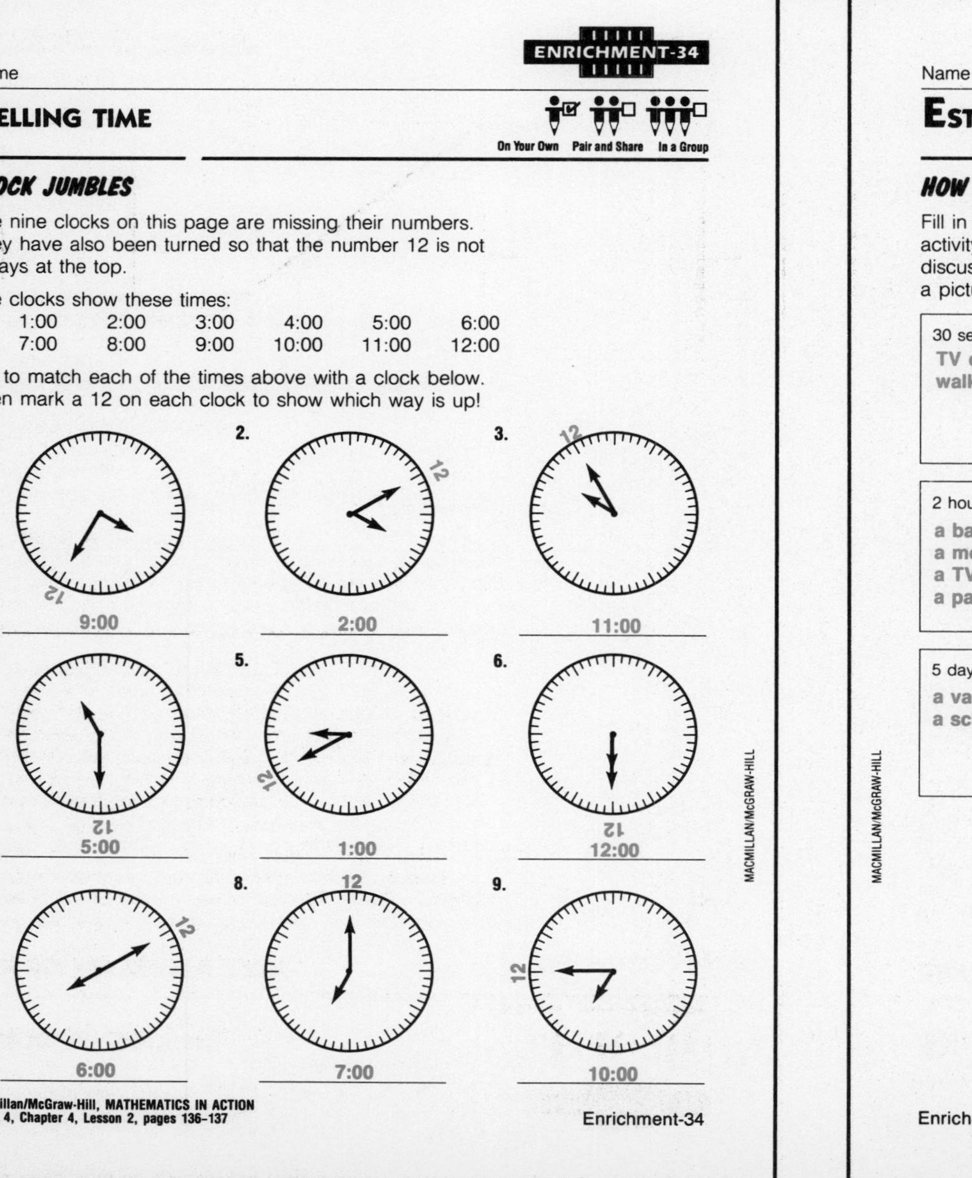

Macmillan/McGraw-Hill, MATHEMATICS IN ACTION
Grade 4, Chapter 4, Lesson 2, pages 136–137

Name

ENRICHMENT-33

ESTIMATING TIME

On Your Own Pair and Share In a Group

HOW THE TIME FLIES

Fill in each box with one or more examples of an event or activity that could take that amount of time. Compare and discuss what you wrote in a group. Pick one box and draw a picture for it. **Answers will vary. Samples are given.**

30 seconds	4 minutes	50 minutes
TV commercial **walking upstairs**	**a phone call** **brushing teeth** **a race** **a speech** **a pop song**	**dinner** **walk home** **a school class**
2 hours	12 hours	1 day
a baseball game **a movie** **a TV program** **a parade**	**a hike** **a car trip** **sleeping** **a day at the beach**	**a holiday** **a train trip** **a birthday** **reading a book**
5 days	1 year	100 years
a vacation **a school week**	**Earth going around Sun** **building a house**	**a tree to grow** **a very old person**

Macmillan/McGraw-Hill, MATHEMATICS IN ACTION
Grade 4, Chapter 4, Lesson 1, pages 134–135

ENRICHMENT-36

Name

PROBLEM SOLVING

On Your Own Pair and Share In a Group

HOW OLD ARE YOU? I'M 3,728!

Answers will vary.

When someone asks how old you are, you probably respond in *years*. But you can measure your age in any unit of time. Use this worksheet to help you find your age in days.

1. Use a calculator to multiply your age in years by 365. Press 365 × [your age in years] = ☐ Write the answer at the right. ___ ___ ___ ___
2. Don't forget about leap years! Every four years we add one day to our calendars. For example, 1972, 1976, 1980, 1984, 1988, and 1992 are all leap years. How many leap years have occurred *since* you were born? Write this number at the right. ___
3. Now you have to find out how many days have passed since your last birthday. You may want to use a calendar to help you count. Start by counting the number of days from your birth date to the end of that month. Write the number at the right. ___ ___
4. Now add the number of days in complete months that have passed. ___ ___
5. Finally, add today's date. ___ ___
6. Add all of the columns, and that's how many days you've been alive! ___ ___ ___ ___
7. For another challenge, try to find how old you will be in days on your next birthday.

ENRICHMENT-35

Name

ELAPSED TIME

On Your Own Pair and Share In a Group

FROM TIME TO TIME

Cut out the digits at the bottom of this page. Place them in the digital clock displays. Compare your answers with another student.

From ___ : ___ ___ A.M.

To ___ : ___ ___ A.M.

Answers will vary. Sample answers below.

1. How close can you get to showing one hour of elapsed time?
   6:59 to 8:01 (one hour and two minutes)
2. How close can you get to showing three hours of elapsed time?
   2:59 to 6:01 (3 hours and 2 minutes)
3. What is the shortest period of time you can form using the digits?
   2 minutes; 7:59 to 8:01
4. Can you find a way to show more than 10 hours of elapsed time?
   9:01 A.M. to 4:35 A.M., for example
5. What is the longest period of time you can form using the digits?
   8:01 A.M. to 7:59 P.M. (next day) (23 hours, 58 min)

0 1 2 3 4 5 6 7 8 9

Name

ENRICHMENT-38

MAKING LINE GRAPHS

On Your Own Pair and Share In a Group

GRAPHIC LOGIC

Use the clues and the points given on the graphs to help you complete each line graph.

A. Ray shampoos dogs at a pet beauty shop. This graph shows how many dog shampoos he gave from Monday to Friday last week.

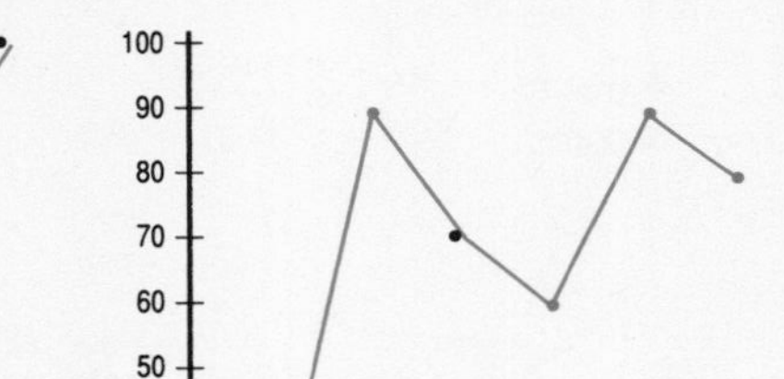

1. Ray shampooed 5 fewer dogs on Monday than he did on Tuesday. 5
2. He shampooed twice as many dogs on Wednesday as on Monday. 10
3. On Thursday, Ray shampooed three times as many dogs as on Monday. 15

B. Ray also walks dogs. This graph shows how many dogs Ray walked each month from January to June.

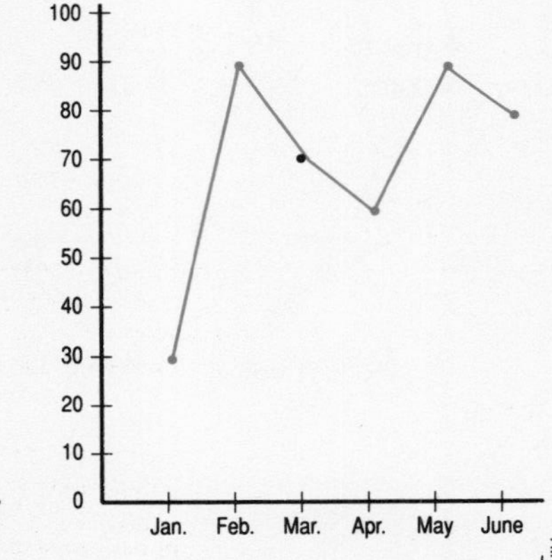

1. Ray walked 10 more dogs in June than in March. 80
2. In February, Ray walked as many dogs as in January and April combined. 90
3. He walked 20 fewer dogs in April than in June. 60
4. In January, Ray walked half as many dogs as he walked in April. 30
5. He walked the same number of dogs in February and May. 90

Name

ENRICHMENT-37

ORDERED PAIRS

On Your Own Pair and Share In a Group

MAKING CONNECTIONS

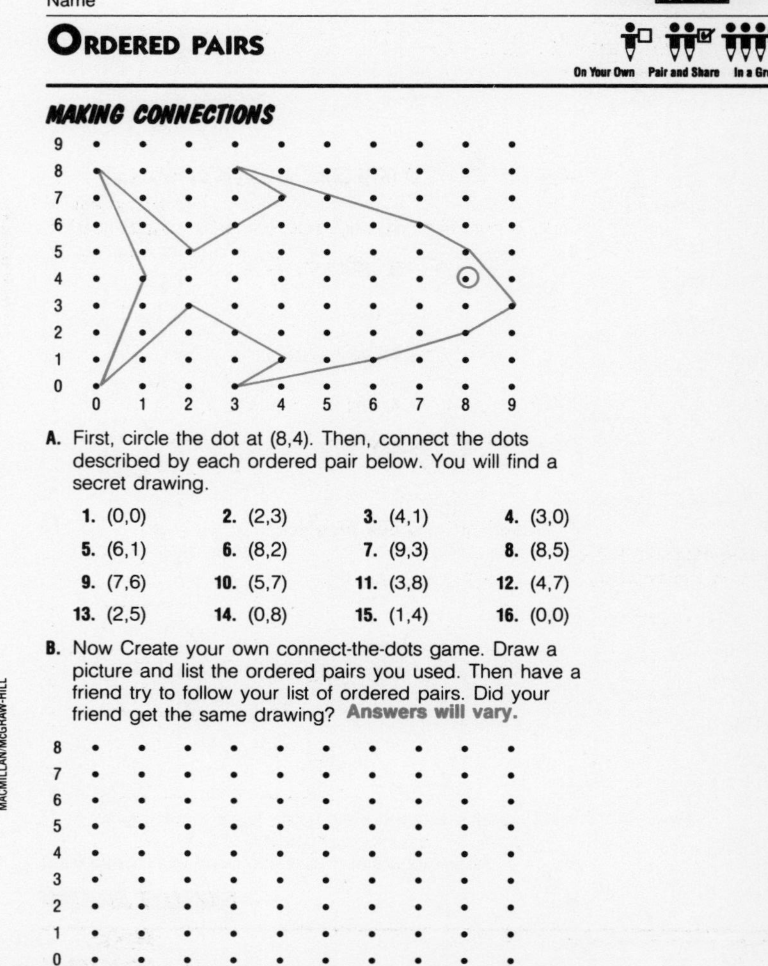

A. First, circle the dot at (8,4). Then, connect the dots described by each ordered pair below. You will find a secret drawing.

1. (0,0)	**2.** (2,3)	**3.** (4,1)	**4.** (3,0)
5. (6,1)	**6.** (8,2)	**7.** (9,3)	**8.** (8,5)
9. (7,6)	**10.** (5,7)	**11.** (3,8)	**12.** (4,7)
13. (2,5)	**14.** (0,8)	**15.** (1,4)	**16.** (0,0)

B. Now Create your own connect-the-dots game. Draw a picture and list the ordered pairs you used. Then have a friend try to follow your list of ordered pairs. Did your friend get the same drawing? Answers will vary.

8
7
6
5
4
3
2
1
0
0 1 2 3 4 5 6 7 8 9

ENRICHMENT-40

Name

MASS

On Your Own Pair and Share In a Group

BALANCING ACT

Cut out the weights at the bottom of this page. Place one or more weights on the empty end or ends of each seesaw to balance the seesaw. Use each weight only once. Move the weights around until you are able to balance the seesaw.

Seesaw	Weight shown	Answer
1	75 g	50 g + 25 g
2	(empty)	4 kg / 4,000 g
3	10 g	8 g + 2 g
4	30 g	18 g + 12 g
5	1 kg	1,000 g
6	2 kg	1,500 g + 500 g
7	50 g	40 g + 10 g
8	18 g	7 g + 11 g
9	(empty)	5 kg / 2,000 g, 3,000 g

- - - - - - - - - - - - - - - - - - - -

1,000 g	40 g	7 g	1,500 g	4 kg	11 g
50 g	8 g	500 g	5 kg	25 g	2,000 g
10 g	3,000 g	2 g	18 g	4,000 g	12 g

Macmillan/McGraw-Hill, MATHEMATICS IN ACTION
Grade 4, Chapter 4, Lesson 9, pages 150-151

ENRICHMENT-39

Name

CAPACITY

On Your Own Pair and Share In a Group

HOLDING PATTERNS

Imagine that this cube can hold one liter of water.

How many liters of water could each of these shapes hold?

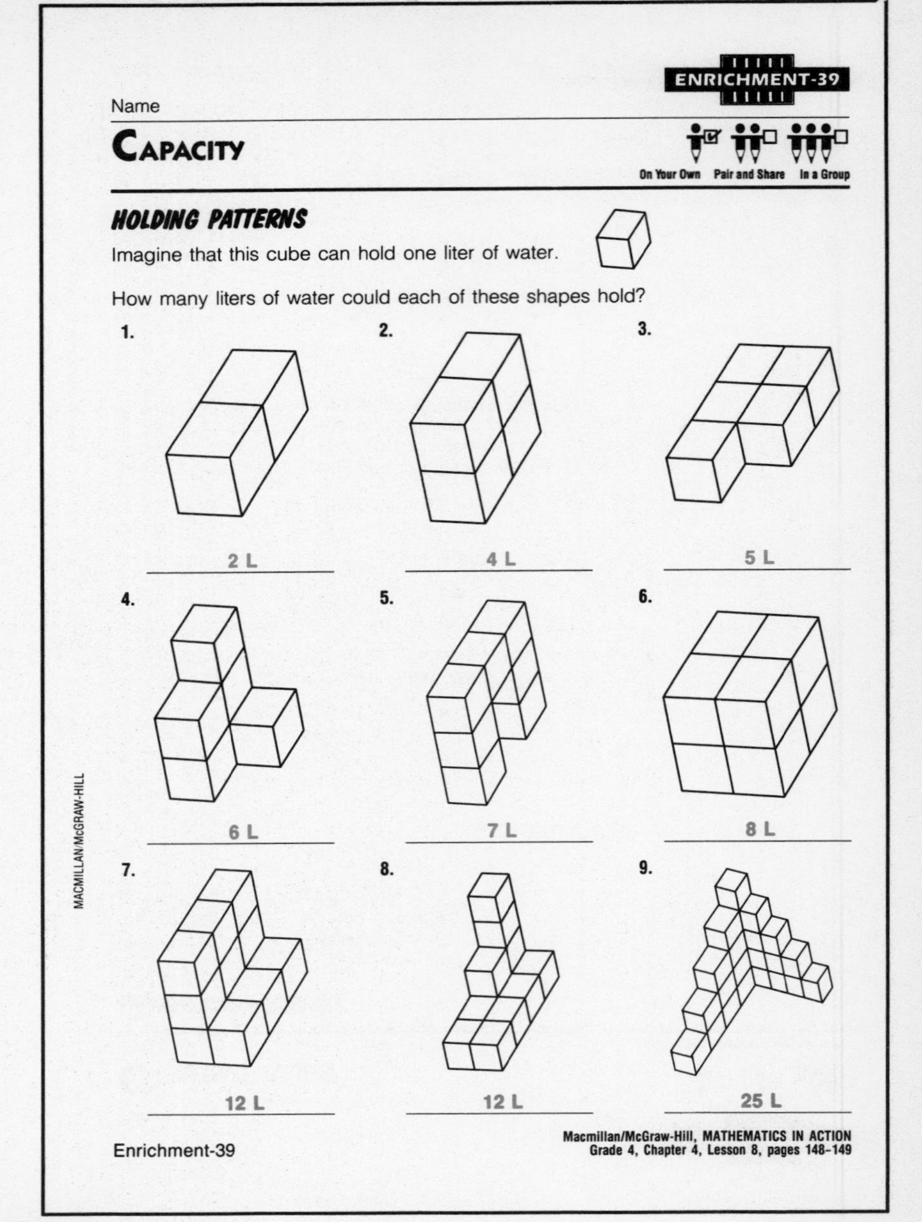

1. 2 L
2. 4 L
3. 5 L
4. 6 L
5. 7 L
6. 8 L
7. 12 L
8. 12 L
9. 25 L

Macmillan/McGraw-Hill, MATHEMATICS IN ACTION
Grade 4, Chapter 4, Lesson 8, pages 148-149

ENRICHMENT-42

Name

TEMPERATURE

On Your Own · Pair and Share · In a Group

UNITS TO FIT

Complete the crossword puzzle below. The words that appear in the puzzle are printed upside down at the bottom of the page. Look if you need help.

ACROSS

2. 60 minutes in 1 ____
4. 1,000 ____ in 1 liter
8. What grams measure
10. 100 ____ in 1 meter
12. What liters measure
14. 60 seconds in 1 ____
15. Water boils at 100 degrees ____

DOWN

1. 1,000 ____ in 1 kilogram
3. 1 ____ equals 1,000 grams
5. What a thermometer measures
6. 10 centimeters in 1 ____
7. 1,000 milliliters equals 1 ____
9. What meters measure
11. 10 decimeters in 1 ____
13. 100 years equal 1 ____

temperature
minute
milliliter
meter
mass
liter
length
kilogram
hour
gram
decimeter
century
centimeter
Centigrade
capacity

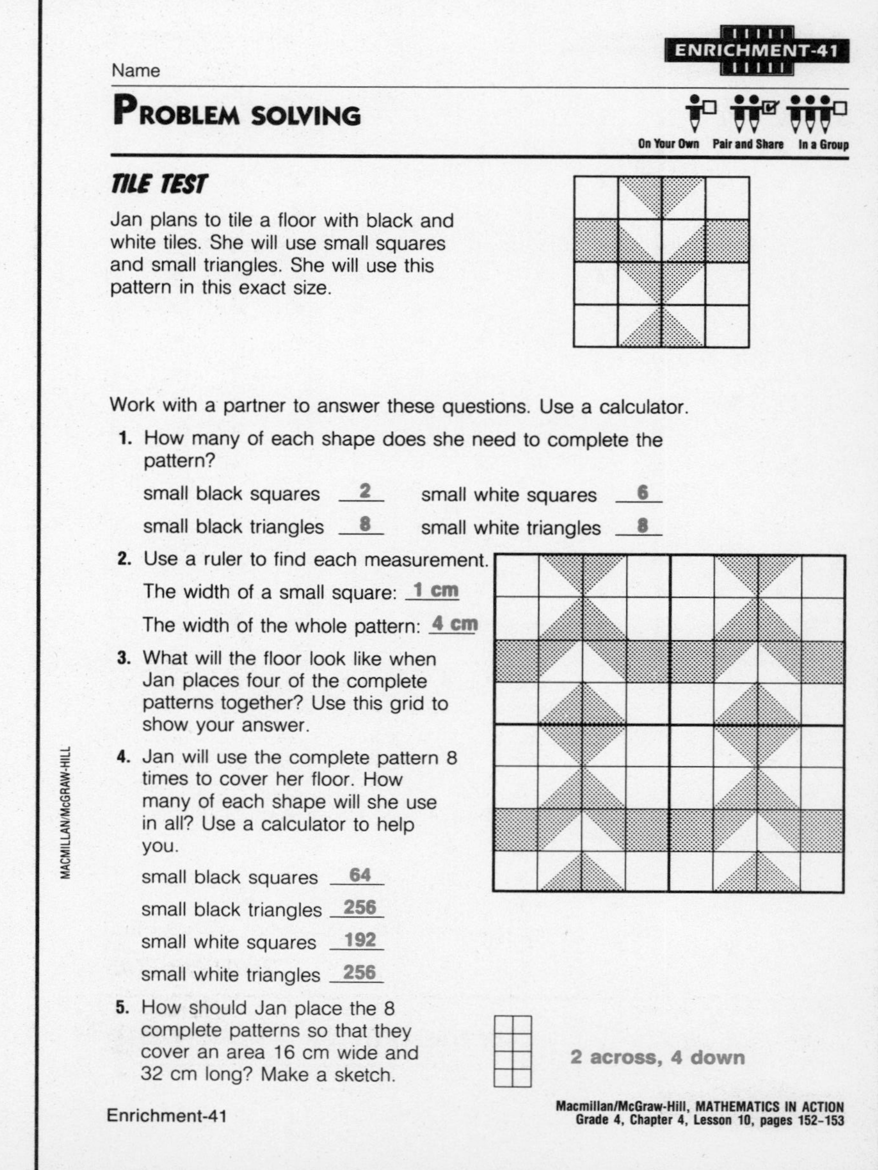

ENRICHMENT-41

Name

PROBLEM SOLVING

On Your Own · Pair and Share · In a Group

TILE TEST

Jan plans to tile a floor with black and white tiles. She will use small squares and small triangles. She will use this pattern in this exact size.

Work with a partner to answer these questions. Use a calculator.

1. How many of each shape does she need to complete the pattern?

   small black squares 2 small white squares 6

   small black triangles 8 small white triangles 8

2. Use a ruler to find each measurement.

   The width of a small square: 1 cm

   The width of the whole pattern: 4 cm

3. What will the floor look like when Jan places four of the complete patterns together? Use this grid to show your answer.

4. Jan will use the complete pattern 8 times to cover her floor. How many of each shape will she use in all? Use a calculator to help you.

   small black squares 64

   small black triangles 256

   small white squares 192

   small white triangles 256

5. How should Jan place the 8 complete patterns so that they cover an area 16 cm wide and 32 cm long? Make a sketch.

   2 across, 4 down

Name

ENRICHMENT-44

On Your Own · Pair and Share · In a Group

THE MEANING OF DIVISION

STEFFI'S STUFF

Steffi collects objects in sets.
She collects:

stamps · flowers · books · rocks · piggy banks · teddy bears · baseballs

Steffi collects in sets of twos, threes, fours, fives, sixes, sevens, and eights. She uses a different number for each object.

For example, she collects teddy bears in sets of twos. As you can see in the drawing, Steffi has six teddy bears, or three sets of two bears.

Work with a partner. Discuss what you see in the drawing. Use the drawing of Steffi's collection to help you fill in her collection chart at the bottom of this page. Remember that each object has a different-sized set.

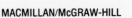

MY COLLECTION

Item	How Many I Have In All	In Sets Of	How Many Sets I Have
Teddy Bears	6	2	3
Piggy Banks	3	3	1
Baseballs	12	4	3
Books	10	5	2
Stamps	18	6	3
Rocks	7	7	1
Flowers	8	8	1

Name

ENRICHMENT-43

On Your Own · Pair and Share · In a Group

THE MEANING OF MULTIPLICATION

DOTS THE POINT

You know that you can represent 3 × 5 with this dot drawing:

These nine multiplication sets can be found in the drawing below:

3 × 3	2 × 14	4 × 4
5 × 5	3 × 9	2 × 5
5 × 6	4 × 6	2 × 15

Can you find them all? Each dot is used only once.
No sets overlap. There is only one complete solution!

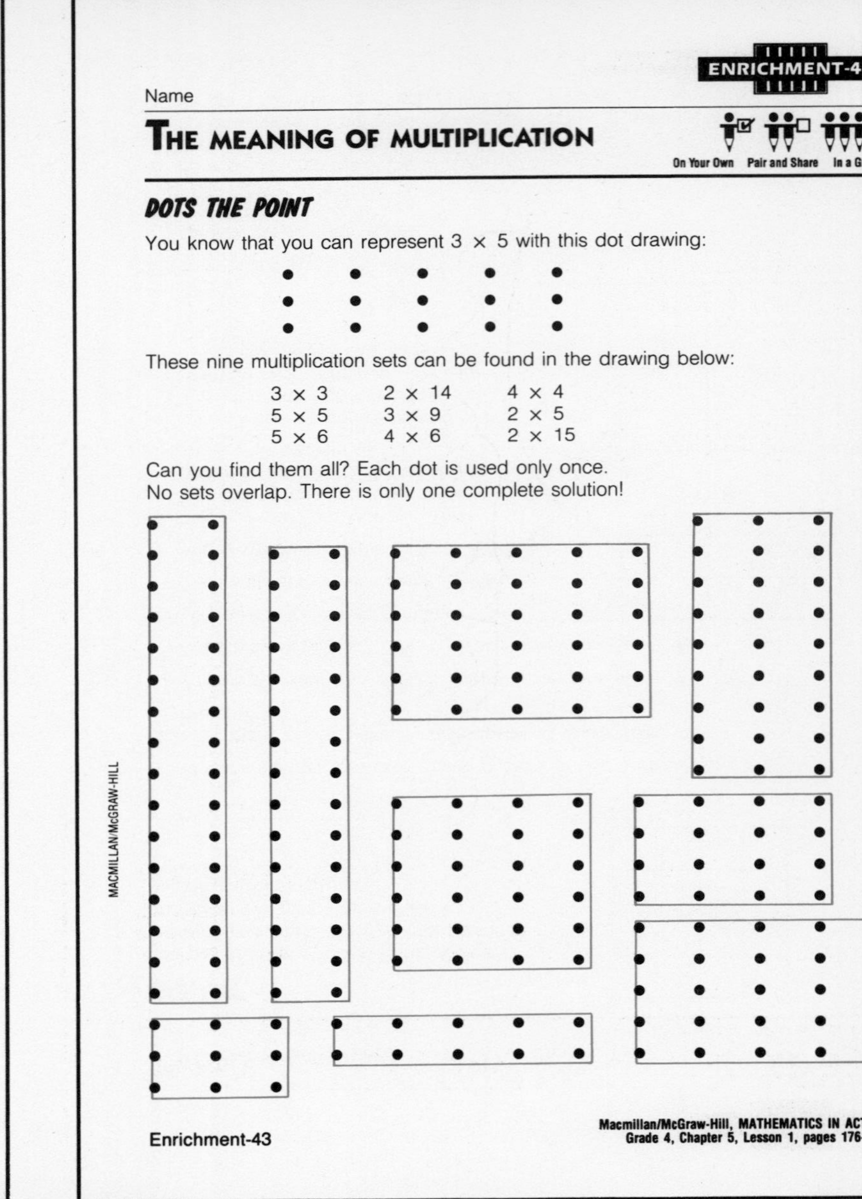

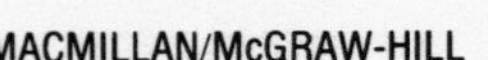

ENRICHMENT-46

Name

Fact Families

On Your Own · Pair and Share · In a Group

BOXED IN

Can you find the numbers that complete each multiplication box? All the information you need is in the boxes.

1.

×	4	7	8	2	5
6	24	42	48	12	30
7	28	49	56	14	35
3	12	21	24	6	15
4	16	28	32	8	20

2.

×	3	8	6	2	4
9	27	72	54	18	36
1	3	8	6	2	4
2	6	16	12	4	8
8	24	64	48	16	32

3.

×	9	1	7	6	4
5	45	5	35	30	20
7	63	7	49	42	28
6	54	6	42	36	24
0	0	0	0	0	0

4.

×	2	0	9	5	8
0	0	0	0	0	0
3	6	0	27	15	24
1	2	0	9	5	8
4	8	0	36	20	32

Macmillan/McGraw-Hill, MATHEMATICS IN ACTION
Grade 4, Chapter 5, Lesson 4, pages 182–183

ENRICHMENT-45

Name

Multiplication and Division Properties

On Your Own · Pair and Share · In a Group

MIX 'N' MATCH

Match each equal quantity. Then look at the letters under the quantities you do not use. Rearrange the letters to answer this riddle:

"Why was the barn so noisy?"

3 × 5 × 6 A	9 × 2 D	4 × 7 × 8 C	8 U
8 × 7 × 4 E	3 ÷ 1 R	2 ÷ 2 I	
1 T	3 M	5 × 6 × 3 N	2 × 8 H
7 × 8 × 4 W	8 ÷ 1 H	4 × 5 N	2 × 9 Y
8 × 3 O	7 ÷ 1 K	7 × 2 × 10 N	10 × 7 × 3 R
	5 × 8 S	3 × 6 × 5 T	7 I

Because the cows had H O R N S.

Macmillan/McGraw-Hill, MATHEMATICS IN ACTION
Grade 4, Chapter 5, Lesson 3, pages 180–181

Name

ENRICHMENT-48

On Your Own · Pair and Share · In a Group

DIVIDING BY 2 THROUGH 9

SORTING CENTS

Ray has a coin collection. Here are the coins in his collection.

36 pennies · 24 buffalo nickels · 48 dimes · 12 silver dollars

Ray wants to sort his collection. He plans to choose from envelopes, sacks, and boxes. He will put the same kinds of coins in each container.

- Each envelope can hold 3 coins.
- Each sack can hold 4 coins.
- Each box can hold 6 coins.

How will he divide his collection if he uses only envelopes? sacks? boxes?

If Ray uses only envelopes:

1. He will fill 12 with pennies, 8 with nickels, 16 with dimes, and 4 with silver dollars.
2. He will use 40 envelopes in all.

If he uses only sacks:

3. He will fill 9 with pennies, 6 with nickels, 12 with dimes, and 3 with silver dollars.
4. He will use 30 sacks in all.

If he uses only boxes:

5. He will fill 6 with pennies, 4 with nickels, 8 with dimes, and 2 with silver dollars.
6. He will use 20 boxes in all.

Macmillan/McGraw-Hill, MATHEMATICS IN ACTION
Grade 4, Chapter 5, Lesson 6, pages 186–187

Name

ENRICHMENT-47

On Your Own · Pair and Share · In a Group

2 THROUGH 9 AS FACTORS

SOME PRODUCTS!

A. Work with a group of friends. Take turns reading the riddles below to the group.

Can you find each pair of numbers described?

I'm thinking of two numbers that . . .

. . . have a sum of 5 and a product of 6. (3, 2)
. . . have a sum of 6 and a product of 9. (3, 3)
. . . have a sum of 12 and a product of 32. (8, 4)
. . . have a sum of 13 and a product of 40. (5, 8)
. . . have a difference of 1 and a product of 42. (6, 7)
. . . have a difference of 2 and a product of 24. (6, 4)
. . . are equal and have a product of 81. (9, 9)
. . . have a difference of 5 and a product of 14. (7, 2)
. . . have a difference of 7 and a product of 18. (2, 9)
. . . are less than 6 and have a product of 12. (3, 4
. . . have a sum of 15 and a product of 56. (7, 8)
. . . have the same number of letters in their names and a product of 21. (7, 3)

B. Have each member of the group make up 3 riddles. Try solving each other's riddles.

Macmillan/McGraw-Hill, MATHEMATICS IN ACTION
Grade 4, Chapter 5, Lesson 5, pages 184–185

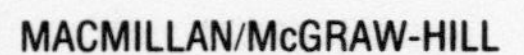

Name

ENRICHMENT-50

MISSING FACTORS

On Your Own · Pair and Share · In a Group

PRODUCT PYRAMIDS

In these pyramids, each number is the product of the two numbers directly below it. Can you complete all of the pyramids?

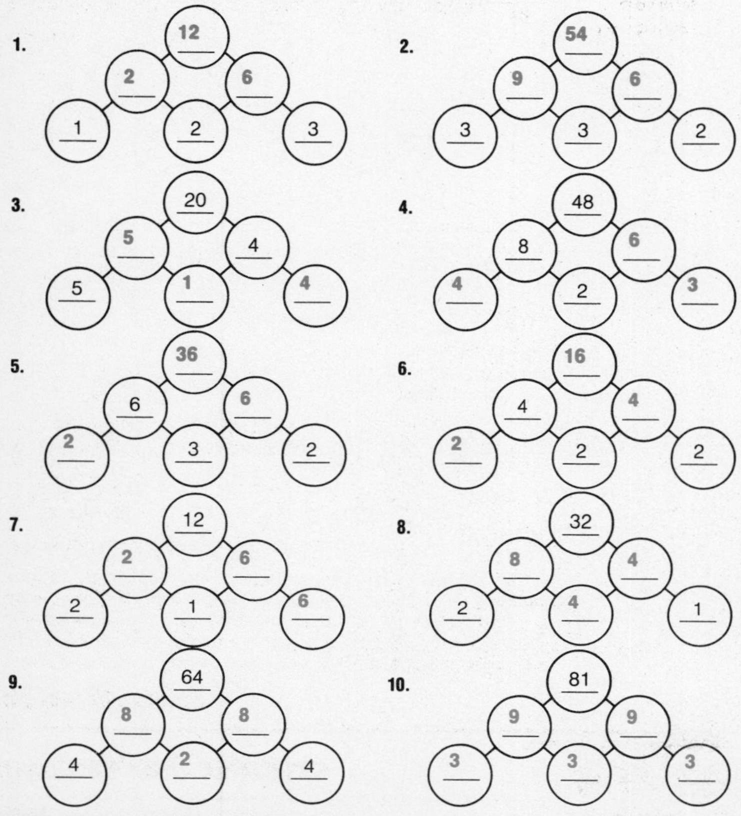

1. 12 / 2, 6 / 1, 2, 3
2. 54 / 9, 6 / 3, 3, 2
3. 20 / 5, 4 / 5, 1, 4
4. 48 / 8, 6 / 4, 2, 3
5. 36 / 6, 6 / 2, 3, 2
6. 16 / 4, 4 / 2, 2, 2
7. 12 / 2, 6 / 2, 1, 6
8. 32 / 8, 4 / 2, 4, 1
9. 64 / 8, 8 / 4, 2, 4
10. 81 / 9, 9 / 3, 3, 3

Macmillan/McGraw-Hill, MATHEMATICS IN ACTION
Grade 4, Chapter 5, Lesson 9, pages 192–193

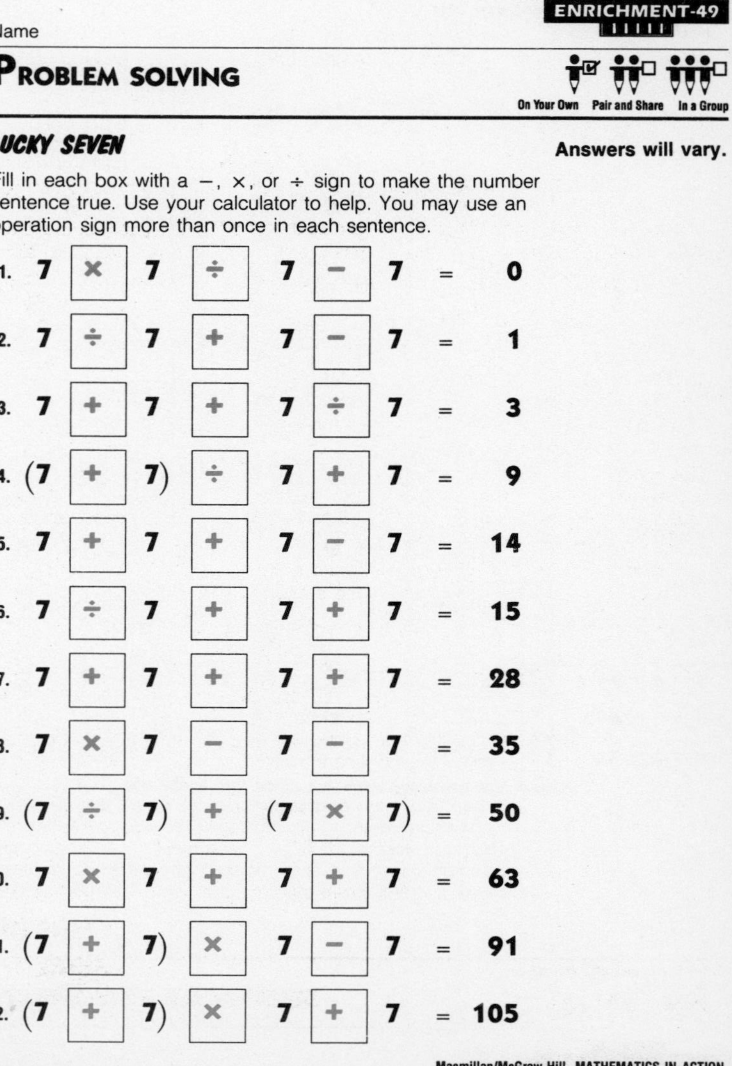

Name

ENRICHMENT-49

PROBLEM SOLVING

On Your Own · Pair and Share · In a Group

LUCKY SEVEN

Answers will vary.

Fill in each box with a −, ×, or ÷ sign to make the number sentence true. Use your calculator to help. You may use an operation sign more than once in each sentence.

1. 7 × 7 ÷ 7 − 7 = 0
2. 7 ÷ 7 + 7 − 7 = 1
3. 7 + 7 + 7 ÷ 7 = 3
4. (7 + 7) ÷ 7 + 7 = 9
5. 7 + 7 + 7 − 7 = 14
6. 7 ÷ 7 + 7 + 7 = 15
7. 7 + 7 + 7 + 7 = 28
8. 7 × 7 − 7 − 7 = 35
9. (7 ÷ 7) + (7 × 7) = 50
10. 7 × 7 + 7 + 7 = 63
11. (7 + 7) × 7 − 7 = 91
12. (7 + 7) × 7 + 7 = 105

Macmillan/McGraw-Hill, MATHEMATICS IN ACTION
Grade 4, Chapter 5, Lesson 7, pages 188–189

ENRICHMENT-52

Name

FACTORS AND MULTIPLES

On Your Own Pair and Share In a Group

SALTWATER TOUGHIE

Use the numbers below to complete the problems. When you find a number, write it in the space and cross it and its letter out. Be sure to do the problems in order! When you are done, the remaining letters, written in order from left to right and top to bottom, will spell out the answer to this riddle:

"What do you use to cut through the ocean?"

1. Factors of 12: 1, 2, 3, 4, 6, 12
2. Multiples of 3 that are less than 30: 15, 21, 24, 27
3. Multiples of 5 that are greater than 30: 35, 40, 45
4. Multiples of 2 that are also multiples of 4: 8, 16, 32, 48, 56, 64
5. Multiples of 7 that are greater than 40: 42, 49, 63
6. Multiples of 9: 81

1 E, 2 N, 3 S, 4 W, 6 T, 7 A
8 R, 12 U, 13 S, 15 D, 16 B, 17 E
19 A, 21 R, 24 E, 27 C, 32 M, 35 O
40 P, 42 D, 43 S, 45 I, 48 V, 49 W
53 A, 56 Y, 63 L, 64 F, 71 W, 81 H

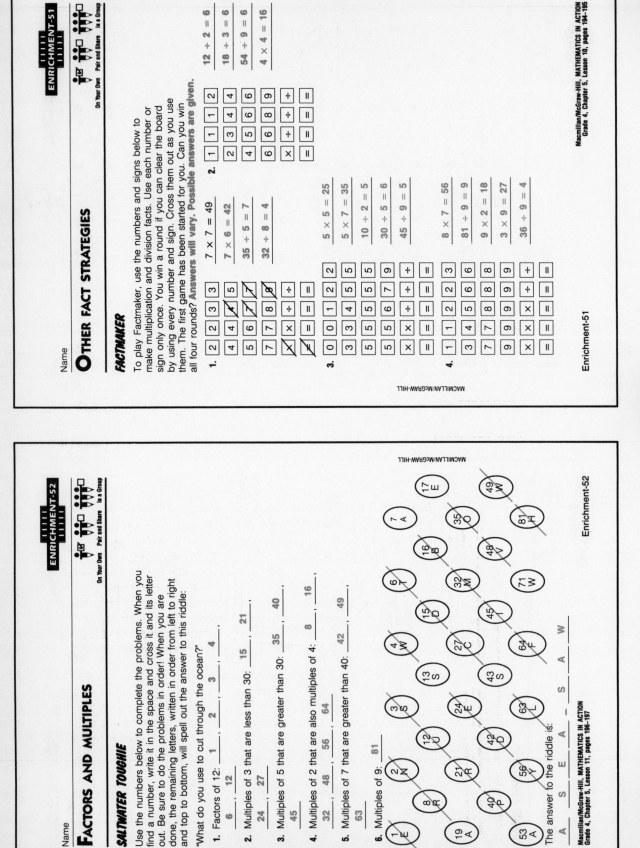

The answer to the riddle is: A S E A - S A W

ENRICHMENT-51

Name

OTHER FACT STRATEGIES

On Your Own Pair and Share In a Group

FACTMAKER

To play Factmaker, use the numbers and signs below to make multiplication and division facts. Use each number or sign only once. You win a round if you can clear the board by using every number and sign. Cross them out as you use them. The first game has been started for you. Can you win all four rounds? **Answers will vary. Possible answers are given.**

1.

2	2	3	3
4	4	4	5
5	6	7	7
7	7	8	9
×	×	÷	÷
=	=	=	=

7 × 7 = 49
7 × 6 = 42
35 ÷ 5 = 7
32 ÷ 8 = 4

2.

1	1	1	2
2	3	4	4
4	5	6	6
6	6	8	9
×	÷	÷	÷
=	=	=	=

12 ÷ 2 = 6
18 ÷ 3 = 6
54 ÷ 9 = 6
4 × 4 = 16

3.

0	0	1	2	2
3	3	4	5	5
5	5	5	5	5
5	5	6	7	9
×	×	÷	÷	÷
=	=	=	=	=

5 × 5 = 25
5 × 7 = 35
10 ÷ 2 = 5
30 ÷ 5 = 6
45 ÷ 9 = 5

4.

1	1	2	2	3
3	4	5	6	6
7	7	8	8	8
9	9	9	9	9
×	×	×	÷	÷
=	=	=	=	=

8 × 7 = 56
81 ÷ 9 = 9
9 × 2 = 18
3 × 9 = 27
36 ÷ 9 = 4

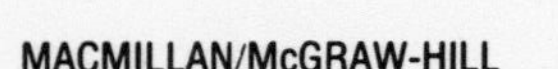

ENRICHMENT-54

Name

AREA

On Your Own | Pair and Share | In a Group

COLOR-BY-AREA

Follow this chart to color each shape in the grid below.

Key: One □ = one square centimeter

If the shape has an area of:	Color it:
1 sq cm	black
7 sq cm	brown
8 sq cm	red
9 sq cm	blue
10 sq cm or greater	green

What does your picture show? A butterfly

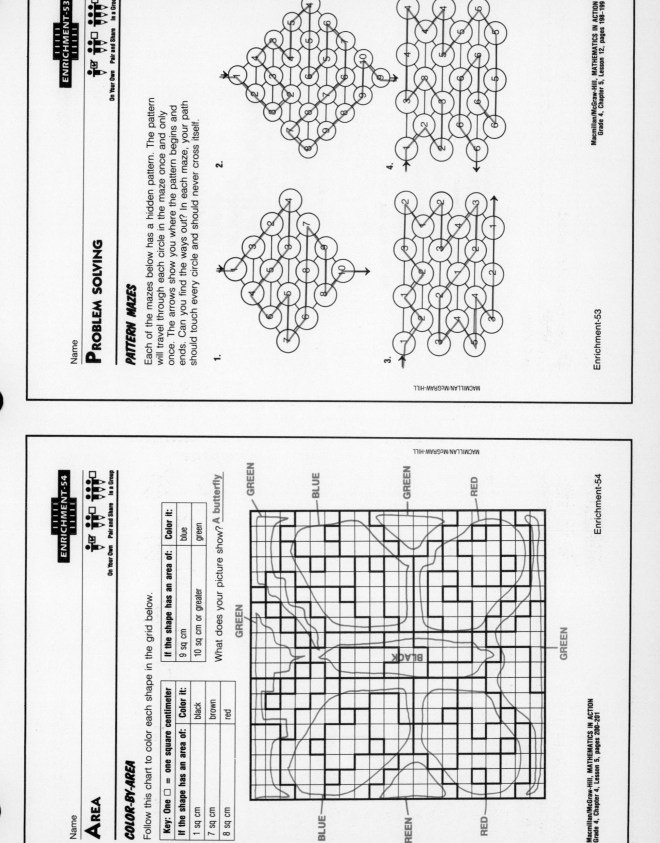

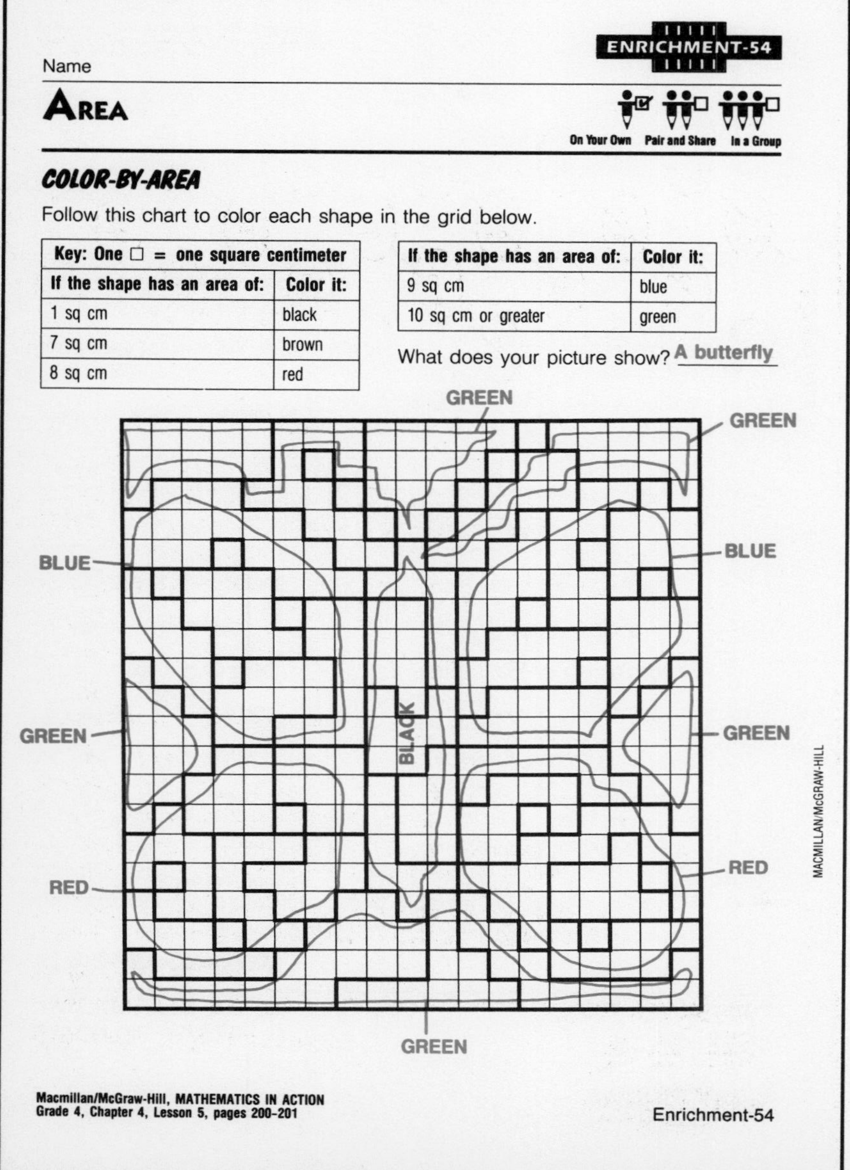

ENRICHMENT-53

Name

PROBLEM SOLVING

On Your Own | Pair and Share | In a Group

PATTERN MAZES

Each of the mazes below has a hidden pattern. The pattern will travel through each circle in the maze once and only once. The arrows show you where the pattern begins and ends. Can you find the ways out? In each maze, your path should touch every circle and should never cross itself.

1.

2.

3.

4.

ENRICHMENT-56

Name

MENTAL MATH: MULTIPLYING BY 10s AND 100s

On Your Own · Pair and Share · In a Group

GEOGRAPHY GROANERS

Fill in each box. Then find the letter in the grid that matches each answer. Write the letter that goes with each exercise number and solve the riddles.

1. 300 × [9] = 2,700
2. 600 × [8] = 4,800
3. [6]00 × 4 = 2,400
4. [2]00 × 9 = 1,800
5. 700 × [6] = 4,200
6. 800 × 5 = 4,[0]00
7. [4],000 × 2 = 8,000
8. [7],000 x 7 = 49,000
9. 4 × 8,000 = 3,[2]00
10. [1],000 × 6 = 6,000
11. [3]00 × 3 = 900
12. [4] × 500 = 2,000
13. [5],000 × 5 = 25,000
14. 8,000 × [2] = 16,000

Answer	0	1	2	3	4	5	6	7	8	9
Letter	A	C	E	H	I	L	M	N	O	R

What city likes to wander? R (1.) O (2.) M (3.) E (4.)

What state reminds you of part of a lion? M (5.) A (6.) I (7.) N (8.) E (9.)

What country is always cold? C (10.) H (11.) I (12.) L (13.) E (14.)

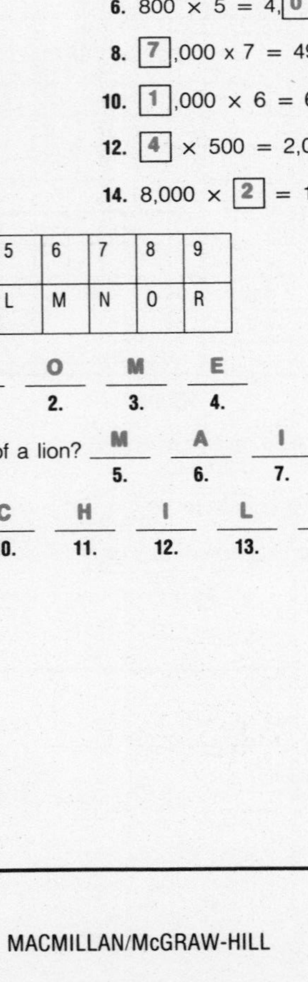

Macmillan/McGraw-Hill, MATHEMATICS IN ACTION
Grade 4, Chapter 6, Lesson 1, pages 220–221

ENRICHMENT-55

Name

MAKING PICTOGRAPHS

On Your Own · Pair and Share · In a Group

WHICH FISH?

Work with a partner. Use the clues to complete each pictograph.

1.

FISH IN FIVE STUDENTS' AQUARIUMS	
Student	Number of Fish
Bob	
Claire	
Dennis	
Edith	
Fred	
Each = 4 fish	

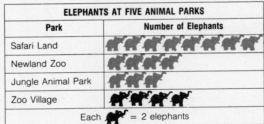

Clue 1 Bob has four more fish than Edith, but four fewer than Fred.

Clue 2 If Claire had four more fish, she would have twice as many as Bob.

Clue 3 Dennis has two more fish than Fred does.

1.

ELEPHANTS AT FIVE ANIMAL PARKS	
Park	Number of Elephants
Safari Land	
Newland Zoo	
Jungle Animal Park	
Zoo Village	
Each = 2 elephants	

Clue 1 There are twice as many elephants at Safari Land as there are at Zoo Village.

Clue 2 There are two more elephants at Newland Zoo than at Jungle Animal Park.

Clue 3 Newland Zoo and Zoo Village have the same number of elephants.

Macmillan/McGraw-Hill, MATHEMATICS IN ACTION
Grade 4, Chapter 5, Lesson 14, pages 202–203

ENRICHMENT-58

Name

Problem Solving

On Your Own | Pair and Share | In a Group

PATH PATTERNS

You can use a +, −, or × in any box. Find a path of correct number sentences through the maze. There is a pattern that can help you. What is the pattern?

Pattern: order of operations is +, −, +, ×.

ENTER

3	+	7	=	10	□	170	=	190	+	210	=	400
□				−				=				−
2				2				10				300
=				=				×				=
4	=	2	□	8	□	3	=	19	□	72	=	100
□				+				=				+
5				10				16				50
=				=				+				=
180	=	10	×	18	=	4	□	3	□	151	=	150
+				□				=				×
5				105				224				2
=				=				−				=
185	□	25	=	220	+	7	=	227	=	6	□	300
−				=				□				+
175				20				20				12
=				×				=				=
10	+	1	=	11	□	5	=	5	□	40	=	312

LEAVE

ENRICHMENT-57

Name

Estimating Products

On Your Own | Pair and Share | In a Group

BOOK NOOKS

Imagine that you belong to a Science Club. Your club has decided to buy new bookcases. Work with a group of friends to decide which bookcases to buy.

Here are some things to consider:

- Your club has 1,000 books.
- You may buy more books in the future.
- You want to use as little floor space as possible.

You can purchase any combination of these bookcase styles:

A — 3 ft

B — 4 ft

C — 6 ft

Answer these questions to help you estimate how many books each case will hold:

1. About how many books will fit on 1 ft of shelf space?
   Answers will vary, 10 to 20 books might be a reasonable estimate.
2. How many feet of shelf space are in each case?
   Answers will vary depending on whether top of bookcase is used.
   Bookcase A: **12 ft** Bookcase B: **24 ft** Bookcase C: **24 ft**
3. About how many books will each case hold?
   Answers will vary.
   Bookcase A: **200** Bookcase B: **300–400** Bookcase C: **300–400**
4. Which bookcases will your club order? Why?
   3 of Bookcase C, 3 of Bookcase B, and 1 of Bookcase A; etc.

ENRICHMENT-60

Name

MULTIPLYING 2-DIGIT NUMBERS: REGROUPING TWICE

On Your Own · Pair and Share · In a Group

JOIN THE CLUB

Work with a partner to complete this page. The Gleeful Club chose this design for their new T-shirts:

They will cut each shape out of felt and then glue the shapes onto the shirts.

1. Complete this chart to show how many of each shape they will have to cut to make each number of T-shirts:

Number of T-shirts	Diamonds	Hearts	Stars
10	20	30	50
16	32	48	80
25	50	75	125
48	96	144	240
67	134	201	335
89	178	267	445

2. The club has enough felt to cut 161 diamonds, 244 hearts, and 322 stars. What is the greatest number of T-shirts they can make with this felt?

   64

3. How might they change their design to be able to make more T-shirts?

   Use only 4 stars to make 80 T-shirts.

   (Answers will vary.)

4. Draw and color your new design on another sheet of paper. Work with your partner to make up a chart like the one above. Decide on several numbers for the first column (Number of T-shirts). Ask some friends to complete the other columns based on the shapes in your design.

ENRICHMENT-59

Name

MULTIPLYING 2-DIGIT NUMBERS: REGROUPING ONCE

On Your Own · Pair and Share · In a Group

NUMBER JUMBLES

For each problem, use the numbers in the box to complete the multiplication problem. Use a calculator to help you check your answers.

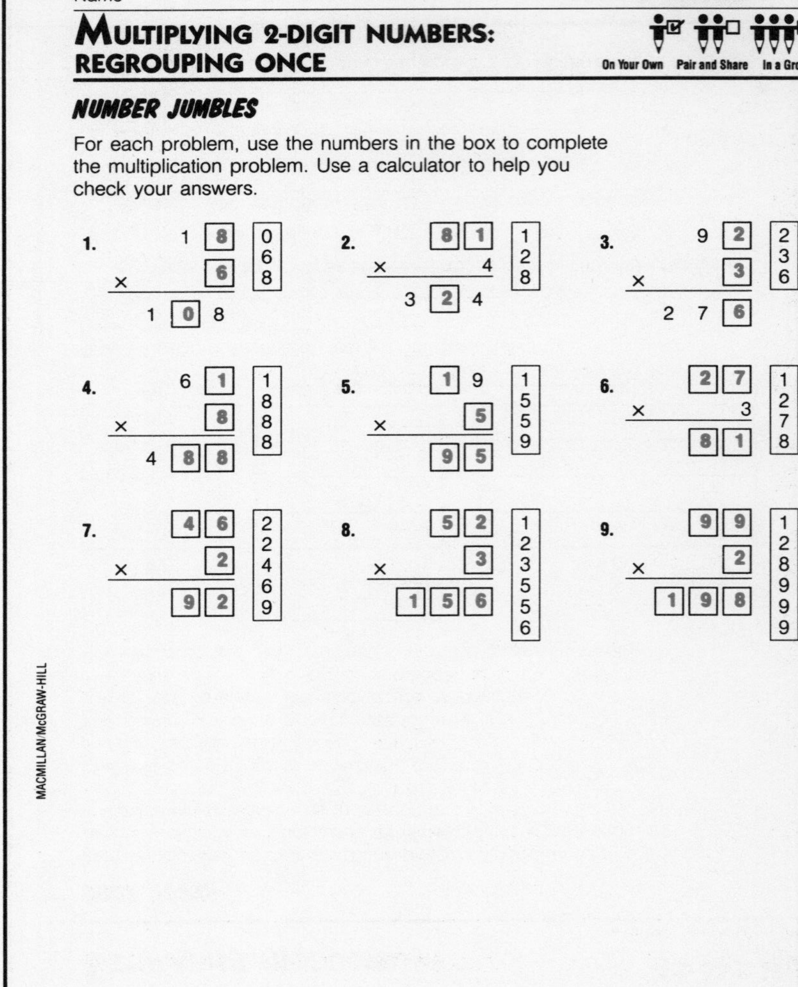

1. 1 [8] × [6] = 1 [0] 8 — Box: 0, 6, 8
2. [8][1] × 4 = 3 [2] 4 — Box: 1, 2, 8
3. 9 [2] × [3] = 2 7 [6] — Box: 2, 3, 6
4. 6 [1] × [8] = 4 [8][8] — Box: 1, 8, 8, 8
5. [1] 9 × [5] = [9][5] — Box: 1, 5, 5, 9
6. [2][7] × 3 = [8][1] — Box: 1, 2, 7, 8
7. [4][6] × [2] = [9][2] — Box: 2, 2, 4, 6, 9
8. [5][2] × [3] = [1][5][6] — Box: 1, 2, 3, 5, 5, 6
9. [9][9] × [2] = [1][9][8] — Box: 1, 2, 8, 9, 9, 9

Name

ENRICHMENT-62

MULTIPLYING MONEY

On Your Own · Pair and Share · In a Group

MONEY MAZES

Can you find the path from top to bottom of each maze that results in the greatest amount of money? You may only travel downward in each maze. Use estimation to help you.

1.

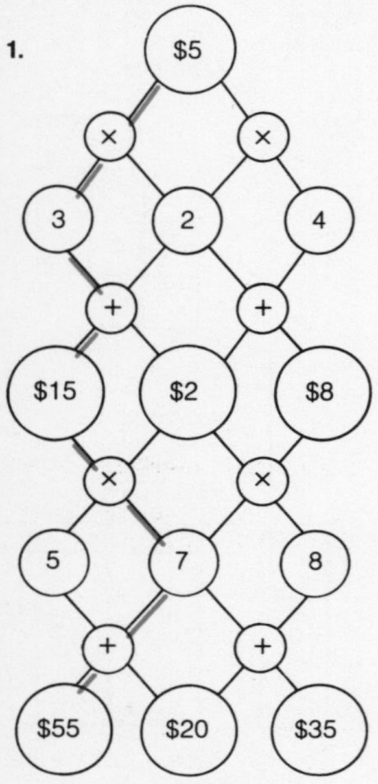

$5

× ×

3 2 4

+ +

$15 $2 $8

× ×

5 7 8

+ +

$55 $20 $35

Total $265.00

2.

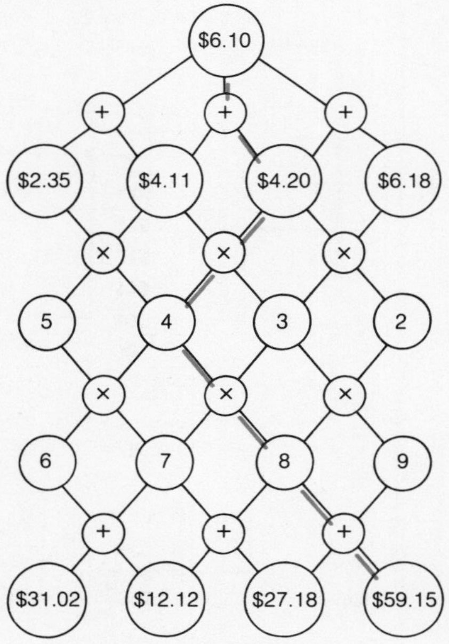

$6.10

+ + +

$2.35 $4.11 $4.20 $6.18

× × ×

5 4 3 2

× × ×

6 7 8 9

+ + +

$31.02 $12.12 $27.18 $59.15

Total $388.75

Name

ENRICHMENT-61

MULTIPLYING 3-DIGIT NUMBERS

On Your Own · Pair and Share · In a Group

HIGH OR LOW

Play this game with a partner. One player is High, the other is Low. Cut out the cards along the side of this page and turn them upside down. You may combine two sets of cards. Players take turns picking a card and placing it on the board. When the board is filled, find the product by multiplying. If the product is greater than 2,500, High wins a point. If the product is less than 2,500, Low wins a point. The player with the most points at the end of 10 rounds is the winner. If the score is tied, play another tie-breaking round.

Gameboard

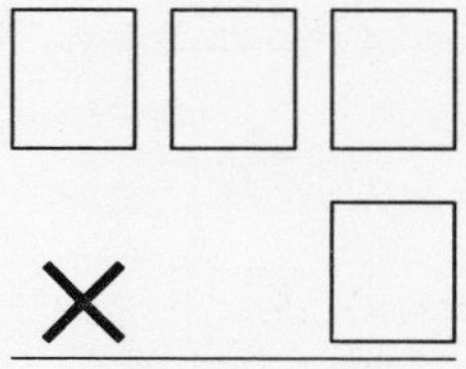

□ □ □

× □

1 2 3 4 5 6 7 8 9

SCORESHEET

	Problem	Product	High	Low
Sample	672 × 3	2,016		1
Round 1				
Round 2				
Round 3				
Round 4				
Round 5				
Round 6				
Round 7				
Round 8				
Round 9				
Round 10				
		Total		

ENRICHMENT-64

Name

Dividing with Remainders

On Your Own · Pair and Share · In a Group

CUT UPS

Cut out the shapes below. Then divide the shape into the given number of pieces. Cut only on the lines.

Into 2 equal pieces:

Into 3 equal pieces:

Into 4 equal pieces:

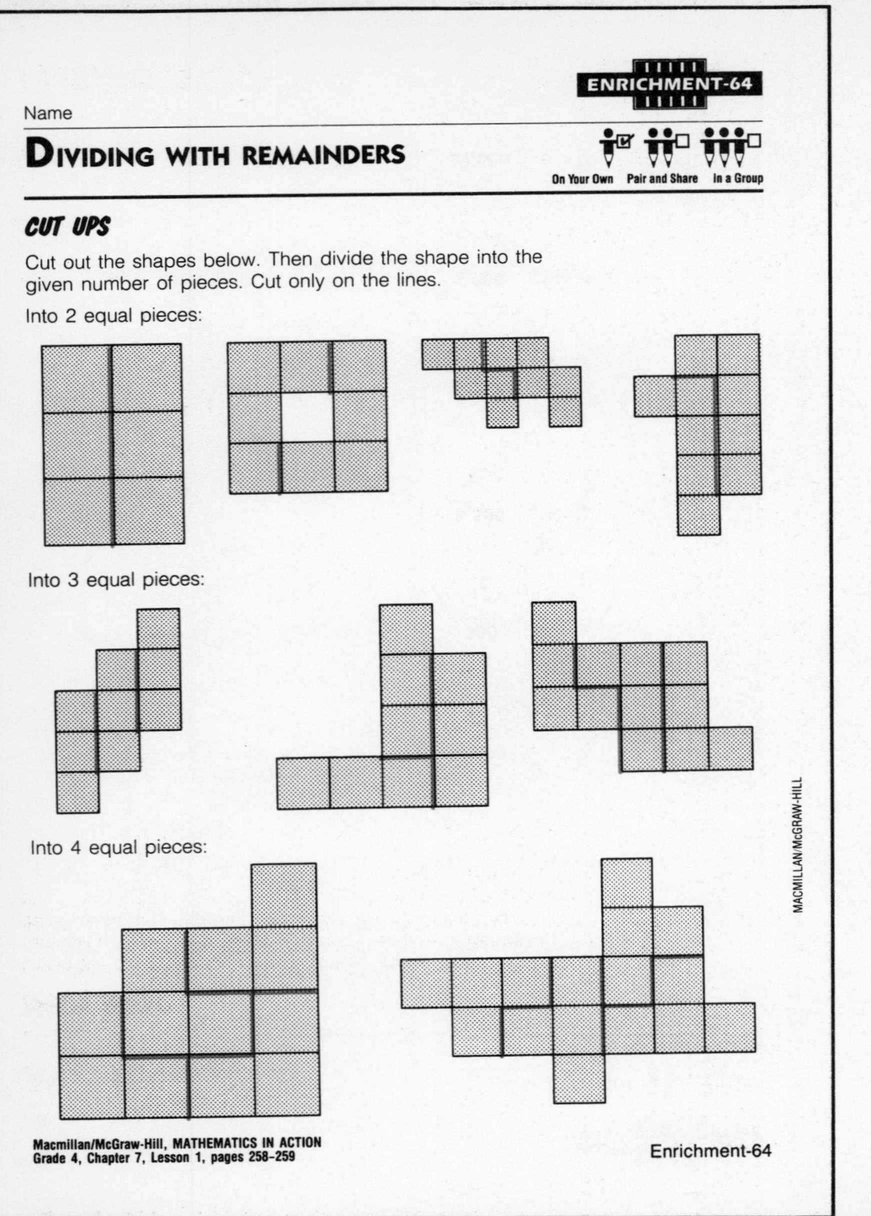

Macmillan/McGraw-Hill, MATHEMATICS IN ACTION
Grade 4, Chapter 7, Lesson 1, pages 258–259

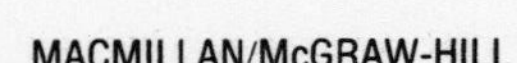

ENRICHMENT-63

Name

Problem Solving

On Your Own · Pair and Share · In a Group

FUN FUND RAISING

Imagine that your class has decided to raise some money for a school or class trip. Choose one of the activities below and work with your group to estimate how much money you will be able to earn.

For each quantity, decide if you will overestimate, underestimate, or find an exact amount. Write over, under, or exact in the blank to the left of each item. Be prepared to give reasons.

Answers will vary. Accept answers that students can justify.

Bake Sale

over How many products will you sell?

exact How much will you charge for a cookie?

exact How much will you charge for a cake?

over How many people will come?

over How many people will sell the goods?

exact How many hours will the bake sale last?

under How much money will the bake sale earn?

Car Wash

over How long will it take to wash one car?

exact How much will you charge for washing each car?

under How many people will want their cars washed?

over How many people will wash each car?

under How many cars will you be able to wash during the day?

exact How many hours will the car wash last?

under How much money will the car wash earn?

Dog Wash

over How long will it take to wash each dog?

exact How much will you charge for washing one dog?

under How many people will want their dogs washed?

over How many people will be needed as washers?

under How many dogs will you be able to wash?

exact How many hours will your dog wash last?

under How much money will the dog wash earn?

What other considerations, such as time, place, and advertising, will affect the success of your event? Compare your estimates with those of other groups.

Work together as a class to decide on the best activity or activities. Do you think your class could sponsor more than one event? Can you think of another event that might be more successful? Could you earn enough to take a class trip? How will you know?

Macmillan/McGraw-Hill, MATHEMATICS IN ACTION
Grade 4, Chapter 6, Lesson 11, pages 240–241

ENRICHMENT-66

Name

ESTIMATING QUOTIENTS

On Your Own Pair and Share In a Group

CHAIN REACTION

Circle the correct answer for the first exercise. Then use the remaining answers to write the next division fact. Repeat those steps until you have finished this page. Use mental math. The first two exercises have been done for you.

1. 900 ÷ 10 = 90
   a. 100 (b.) 90 c. 20

2. 100 ÷ 20 = 5
   (a.) 5 b. 10 c. 40

3. 40 ÷ 10 = 4
   a. 400 (b.) 4 c. 4,000

4. 4,000 ÷ 400 = 10
   a. 6,000 b. 20 (c.) 10

5. 6,000 ÷ 20 = 300
   a. 900 (b.) 300 c. 3

6. 900 ÷ 3 = 300
   a. 120 b. 30 (c.) 300

7. 120 ÷ 30 = 4
   (a.) 4 b. 70 c. 5,600

8. 5,600 ÷ 70 = 80
   a. 800 (b.) 80 c. 64,000

9. 64,000 ÷ 800 = 80
   a. 8 b. 8,000 (c.) 80

10. 8,000 ÷ 8 = 1,000
    (a.) 1,000 b. 50 c. 10,000

11. 10,000 ÷ 50 = 200
    a. 2,000 b. 40 (c.) 200

12. 2,000 ÷ 40 = 50
    a. 500 b. 3,500 (c.) 50

13. 3,500 ÷ 500 = 7
    a. 70 (b.) 7 c. 49,000

14. 49,000 ÷ 70 = 700
    a. 7 b. 70 (c.) 700

Macmillan/McGraw-Hill, MATHEMATICS IN ACTION
Grade 4, Chapter 7, Lesson 3, pages 262–263

ENRICHMENT-65

Name

MENTAL MATH: DIVIDING 10s AND 100s

On Your Own Pair and Share In a Group

WHAT'S LEFT?

Q: What kind of food reminds you of remainders?

Complete each division problem. Use the numbers at the bottom of the page. When you use a number, cross it out. Then cross out the letter underneath it. When you have finished, the remaining letters will spell out an answer to the riddle.

1. 5)36 = 7 R 1
2. 6)10 = 1 R4
3. 4)14 = 3 R2
4. 7)50 = 7 R1
5. 8)70 = 8 R6
6. 3)27 = 9 R0
7. 4)19 = 4 R 3
8. 7)55 = 7 R 6
9. 8)22 = 2 R6
10. 9)62 = 6 R8
11. 6)35 = 5 R5
12. 9)25 = 2 R7

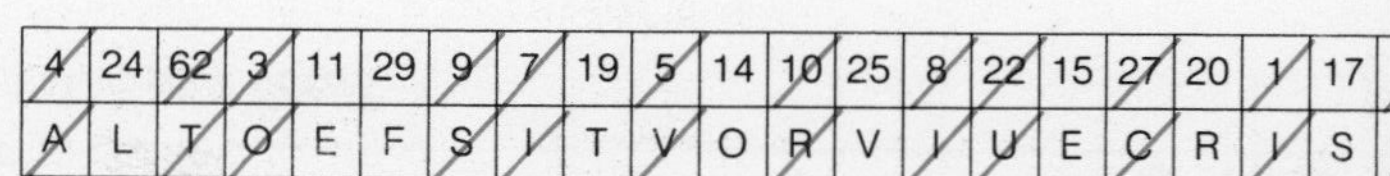

4	24	62	3	11	29	9	7	19	5	14	10	25	8	22	15	27	20	1	17	6
A	L	T	O	E	F	S	I	T	V	O	R	V	I	U	E	C	R	I	S	G

Write the answer here:
L E F T O V E R S

Macmillan/McGraw-Hill, MATHEMATICS IN ACTION
Grade 4, Chapter 7, Lesson 2, pages 260–261

Name

ENRICHMENT-68

DIVIDING 2-DIGIT NUMBERS

On Your Own   Pair and Share   In a Group

RIGHTING WRONGS

None of the division problems below are correct! But you can fix them all by swapping numbers. You can exchange two divisors, two dividends, or two quotients. Circle the numbers you will change and draw a line connecting them. Make only one change in each problem. The first one is done for you.

1. 2)61 = 18 R1
2. 6)11 = 5 R1
3. 7)24 = 5 R2
4. 3)17 = 3 R3
5. 2)18 = 3 R0
6. 5)6 = 3 R2
7. 4)15 = 10 R1
8. 8)37 = 7 R5
9. 4)14 = 1 R1
10. 4)41 = 3 R3
11. 6)77 = 8 R5
12. 9)82 = 13 R4
13. Try writing a set of six mixed-up division problems of your own. Try them out on a friend.

Name

ENRICHMENT-67

PROBLEM SOLVING

On Your Own   Pair and Share   In a Group

DIVIDE AND COLOR

Estimate each quotient. Then follow this chart to color the picture.

If the quotient is . . .	Color that section
Less than 10	Red
Greater than 10 but less than 50	Dark blue
Greater than 50 but less than 600	Light blue
Greater than 600 but less than 1,500	Green
Greater than 1,500	Yellow

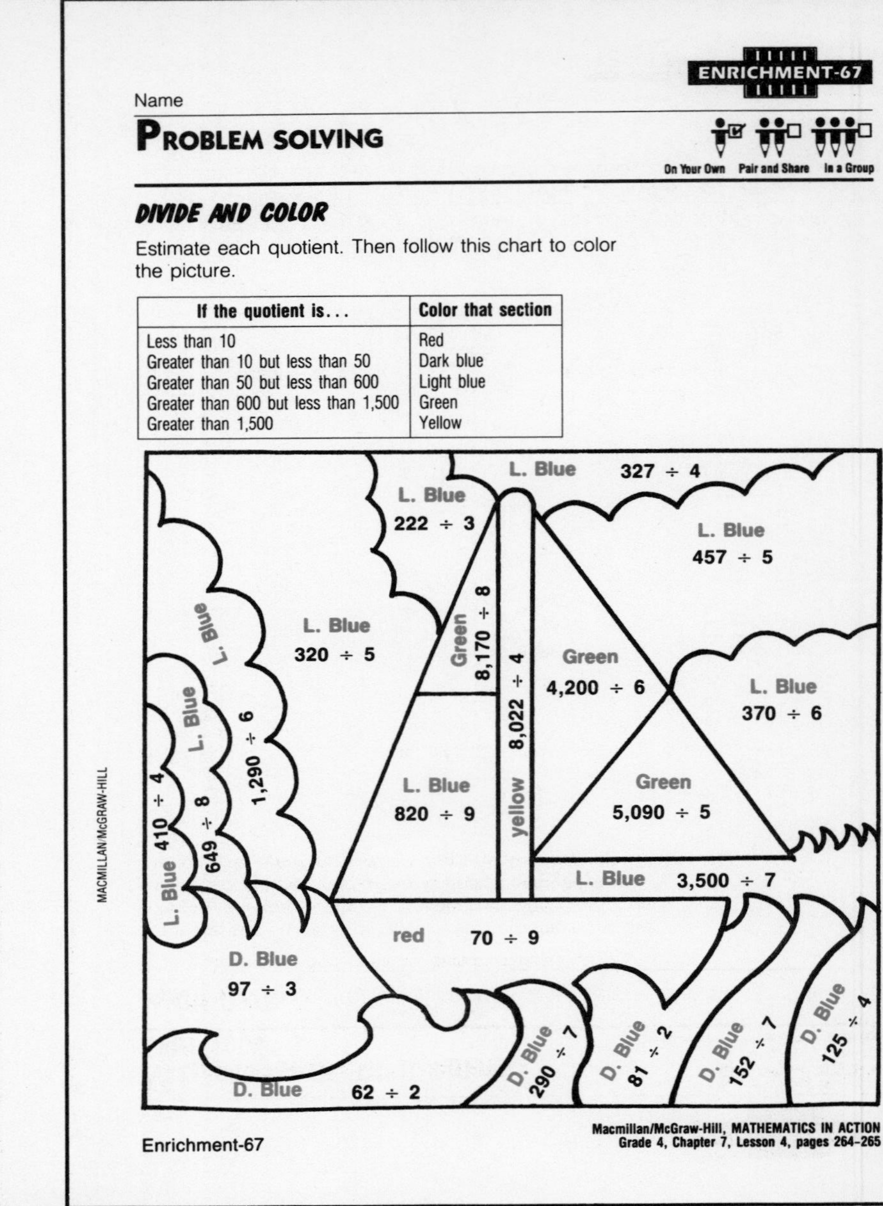

Name

ENRICHMENT-70

MORE DIVIDING 3-DIGIT NUMBERS

On Your Own · Pair and Share · In a Group

DIVIDED ATTENTIONS

Complete each division problem using the digits in the box to the right.

1. 8) 120 = 15
− 8
40
− 40
0

Digits: 0 0 0 0 / 1 1 2 4 / 4 5 8

2. 7) 497 = 71
− 49
07
− 7
0

Digits: 0 0 1 4 / 7 7 7 7 / 7 9

3. 3) 999 = 333
− 9
09
− 9
09
− 9
0

Digits: 0 0 0 3 / 3 3 3 9 / 9 9 9 9 / 9 9 9

4. 5) 680 = 136
− 5
18
− 15
30
− 30
0

Digits: 0 0 0 1 / 1 1 3 3 / 5 5 5 6 / 6 8 8

5. 6) 738 = 123
− 6
13
− 12
18
− 18
0

Digits: 0 1 1 1 / 1 1 2 2 / 3 3 3 6 / 6 7 8 8 / 8

Name

ENRICHMENT-69

DIVIDING 3-DIGIT NUMBERS

On Your Own · Pair and Share · In a Group

MISSING ELEMENTS

Can you find all of the possible sets of divisors and dividends for each quotient and remainder?

The first four exercises tell you how many sets you need to find. In the last four, you have to decide how many sets you can find. (Do not use 1 as a divisor). Work with a partner to solve the problems.

1. ?) ??? = 1 2 4
868 ÷ 7
992 ÷ 8

2. ?) ??? = 1 0 1 R 5
611 ÷ 6
711 ÷ 7
813 ÷ 8
914 ÷ 9

3. ?) ??? = 3 0 5
610 ÷ 2
915 ÷ 3

4. ?) ??? = 2 4 4 R 2
734 ÷ 3
978 ÷ 4

5. ?) ??? = 2 7 7 R 1
555 ÷ 2; 832 ÷ 3

6. ?) ??? = 1 2 2 R 3
491 ÷ 4; 613 ÷ 5

7. ?) ??? = 2 8 9 R 2
868 ÷ 3

8. ?) ??? = 1 0 7 R 2
323 ÷ 3; 430 ÷ 4;
537 ÷ 5; 644 ÷ 6;
751 ÷ 7; 858 ÷ 8; 965 ÷ 9

Name

DIVIDING MONEY

BAND AID

Jill's band, Sound-Off, is choosing among the three concert halls described below:

Memorial Auditorium	Sound Stage	New Variety Theater
600 seats 24 rows Rental fee: $525/night	630 seats 30 rows Rental fee: $577/night	532 seats 28 rows Rental fee: $418/night

Jill makes several calculations to compare each space. Use a calculator to help you. Round your answers. Then discuss your answers in a group.

1. There are an equal number of seats in every row. How many seats are in each row?

Memorial Auditorium **25**

Sound Stage **21**

New Variety Theater **19**

2. Jill wants to sell at least $2,000 worth of tickets. Assume that she can sell out any of the theaters. What is the lowest price she can charge for tickets?

Memorial Auditorium **$3.34**

Sound Stage **$3.18**

New Variety Theater **$3.76**

3. What is Jill's cost per seat for renting each hall?

Memorial Auditorium **$0.88** Sound Stage **$0.92** New Variety Theater **$0.79**

4. Suppose that Jill decides to charge $4 for each ticket. How much will she take in if she sells all of the tickets? How much will she earn (have left)?

	Take In	Earn
Memorial Auditorium	**$2,400**	**$1,875**
Sound Stage	**$2,520**	**$1,943**
New Variety Theater	**$2,128**	**$1,710**

5. Which space do you think Jill should rent? Why?

Answers will vary. The most money can be earned at Sound Stage, but New Variety offers the least risk.

Macmillan/McGraw-Hill, MATHEMATICS IN ACTION
Grade 4, Chapter 7, Lesson 11, pages 278-279

Name

ENRICHMENT-71

On Your Own Pair and Share In a Group

ZEROS IN THE QUOTIENT

EDWARDS' LETTERS

Each digit has been replaced with a specific letter in the problem below. For example, every 1 might be replaced with a V. Can you find out what digit each letter stands for? When you do, write each division problem. Then use the letter values you've found to answer the riddle at the bottom of the page.

Q: Why did the man name two of his children Edward? (*Hint:* T = 5)

Problem	Answer	Problem	Answer	Problem	Answer
1. RES / T)TOE	**108 / 5)540**	**2.** REA / B)BTO	**109 / 6)654**	**3.** WER / W)OEW	**201 / 2)402**
4. RER / W)WEW	**101 / 2)202**	**5.** REE / N)NEE	**100 / 3)300**	**6.** RED / D)DOA	**107 / 7)749**
7. WED / O)SWS	**207 / 4)828**	**8.** RER / N)NEN	**101 / 3)303**	**9.** NEN / W)BEB	**303 / 2)606**

Edward #1

Edward #2

A: **T W O E D S A R E**
5 2 4 0 7 8 9 1 0

B E T T E R ' N O N E
6 0 5 5 0 1 3 4 3 0

Macmillan/McGraw-Hill, MATHEMATICS IN ACTION
Grade 4, Chapter 7, Lesson 10, pages 276-277

ENRICHMENT-74

Name

MORE MEDIAN, RANGE, AND AVERAGE

On Your Own · Pair and Share · In a Group

ABOUT AVERAGES

Solve the problems. You may want to have a calculator handy.

1. Ms. Daley dropped the test papers from two of her classes after she had scored them. These are the scores:

70	70	70	72	73	74	75	80
81	82	87	91	91	92	92	96

- Each class has the same number of students.
- The test scores for Class 1 had a range of 70 to 96 and an average of 83.
- The test scores for Class 2 had a range of 70 to 91 and an average of 79.

Can you find which scores were in each class?

Class 1: 70, 70, 75, 82, 87, 92, 92, 96

Class 2: 70, 72, 73, 74, 80, 81, 91, 91

2. Use the numbers in this box:

$12.00	$12.25	$12.50	$12.75
$13.00	$13.50	$13.55	$13.75
$14.00	$14.50		

Form two sets.

- Each set has 5 numbers.
- Set 1 has a range of $12.00 to $13.50. It has a median of $12.75.
- Set 2 has a range of $12.50 to $14.50. It has a median of $13.75.

Find each set and its average.

Set 1: $12.00, $12.25, $12.75, $13.00, $13.50

Average: $12.70

Set 2: $12.50, $13.55, $13.75, $14.00, $14.50

Average: $13.66

3. Think about the counting numbers 1 to 20.

1 2 3 4 5 6 7 8 9 10 11 12 13 14 15 16 17 18 19 20

What is the average of the first 5 numbers? 3

The median? 3

ENRICHMENT-73

Name

PROBLEM SOLVING

On Your Own · Pair and Share · In a Group

MATT'S LOST HIS MARBLES!

Matt has an ENORMOUS marble collection. He keeps it in an old bathtub he found in a junkyard. The tub holds 100,555 marbles!

Matt also holds marbles in these containers:

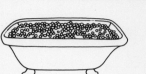

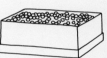

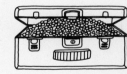

39 marbles · 1,000 marbles · 2,500 marbles

167 marbles · 2,111 marbles · 14,800 marbles

Work with a partner. Using the clues below, can you find out how many marbles each container holds? A calculator will help!

- Matt fills the bucket 47 times with marbles from the bathtub, and there are 1,338 left over.
- He fills the jug twice with the marbles in one bucket, and there are 111 marbles left over.
- If the jug could hold 2 more marbles, Matt could fill the vase 6 times with the marbles in the jug.
- Matt uses 6 suitcases, 4 shoeboxes, and 45 glasses to fill the bathtub completely.
- The shoebox holds 389 more marbles than the bucket.
- Matt fills the vase with 4 glasses of marbles, but needs 11 more marbles to fill the vase all the way.

ENRICHMENT-76

Name

ANGLES

On Your Own · Pair and Share · In a Group

THREE-IN-ONE

The shape below contains answers to three different riddles! Sort the angles into the groups listed below. Then rearrange the letters in each group to answer each riddle.

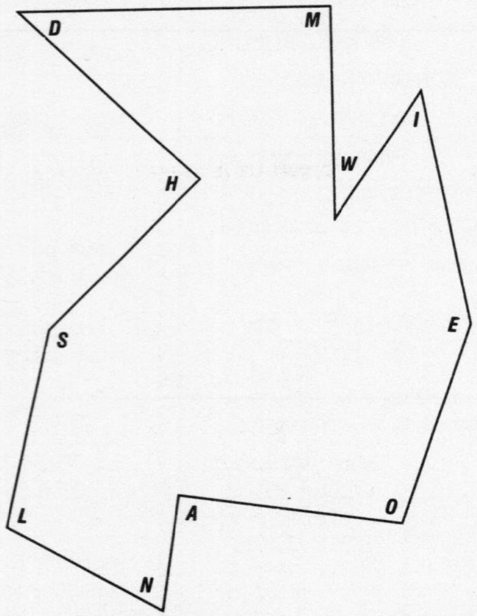

D M I W H S E L A O N

1. Less than a right angle:
   N
   W
   I
   D

   Q: What can be felt but never seen?

   A: W I N D

2. Right angle:
   M
   H
   A

   Q: What kind of food overacts?

   A: H A M

3. Greater than a right angle:
   L
   O
   E
   S

   Q: What kind of fish can you find on your shoe?

   A: S O L E

Macmillan/McGraw-Hill, MATHEMATICS IN ACTION
Grade 4, Chapter 8, Lesson 3, pages 308–309

ENRICHMENT-75

Name

LINES, LINE SEGMENTS, AND RAYS

On Your Own · Pair and Share · In a Group

PICTURE THIS

Draw these lines, line segments, and rays to complete this picture.

Lines

ST
YZ

Line Segments

AB	*OQ*
BC	*UV*
AC	*RP*
CT	*OP*
SB	*VW*
XW	*UX*

Rays

DE	*DJ*
DF	*DK*
DG	*DL*
DH	*DM*
DI	*DN*

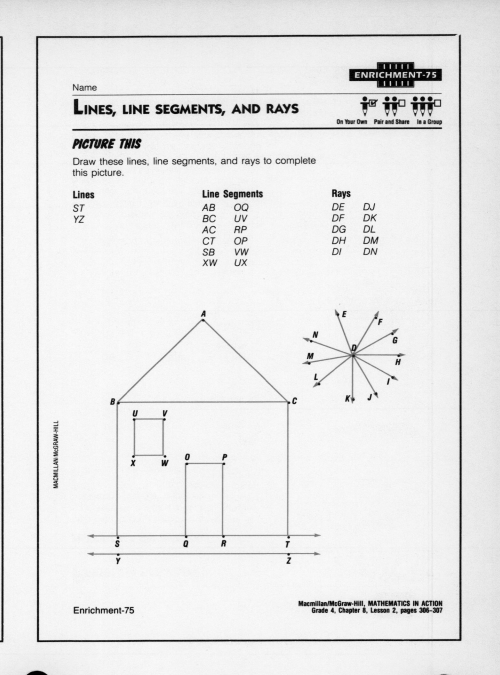

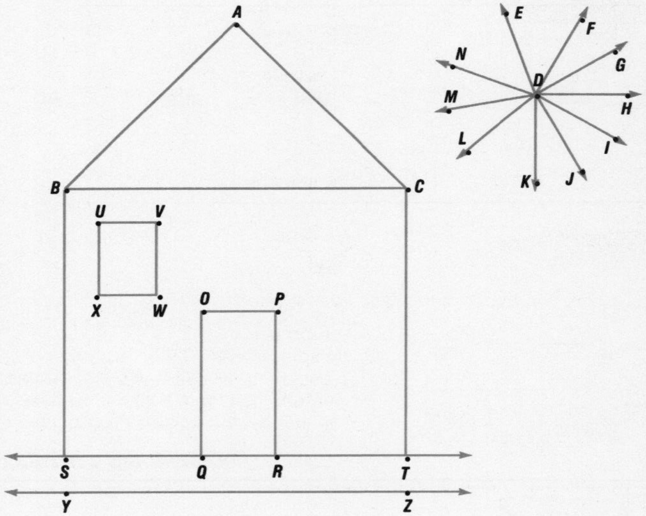

A B C U V X W O P S Q R T Y Z E F N G D M H L I K J

Macmillan/McGraw-Hill, MATHEMATICS IN ACTION
Grade 4, Chapter 8, Lesson 2, pages 306–307

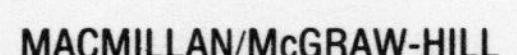

Name

ENRICHMENT-78

PROBLEM SOLVING

On Your Own Pair and Share In a Group

BUNCHES and BAGS

This is Frieda's Fruit Store. Use information in the drawing to help you answer the questions below.

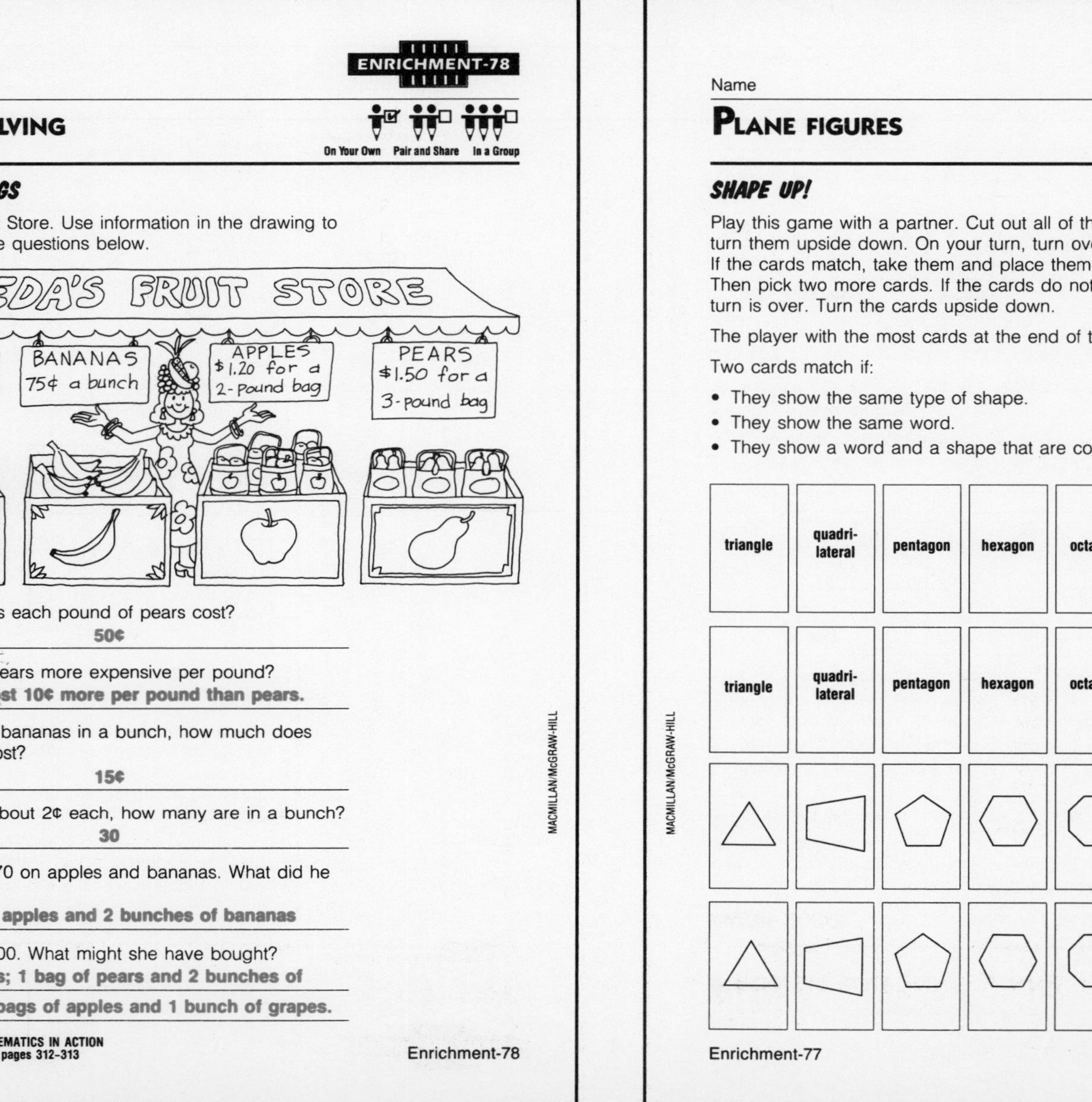

1. How much does each pound of pears cost?
   50¢
2. Are apples or pears more expensive per pound?
   Apples cost 10¢ more per pound than pears.
3. If there are five bananas in a bunch, how much does each banana cost?
   15¢
4. If grapes cost about 2¢ each, how many are in a bunch?
   30
5. Allen spent $2.70 on apples and bananas. What did he buy?
   1 bag of apples and 2 bunches of bananas
6. Edna spent $3.00. What might she have bought?
   2 bags of pears; 1 bag of pears and 2 bunches of bananas; or 2 bags of apples and 1 bunch of grapes.

Macmillan/McGraw-Hill, MATHEMATICS IN ACTION
Grade 4, Chapter 8, Lesson 5, pages 312-313

Name

ENRICHMENT-77

PLANE FIGURES

On Your Own Pair and Share In a Group

SHAPE UP!

Play this game with a partner. Cut out all of the cards and turn them upside down. On your turn, turn over two cards. If the cards match, take them and place them in your pile. Then pick two more cards. If the cards do not match, your turn is over. Turn the cards upside down.

The player with the most cards at the end of the game is the winner.

Two cards match if:

- They show the same type of shape.
- They show the same word.
- They show a word and a shape that are correctly matched.

Macmillan/McGraw-Hill, MATHEMATICS IN ACTION
Grade 4, Chapter 8, Lesson 4, pages 310-311

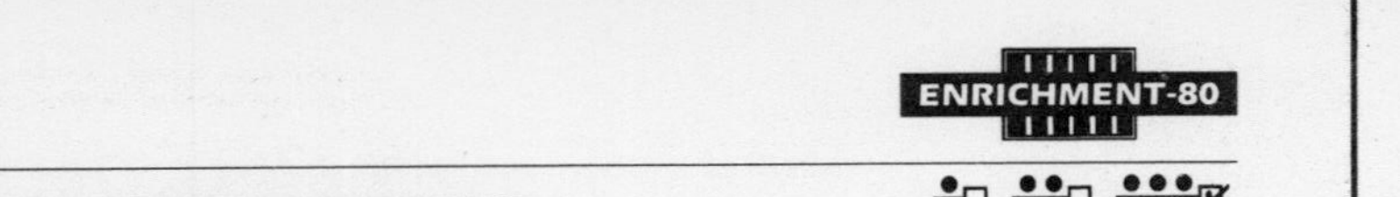

ENRICHMENT-80

Name

SLIDES, FLIPS, AND TURNS

On Your Own | Pair and Share | In a Group

SHAPE TWISTS

Work with a group of friends. Use the shapes and cards below to create puzzles. Cut out the four shapes and three cards. Turn the cards upside down.

Choose one shape. On another sheet of paper, trace the shape. Then pick one of the cards. Follow the instructions on the card. Return the card and pick again. After you have picked four cards, pass your artwork to your friends. See if they can guess what cards you picked to create it.

Can you guess what cards were picked to draw these pictures?

1. 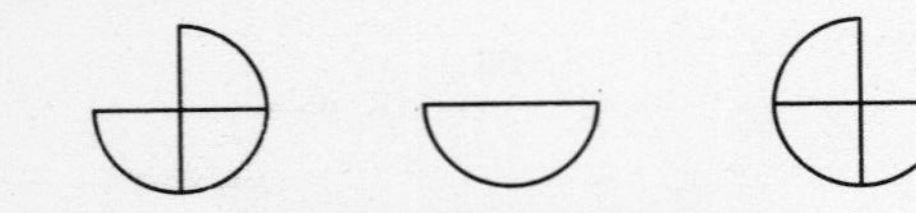

turn, slide, slide, turn

2. 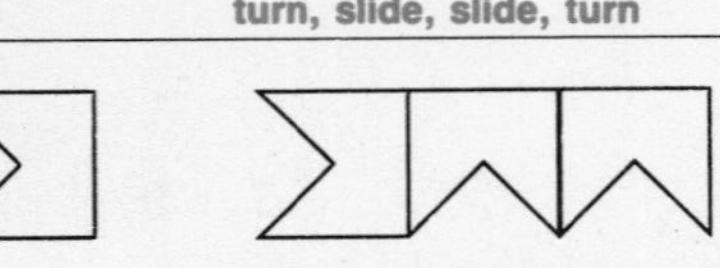

slide, turn, flip, slide

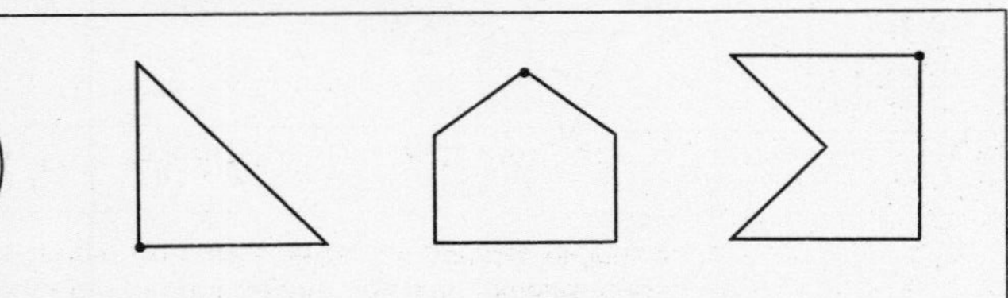

Slide
Slide your shape one inch to the right and trace it again.

Flip
Flip your shape over to the right and trace it again.

Turn
Turn your shape around the point shown and trace it again.

ENRICHMENT-79

Name

PROBLEM SOLVING

On Your Own | Pair and Share | In a Group

ARTFUL ROGER

Roger and his friends worked on their art projects together. Use the clues and the chart to help you find out which materials each friend used. Put a ✓ for yes and an X for no.

- Roger and the person who made a clay sculpture are best friends.
- Tina did not use clay or paint.
- The photographer took a photo of Ed and Cleo.
- In the background of the photo, you can see Tina using her crayons.
- Ed painted a picture of his goldfish.

	Crayons	Paint	Photographs	Clay
Roger	X	X	✓	X
Tina	✓	X	X	X
Ed	X	✓	X	X
Cleo	X	X	X	✓

After making their artworks, the friends had a contest to see who could clean up the fastest.

- Roger was faster than Tina.
- Cleo was slower than Tina, but faster than Ed.

Can you find the order of the four friends? Put a ✓ for yes and an X for no.

	First (fastest)	Second	Third	Fourth (slowest)
Roger	✓	X	X	X
Tina	X	✓	X	X
Ed	X	X	X	✓
Cleo	X	X	✓	X

Name

ENRICHMENT-82

LINE OF SYMMETRY

On Your Own | Pair and Share | In a Group

ANOTHER SIDE OF SYMMETRY

Complete this page to find a pattern. For each shape, draw every possible line of symmetry. Write the number of lines in the chart.

Shape	Number of lines of symmetry
triangle	3
square	4
pentagon	5
hexagon	6
octagon	8
decagon	10

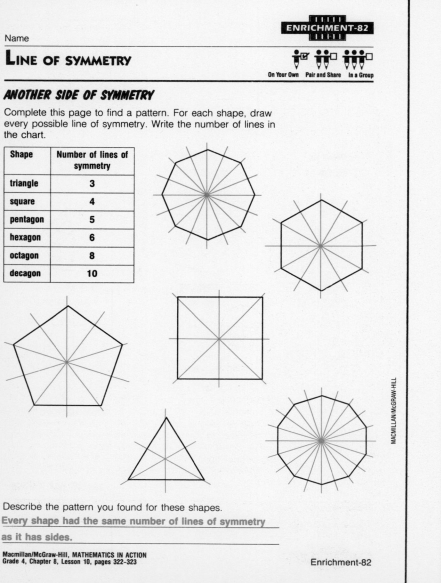

Describe the pattern you found for these shapes.

Every shape had the same number of lines of symmetry as it has sides.

Macmillan/McGraw-Hill, MATHEMATICS IN ACTION
Grade 4, Chapter 8, Lesson 10, pages 322-323

Name

ENRICHMENT-81

CONGRUENCE AND SIMILARITY

On Your Own | Pair and Share | In a Group

MATCHWORKS

Each of the drawings below contains similar and congruent shapes. Can you find them all?

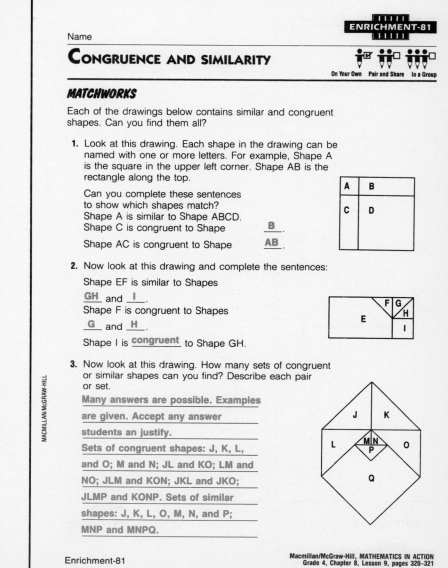

1. Look at this drawing. Each shape in the drawing can be named with one or more letters. For example, Shape A is the square in the upper left corner. Shape AB is the rectangle along the top.

   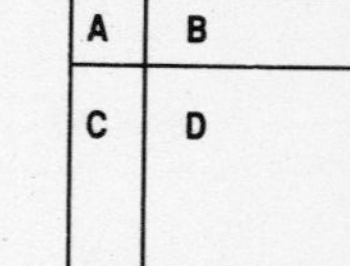

   Can you complete these sentences to show which shapes match?
   Shape A is similar to Shape ABCD.
   Shape C is congruent to Shape __B__.
   Shape AC is congruent to Shape __AB__.

2. Now look at this drawing and complete the sentences:
   Shape EF is similar to Shapes __GH__ and __I__.
   Shape F is congruent to Shapes __G__ and __H__.
   Shape I is __congruent__ to Shape GH.

3. Now look at this drawing. How many sets of congruent or similar shapes can you find? Describe each pair or set.

   Many answers are possible. Examples are given. Accept any answer students an justify. Sets of congruent shapes: J, K, L, and O; M and N; JL and KO; LM and NO; JLM and KON; JKL and JKO; JLMP and KONP. Sets of similar shapes: J, K, L, O, M, N, and P; MNP and MNPQ.

Macmillan/McGraw-Hill, MATHEMATICS IN ACTION
Grade 4, Chapter 8, Lesson 9, pages 320-321

Name

ENRICHMENT-84

VOLUME

On Your Own · Pair and Share · In a Group

AROUND THE BLOCK

Imagine that each of the shapes below is made of blocks. What is the volume of each shape in cubic blocks? How much would each shape cost to build if blocks cost 25¢ each? How many sides would you have to paint to completely paint each shape? Write your answers in the lines below each shape.

1. 7 cubic units; $1.75; 24 sides
2. 8 cu; $2; 28 sides
3. 11 cu; $2.75; 36 sides
4. 8 cu; $2; 32 sides
5. 19 cu; $4.75; 56 sides
6. 12 cu; $3; 36 sides
7. 11 cu; $2.75; 41 sides
8. 13 cu; $3.25; 42 sides

Macmillan/McGraw-Hill, MATHEMATICS IN ACTION
Grade 4, Chapter 8, Lesson 12, pages 326–327

Name

ENRICHMENT-83

SPACE FIGURES

On Your Own · Pair and Share · In a Group

NOW IN 3-D

Work on this activity with a group. Each set of shapes could be cut out and formed into a space figure. Can you see which figure each set would form? Write the name of the space figure below each set.

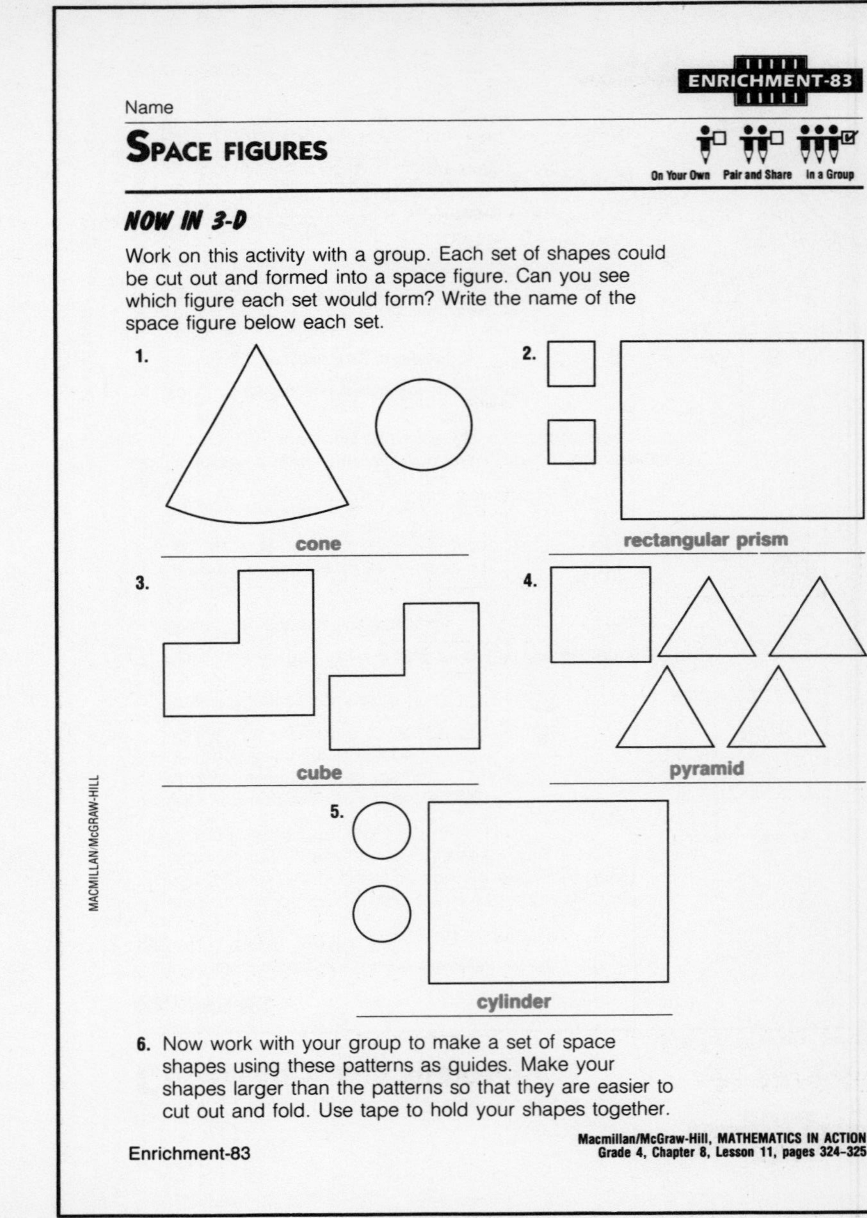

6. Now work with your group to make a set of space shapes using these patterns as guides. Make your shapes larger than the patterns so that they are easier to cut out and fold. Use tape to hold your shapes together.

Macmillan/McGraw-Hill, MATHEMATICS IN ACTION
Grade 4, Chapter 8, Lesson 11, pages 324–325

ENRICHMENT-86

Name

Parts of a Whole

On Your Own | Pair and Share | In a Group

HOW DOES YOUR GARDEN GROW?

Sal is going to plant a vegetable garden this year. These are the vegetables he wants to plant:

Peas	Tomatoes
Carrots	Corn
Lettuce	Broccoli
	Cabbage

This is what he has decided.

- The tomatoes and the lettuce will each take up an equal amount of space in the garden.
- The lettuce needs twice as much space as the cabbage.
- The broccoli needs only half as much space as the lettuce.
- The peas and the carrots will each get as much space in the garden as the broccoli.
- The corn needs as much space as the peas and carrots combined.

Help Sal design his garden. Use the grid below. Show how much space each vegetable should get.

The space needed for the peas, carrots, broccoli, and cabbage is equal. The space needed for the lettuce, tomatoes, and corn is equal. Lettuce needs twice as much space as the cabbage. The lettuce, tomatoes,and cabbage each get 20% of the 40 boxes (8 each) and the other vegetables get 10% (4 boxes).
20% + 20% + 20% + 10% + 10% + 10% + 10% = 100%

SAL'S VEGETABLE GARDEN — **Designs will vary.**

Tomatoes	Lettuce	Corn	Peas	Peas
Tomatoes	Lettuce	Corn	Peas	Peas
Tomatoes	Lettuce	Corn	Carrots	Carrots
Tomatoes	Lettuce	Corn	Carrots	Carrots
Tomatoes	Lettuce	Corn	Broccoli	Broccoli
Tomatoes	Lettuce	Corn	Broccoli	Broccoli
Tomatoes	Lettuce	Corn	Cabbage	Cabbage
Tomatoes	Lettuce	Corn	Cabbage	Cabbage

ENRICHMENT-85

Name

The Meaning of Fractions

On Your Own | Pair and Share | In a Group

FLAG FRACTIONS

1. Color each country's flag below. Use these colors:

B – blue G – green Y – yellow W – white
R – red K – black O – orange

Country	Flag (stripes)
ARGENTINA	B / W / B (horizontal)
AUSTRIA	R / W / R (horizontal)
NIGERIA	G | W | G (vertical)
POLAND	W / R (horizontal)
BELGIUM	K | Y | R (vertical)
SIERRA LEONE	G / W / B (horizontal)
PERU	R | W | R (vertical)
UGANDA	K / Y / R / K / Y / R (horizontal)
HUNGARY	R / W / G (horizontal)
IVORY COAST	O | W | G (vertical)
ITALY	G | W | R (vertical)
BOLIVIA	R / Y / G (horizontal)

Use the flags to answer each question.

2. What fraction of Belgium's flag is yellow? **$\frac{1}{3}$**

3. Name another country whose flag has the same part of red as Peru. **Austria**

4. What fraction of Nigeria's flag is green? **$\frac{2}{3}$**

5. Which country's flag has the greatest part of white? **Poland**

6. Name another country whose flag has the same part of green as Italy. **Answers will vary: Hungary, Ivory Coast, Bolivia, or Sierra Leone**

7. What part of Uganda's flag is yellow? **$\frac{2}{6} = \frac{1}{3}$**

8. Look at a world map or a globe. Find each country whose flag is shown above.

Name

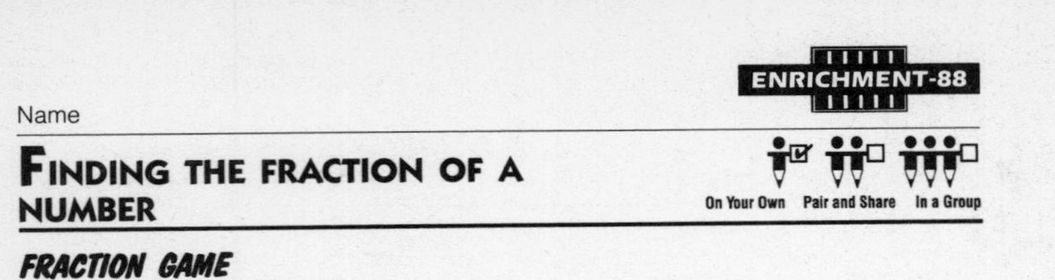

FINDING THE FRACTION OF A NUMBER

ENRICHMENT-88

On Your Own Pair and Share In a Group

FRACTION GAME

Here is a game for two or more players.

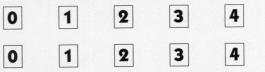

0 **1** **2** **3** **4** **5**

0 **1** **2** **3** **4** **5**

- Make two decks of cards as shown above. Mix each deck and put the deck face down.
- The first player picks the top card from each deck. The player uses the cards to make a fraction no greater than 1.
- The player multiplies the fraction by 60 and writes the answer as the score for that turn.

> For example, if you pick **2** and **4** you would find $\frac{2}{4}$ of 60 = 30
>
> Your score = 30

- Each card is replaced in the deck it came from and the decks are mixed again.
- Players take turns picking cards and adding to their scores.
- If a player picks 0, the player's score is 0 for that turn. If a player picks 0–0, the cards are replaced, and the player picks again.
- The first player whose score totals 100 or more is the winner.

Variations

- Try to score a different total.
- Change the rules for what happens when a player picks 0 or 0–0.
- Play the game using a calculator. Find fractions of 120.

Macmillan/McGraw-Hill, MATHEMATICS IN ACTION
Grade 4, Chapter 9, Lesson 4, pages 350–351

Name

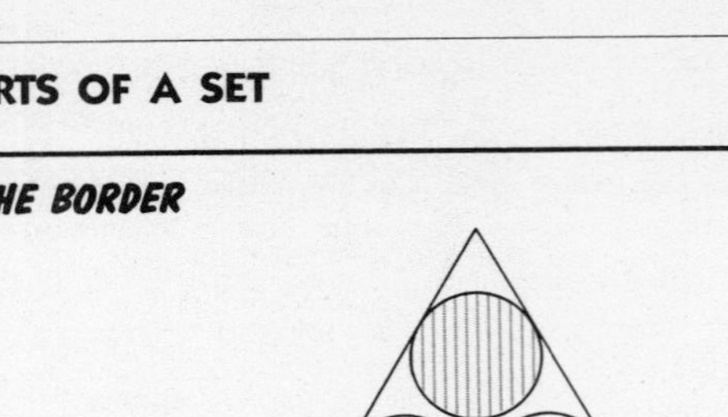

PARTS OF A SET

ENRICHMENT-87

On Your Own Pair and Share In a Group

AT THE BORDER

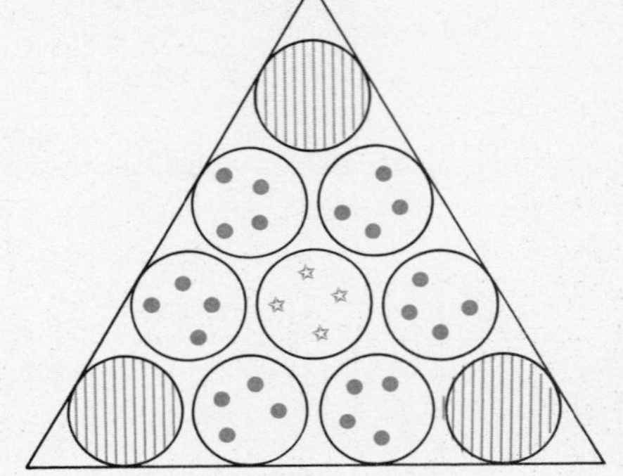

1. Some of the circles touch the border at exactly two points. Draw stripes on these circles. **See drawing.**
2. Some of the circles touch the border at exactly one point. Draw dots on these circles. **See drawing.**
3. Draw stars on any circle that does not touch the border at all. **See drawing.**
4. What fraction of the circles have stripes? $\frac{3}{10}$
5. What fraction of the circles have dots? $\frac{6}{10} = \frac{3}{5}$
6. What fraction of the circles have stars? $\frac{1}{10}$
7. What fraction of the circles touch the border? $\frac{9}{10}$
8. What fraction of the circles do not touch the border? $\frac{1}{10}$
9. What fraction of the circles touch only one other circle? $\frac{0}{10}$ = **zero**

Macmillan/McGraw-Hill, MATHEMATICS IN ACTION
Grade 4, Chapter 9, Lesson 3, pages 348–349

ENRICHMENT-90

Name

FINDING EQUIVALENT FRACTIONS

On Your Own Pair and Share In a Group

CONCENTRATE ON FRACTIONS

$\frac{1}{8}$	$\frac{1}{6}$	$\frac{1}{4}$	$\frac{1}{3}$	$\frac{1}{2}$
$\frac{2}{8}$	$\frac{2}{5}$	$\frac{2}{3}$	$\frac{3}{4}$	$\frac{3}{8}$
$\frac{2}{4}$	$\frac{3}{12}$	$\frac{5}{15}$	$\frac{4}{9}$	$\frac{2}{7}$
$\frac{2}{12}$	$\frac{4}{10}$	$\frac{6}{21}$	$\frac{6}{16}$	$\frac{3}{5}$
$\frac{9}{12}$	$\frac{12}{20}$	$\frac{1}{5}$	LOSE A TURN	$\frac{5}{25}$

Here is a fraction game to play with a friend.

- Make a set of 25 cards as shown above. Shuffle the cards together and place them face down – 5 in each row and 5 in each column.
- The first player turns over two cards. If the fractions are equivalent, the player keeps the cards and goes again.
- If the cards do not show equivalent fractions, the cards are turned face down again and the second player goes.
- If a player picks the LOSE A TURN card, the other player gets to take two turns. The LOSE A TURN card is replaced face down.
- The game continues until all cards except LOSE A TURN have been taken. The player with the most cards is the winner.

**You can make up your own set of equivalent fraction cards and play concentration with them.

ENRICHMENT-89

Name

PROBLEM SOLVING

On Your Own Pair and Share In a Group

LARRY, CAREY, AND HARRY

Solve each problem by using the clues.

1. Larry, Carey and Harry went out for lunch. Each friend ordered a salad: the choices were egg, tuna, and chicken.
   - Carey won't eat egg.
   - Larry never orders tuna.
   - Harry only likes chicken.
   - Each friend ate something different.

   What did each friend order for lunch?

   Larry ordered egg

   Carey ordered tuna

   Harry ordered chicken

2. Larry, Carey, and Harry live in the same apartment building as Barry and Mary.
   - Carey's apartment is on a higher floor than Mary's, but it is lower than Larry's apartment.
   - Barry's apartment is between Larry's and Carey's.
   - The only friend who lives on a lower floor than Harry is Mary.

List the names of the friends in the chart at the right.

Larry	HIGHEST
Barry	
Carey	
Harry	
Mary	LOWEST

ENRICHMENT-92

On Your Own Pair and Share In a Group

Name

WHOLE NUMBERS AND MIXED NUMBERS

FRACTION BINGO

Write each fraction as a mixed number or whole number. The fraction part of each mixed number should be in simplest form.

Then make BINGO on the gamecard below by drawing an X over each answer that appears on the card. (Some answers do not appear.)

1. $\frac{9}{4}$ $2\frac{1}{4}$	2. $\frac{7}{3}$ $2\frac{1}{3}$	3. $\frac{8}{5}$ $1\frac{3}{5}$	4. $\frac{9}{6}$ $1\frac{1}{2}$
5. $\frac{11}{2}$ $5\frac{1}{2}$	6. $\frac{15}{5}$ 3	7. $\frac{12}{7}$ $1\frac{5}{7}$	8. $\frac{14}{4}$ $3\frac{1}{2}$
9. $\frac{12}{9}$ $1\frac{1}{3}$	10. $\frac{10}{6}$ $1\frac{2}{3}$	11. $\frac{13}{8}$ $1\frac{5}{8}$	12. $\frac{15}{6}$ $2\frac{1}{2}$
13. $\frac{20}{10}$ 2	14. $\frac{22}{7}$ $3\frac{1}{7}$	15. $\frac{12}{10}$ $1\frac{1}{5}$	16. $\frac{18}{3}$ 6
17. $\frac{17}{8}$ $2\frac{1}{8}$	18. $\frac{16}{4}$ 4	19. $\frac{44}{16}$ $2\frac{3}{4}$	20. $\frac{13}{3}$ $4\frac{1}{3}$

B	I	N	G	O
$4\frac{1}{2}$	$1\frac{1}{8}$	$2\frac{1}{4}$ (X)	6 (X)	3 (X)
$3\frac{1}{7}$ (X)	$2\frac{1}{3}$ (X)	$1\frac{2}{3}$ (X)	$4\frac{3}{4}$	$1\frac{5}{8}$ (X)
$3\frac{1}{2}$ (X)	5	FREE SPACE	$1\frac{3}{5}$ (X)	4 (X)
$1\frac{4}{5}$	$2\frac{3}{4}$ (X)	$2\frac{1}{2}$ (X)	$2\frac{5}{6}$	$1\frac{1}{5}$ (X)
$1\frac{1}{3}$ (X)	$5\frac{1}{2}$ (X)	7	$2\frac{1}{8}$ (X)	$4\frac{1}{3}$ (X)

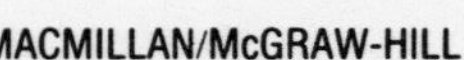

ENRICHMENT-91

On Your Own Pair and Share In a Group

Name

SIMPLIFYING FRACTIONS

AS SIMPLE AS POSSIBLE

My nickname is the Coyote State. People visit me to see Mount Rushmore, where the faces of Presidents Washington, Jefferson, Lincoln, and Theodore Roosevelt are carved. My state tree is the Black Hills spruce. What state am I?

To find out, complete the exercises below. In each exercise, three of the fractions have the simplest form shown at the right. Circle the fraction that does not belong. Then match each letter to its exercise number in the boxes below.

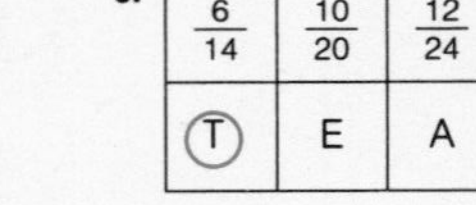

1.

$\frac{8}{12}$	$\frac{6}{8}$	$\frac{4}{6}$	$\frac{6}{9}$	$= \frac{2}{3}$
C	(U)	R	E	

2.

$\frac{12}{16}$	$\frac{6}{8}$	$\frac{8}{10}$	$\frac{9}{12}$	$= \frac{3}{4}$
R	I	(D)	E	

3.

$\frac{4}{20}$	$\frac{3}{24}$	$\frac{5}{40}$	$\frac{2}{16}$	$= \frac{1}{8}$
(S)	O	F	T	

4.

$\frac{4}{16}$	$\frac{6}{15}$	$\frac{4}{10}$	$\frac{10}{25}$	$= \frac{2}{5}$
(H)	A	N	D	

5.

$\frac{3}{18}$	$\frac{5}{30}$	$\frac{2}{12}$	$\frac{8}{24}$	$= \frac{1}{6}$
B	A	N	(K)	

6.

$\frac{6}{14}$	$\frac{10}{20}$	$\frac{12}{24}$	$\frac{25}{50}$	$= \frac{1}{2}$
(T)	E	A	R	

7.

$\frac{50}{80}$	$\frac{20}{32}$	$\frac{36}{48}$	$\frac{40}{64}$	$= \frac{5}{8}$
L	E	(A)	P	

8.

$\frac{18}{42}$	$\frac{12}{21}$	$\frac{15}{35}$	$\frac{9}{21}$	$= \frac{3}{7}$
C	(O)	Z	Y	

Answer:

S	O	U	T	H	D	A	K	O	T	A
3	8	1	6	4	2	7	5	8	6	7

ENRICHMENT-94

Name

MEASURING LENGTH: CUSTOMARY UNITS

On Your Own Pair and Share In a Group

EXPERIMENT TO ESTIMATE

1. What part of the picture do you think is shaded? Write your guess as a fraction.

   Answers will vary.

Now use this method to find an estimate.

2. Close your eyes. Put your pencil down on the picture and make a dot.
3. Repeat 49 times.
4. Count the number of times you made a dot in the shaded part. Write your answer here.

   Answers will vary.

5. Write a fraction as an estimate of the shaded part. Use your answer to question 4 as the numerator. What number will you use as the denominator?

   50

   Fraction $\frac{\square}{50}$ Answers will vary.

6. Compare the fraction you found by experimenting with the guess you wrote for question 1. Was your guess close? Explain?

   Answers will vary.

7. To repeat the experiment, trace the picture. Try it again yourself or ask a friend to try. Compare the results of your experiments.
8. Draw a picture of your own. Use the same method to estimate the part that is shaded.

Macmillan/McGraw-Hill, MATHEMATICS IN ACTION
Grade 4, Chapter 9, Lesson 11, pages 364-365

ENRICHMENT-93

Name

COMPARING FRACTIONS AND MIXED NUMBERS

On Your Own Pair and Share In a Group

POINT THE WAY

Draw arrows in order from the least to the greatest fraction or mixed number in each box. The first problem is started for you.

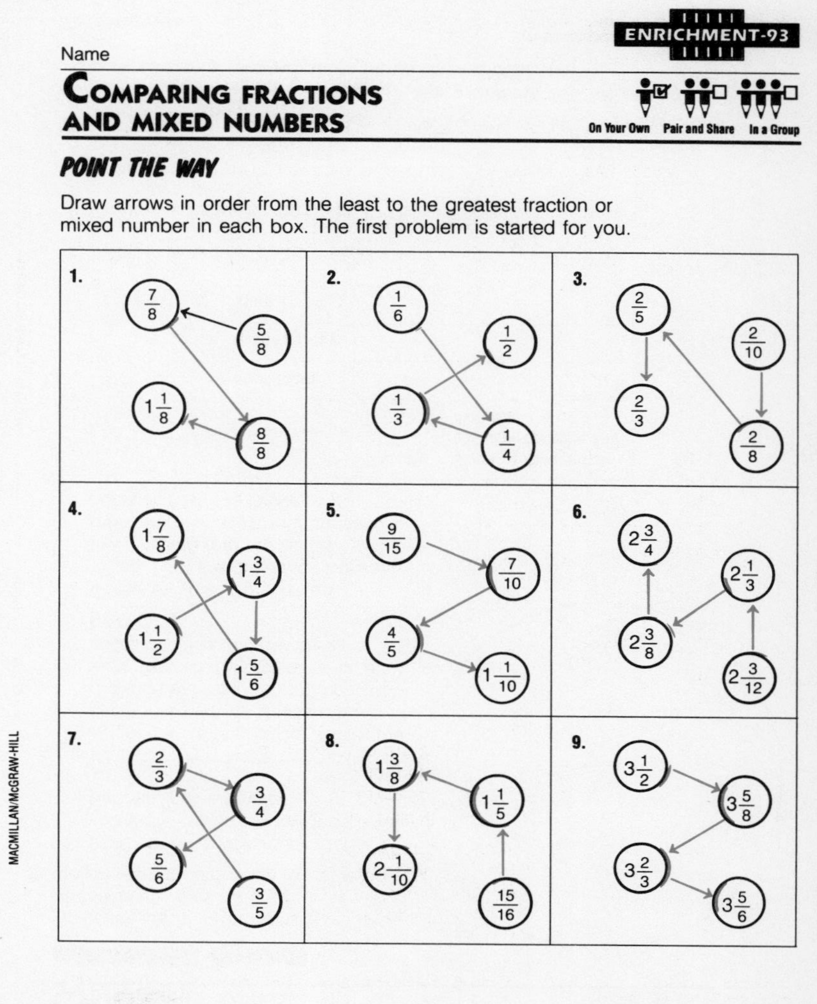

Macmillan/McGraw-Hill, MATHEMATICS IN ACTION
Grade 4, Chapter 9, Lesson 10, pages 362-363

Name

PROBLEM SOLVING

On Your Own Pair and Share In a Group

ANSWER WITH A QUESTION

These problems already have answers. Use the information given and logical thinking to write a question that fits each answer. **Answers may vary.**

Compare your questions with those of some friends.

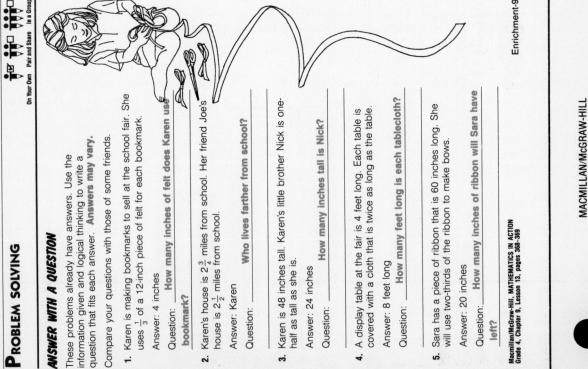

1. Karen is making bookmarks to sell at the school fair. She uses $\frac{1}{3}$ of a 12-inch piece of felt for each bookmark.

   Answer: 4 inches

   Question: **How many inches of felt does Karen use bookmark?**

2. Karen's house is $2\frac{3}{4}$ miles from school. Her friend Joe's house is $2\frac{1}{2}$ miles from school.

   Answer: Karen

   Question: **Who lives farther from school?**

3. Karen is 48 inches tall. Karen's little brother Nick is one-half as tall as she is.

   Answer: 24 inches

   Question: **How many inches tall is Nick?**

4. A display table at the fair is 4 feet long. Each table is covered with a cloth that is twice as long as the table.

   Answer: 8 feet long

   Question: **How many feet long is each tablecloth?**

5. Sara has a piece of ribbon that is 60 inches long. She will use two-thirds of the ribbon to make bows.

   Answer: 20 inches

   Question: **How many inches of ribbon will Sara have left?**

Macmillan/McGraw-Hill, MATHEMATICS IN ACTION
Grade 4, Chapter 9, Lesson 13, pages 368–369

Name

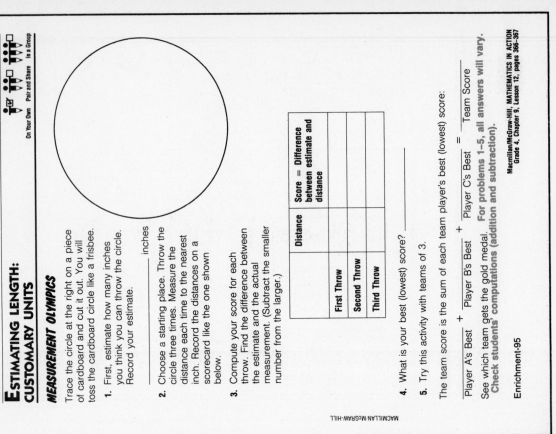

ENRICHMENT-95

ESTIMATING LENGTH: CUSTOMARY UNITS

On Your Own Pair and Share In a Group

MEASUREMENT OLYMPICS

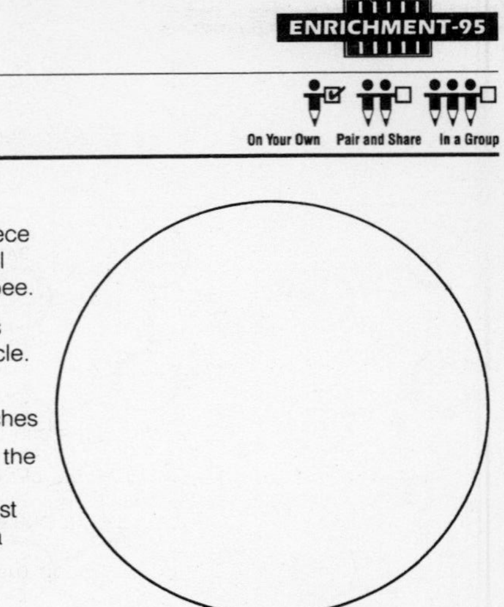

Trace the circle at the right on a piece of cardboard and cut it out. You will toss the cardboard circle like a frisbee.

1. First, estimate how many inches you think you can throw the circle. Record your estimate.

   ______ inches

2. Choose a starting place. Throw the circle three times. Measure the distance each time to the nearest inch. Record the distances on a scorecard like the one shown below.

3. Compute your score for each throw. Find the difference between the estimate and the actual measurement. (Subtract the smaller number from the larger.)

	Distance	Score = Difference between estimate and distance
First Throw		
Second Throw		
Third Throw		

4. What is your best (lowest) score? ______

5. Try this activity with teams of 3.

The team score is the sum of each team player's best (lowest) score:

______ + ______ + ______ = ______
Player A's Best + Player B's Best + Player C's Best = Team Score

See which team gets the gold medal. **For problems 1–5, all answers will vary. Check students' computations (addition and subtraction).**

Macmillan/McGraw-Hill, MATHEMATICS IN ACTION
Grade 4, Chapter 9, Lesson 12, pages 366–367

Name

ENRICHMENT-98

On Your Own Pair and Share In a Group

FINDING GREATER SUMS

FRACTIONS IN ACTION

Each problem below uses this fraction pattern:

$\frac{\square}{\square} + \frac{\square}{\square}$

Write your answers in the last column. The first problem in each table is done for you.

	Arrange these digits:	To get a sum of:	Your answer:
1.	3 4 5 5	$1\frac{2}{5}$	$\frac{4}{5} + \frac{3}{5}$
2.	2 7 7 8	$1\frac{3}{7}$	$\frac{2}{7} + \frac{8}{7}$
3.	2 3 4 8	1	$\frac{2}{8} + \frac{3}{4}$
4.	2 3 4 6	$1\frac{2}{3}$	$\frac{2}{6} + \frac{4}{3}$
5.	2 3 4 6	$1\frac{1}{3}$	$\frac{4}{6} + \frac{2}{3}$
6.	3 4 8 8	$1\frac{3}{4}$	$\frac{3}{4} + \frac{8}{8}$

	Arrange these digits:	To get two sums of:	Your answer:
7.	2 2 3 3 3 4 4 5	$1\frac{2}{3}$ and $1\frac{3}{4}$	$\frac{2}{3} + \frac{3}{3}$ $\frac{2}{4} + \frac{5}{4}$
8.	3 4 5 6 6 6 8 8	$1\frac{1}{6}$ and $1\frac{3}{8}$	$\frac{3}{6} + \frac{4}{6}$ $\frac{5}{8} + \frac{6}{8}$
9.	2 5 5 5 6 7 7 7	$1\frac{4}{5}$ and $1\frac{4}{7}$	$\frac{2}{5} + \frac{7}{5}$ $\frac{5}{7} + \frac{6}{7}$

Macmillan/McGraw-Hill, MATHEMATICS IN ACTION
Grade 4, Chapter 10, Lesson 3, pages 390-391

Name

ENRICHMENT-97

On Your Own Pair and Share In a Group

FINDING SUMS

TINA'S TOYSHOP

This drawing shows some of the toys that Tina sells at her shop. Look at the picture. Then answer the questions below. Write your answers in simplest form.

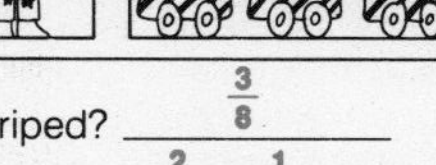
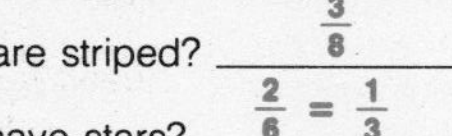

1. What fraction of the balls are striped? $\frac{3}{8}$
2. What fraction of the cars have stars? $\frac{2}{6} = \frac{1}{3}$
3. What fraction of all of the toys are dotted? $\frac{8}{24} = \frac{1}{3}$
4. What fraction of the toy soldiers and the dolls are striped? $\frac{2}{10} = \frac{1}{5}$ are dotted? $\frac{4}{10} = \frac{2}{5}$ $(\frac{4}{10})$ have stars? $\frac{4}{10} = \frac{2}{5}$

Write each fraction described. Then circle the answer that describes the greater fraction.

5. **a.** the fraction of dolls that have stripes $\frac{1}{6}$ — **(b.)** the fraction of dolls and balls that have stripes $\frac{4}{14} = \frac{2}{7}$

6. **a.** the fraction of all toys that have stars $\frac{8}{24} = \frac{1}{3}$ — **(b.)** the fraction of dolls and cars that do not have stars $\frac{7}{12}$

7. **(a.)** the fraction of dolls that do not have stripes $\frac{5}{6}$ — **b.** the fraction of toy soldiers and cars that have dots $\frac{3}{10}$

Macmillan/McGraw-Hill, MATHEMATICS IN ACTION
Grade 4, Chapter 10, Lesson 2, pages 388-389

Name

FINDING DIFFERENCES

ENRICHMENT-100

On Your Own Pair and Share In a Group

FUNNY FRACTIONS

Each subtraction problem has been broken into three parts. Draw lines showing how to connect the problems. The answer to each numbered problem has a letter. Place these letters in the blanks below. Is there something funny about your answer?

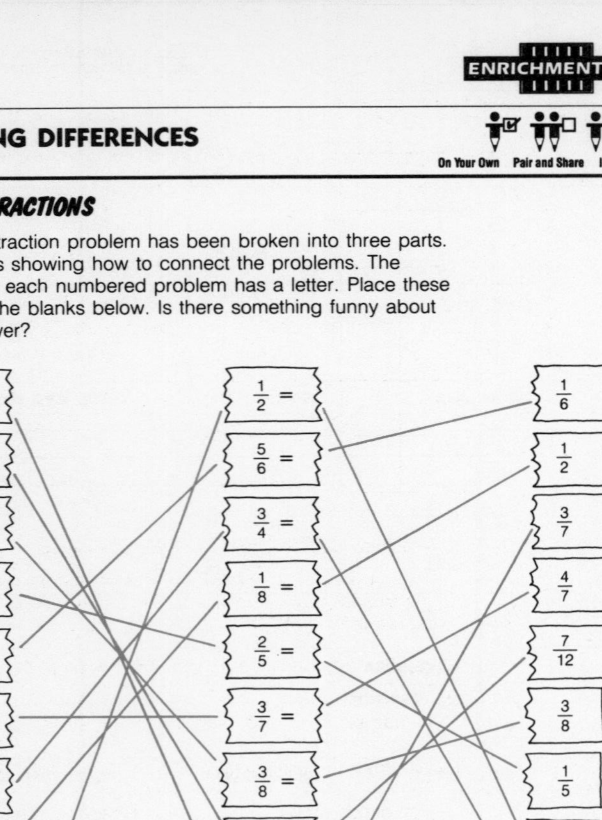

Where do circus clowns eat?

In the L A U G H -A- T E R I A!
1 2 3 4 5 6 7 8 9 10

Macmillan/McGraw-Hill, MATHEMATICS IN ACTION
Grade 4, Chapter 10, Lesson 7, pages 398–399

Name

PROBLEM SOLVING

ENRICHMENT-99

On Your Own Pair and Share In a Group

STRATEGY GRAB BAG

Welcome to Strategy! You and your partner can win the game by answering all of the questions below. You can use any strategy you want to find your answers. If one strategy doesn't work, just try another. The first pair to answer all the questions correctly wins!

Here are some strategies you can use:

- Find a pattern
- Draw a picture
- Guess and test
- Solve a similar problem

1. There is a staircase with 18 steps. You walk halfway up the steps, then down 2 steps, then up 4 steps, then down 7 steps, and then halfway up the remaining steps. What step do you finish on? (1 is the first step, 18 is the last.)
   Step 11

2. You are watching Marvin the Magician pull rabbits from a hat. First he pulls 2 rabbits, then he pulls 6 rabbits. Next he pulls 18 rabbits, and then 54 rabbits! How many rabbits do you think he will pull out of the hat next time? Why?
   162; each time he pulls out 3 times as many rabbits

3. You take a trip to a city 240 miles away. You drive half of the distance in the morning. Then you drive half of the remaining distance before stopping for lunch. Then you drive half of the remaining distance before your car gets a flat tire. How far are you from the city?
   30 miles

4. You are building a playhouse. Plastic bricks cost 27¢ each; wood bricks cost 74¢ each, and stone bricks cost $1.44 each. You can use any combination of the bricks to build the playhouse. Can you find a way to spend exactly $100 on bricks for your playhouse?
   Answers will vary. Possible answer: 100 plastic bricks ($27); 50 wood bricks ($37) and 25 stone bricks ($36)

MACMILLAN/McGRAW-HILL

Macmillan/McGraw-Hill, MATHEMATICS IN ACTION
Grade 4, Chapter 10, Lesson 4, pages 392–393

MACMILLAN/McGRAW-HILL

Name

ENRICHMENT-102

PERIMETER AND AREA

On Your Own | Pair and Share | In a Group

FENCE ME IN

Imagine that your class has been given an 18 foot by 18 foot garden. How will you arrange the garden areas? Work with a group to decide how you will place the fences and the path.

Here are some things to consider:

- You want to plant both vegetables and flowers. You will use a fence to separate the flowers from the vegetables.
- The vegetables need at least twice as much space as the flowers.
- You want to place a fence completely around each garden area.
- You want one path 3 feet wide through your garden.

1. What other factors do you need to consider? **Answers will vary. Examples: How much space to allow for the vegetables; for the path.**

2. After you have designed the shape of your garden and its path and fences, draw them on the grid below. Label the vegetable section V and the flower section F. **(Answers will vary. Check students' grids.)**

3. Find the perimeter and area of each garden section. **Answers will vary.**

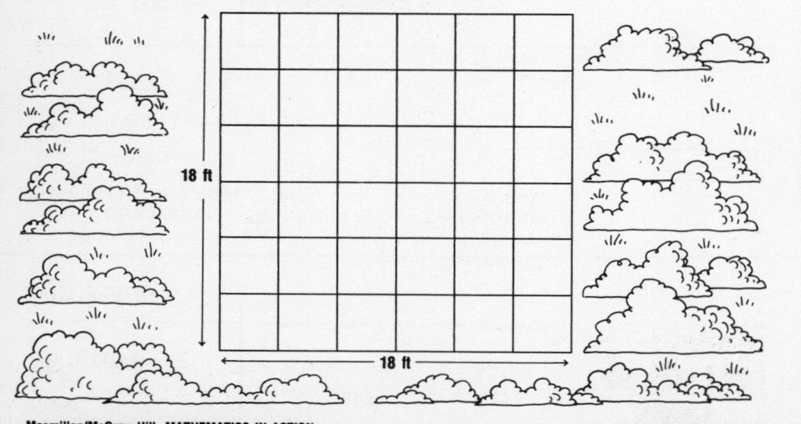

Name

ENRICHMENT-101

PROBLEM SOLVING

On Your Own | Pair and Share | In a Group

HOUSE NUMBER PROJECT

You and a group of students are trying to raise money by building house number boards. You can buy metal numbers at the local hardware store and glue them onto a wooden board.

Work together with your group to plan how you will complete this project.

The wooden board you are going to use costs 5¢ per square inch. The numbers are sold in three different sizes and prices. Here are examples for the number 8.

Which size do you think would be best? Measure the one you choose to the nearest $\frac{1}{8}$ inch.

After you have chosen a size, consider the following:

- How much space will you allow for each number?
- Will every number take the same amount of space?
- How much wood will you allow for a border?

1. Work together to make a model of one of the products you will try to sell. You might use stencils to make sure that your numbers are neatly done. Draw your house number on the back of this worksheet. **(Answers will vary.)**

2. Look at the digits in your house number and the spaces between them. What size board will you need? Draw a board around your numbers. **(Answers will vary.)**

3. How much did the materials (numbers and board) for your project cost? Use a calculator to help you.
Answers will vary. Example for a 5″ × 12″ board with 3 large-sized numbers: $.05 (5 × 12) + 3 × $.95 = $5.85

4. How much should you charge for your completed house number board if you want to make a profit of $2.00 for your classroom? **Answers will vary.**

Name

ENRICHMENT-104

WEIGHT

On Your Own · Pair and Share · In a Group

FISH SCALES

Put the fish in order from lightest to heaviest. Number them 1 (for lightest) to 14 (for heaviest). Write the letter of each fish in the numbered space in the cartoon below. The letters will complete the "fishy" discussion.

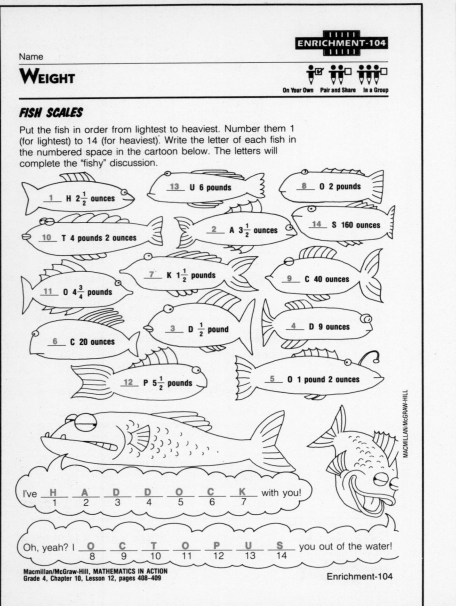

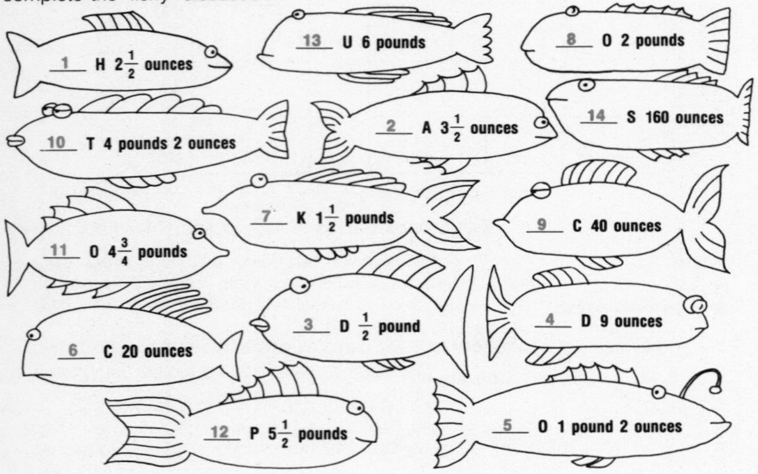

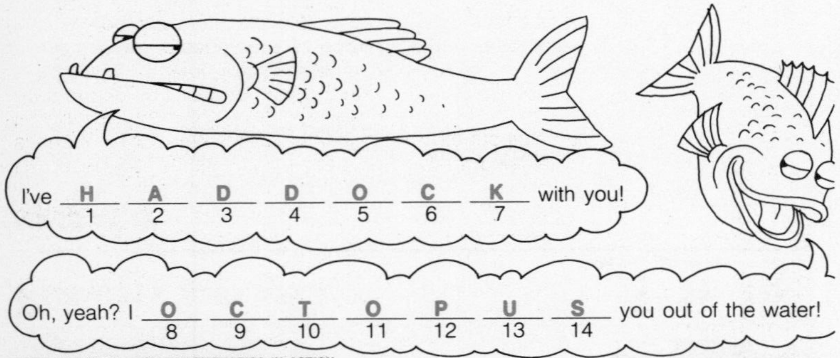

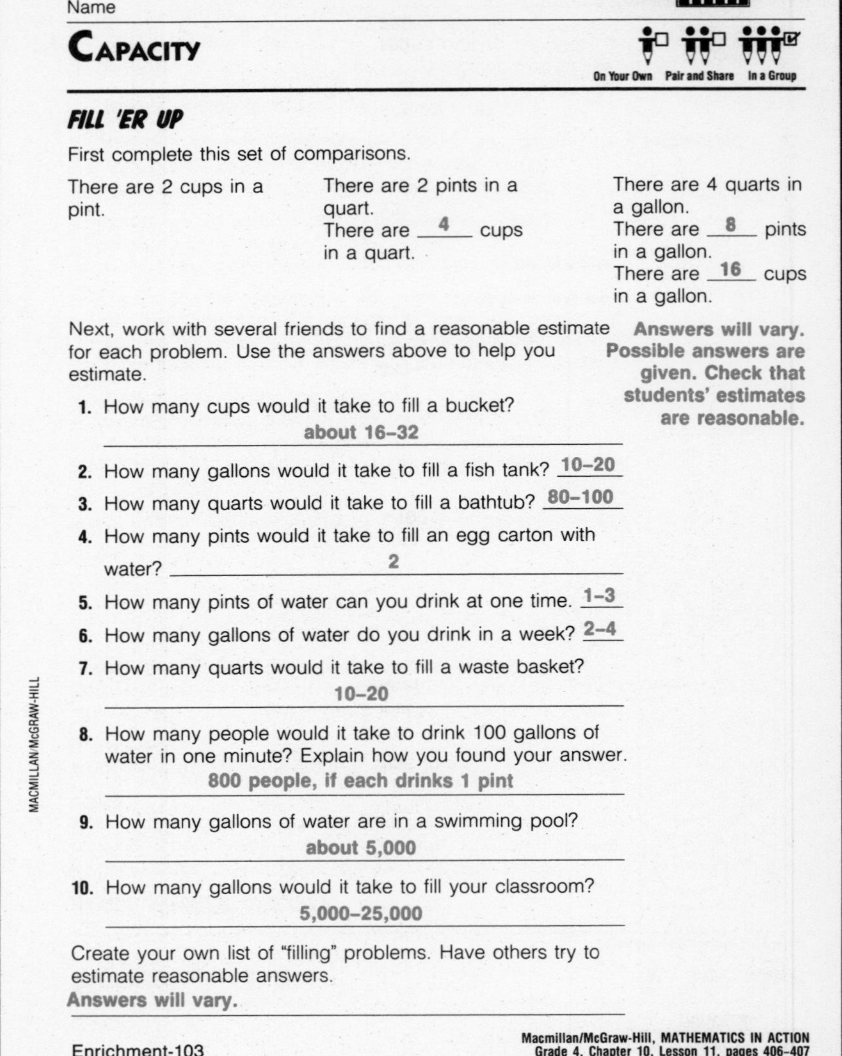

Macmillan/McGraw-Hill, MATHEMATICS IN ACTION
Grade 4, Chapter 10, Lesson 12, pages 408–409

Enrichment-104

Name

ENRICHMENT-103

CAPACITY

On Your Own · Pair and Share · In a Group

FILL 'ER UP

First complete this set of comparisons.

There are 2 cups in a pint.

There are 2 pints in a quart.
There are **4** cups in a quart.

There are 4 quarts in a gallon.
There are **8** pints in a gallon.
There are **16** cups in a gallon.

Next, work with several friends to find a reasonable estimate for each problem. Use the answers above to help you estimate.

Answers will vary. Possible answers are given. Check that students' estimates are reasonable.

1. How many cups would it take to fill a bucket? **about 16–32**
2. How many gallons would it take to fill a fish tank? **10–20**
3. How many quarts would it take to fill a bathtub? **80–100**
4. How many pints would it take to fill an egg carton with water? **2**
5. How many pints of water can you drink at one time. **1–3**
6. How many gallons of water do you drink in a week? **2–4**
7. How many quarts would it take to fill a waste basket? **10–20**
8. How many people would it take to drink 100 gallons of water in one minute? Explain how you found your answer. **800 people, if each drinks 1 pint**
9. How many gallons of water are in a swimming pool? **about 5,000**
10. How many gallons would it take to fill your classroom? **5,000–25,000**

Create your own list of "filling" problems. Have others try to estimate reasonable answers.
Answers will vary.

Enrichment-103

Macmillan/McGraw-Hill, MATHEMATICS IN ACTION
Grade 4, Chapter 10, Lesson 11, pages 406–407

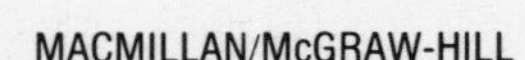

ENRICHMENT-106

Name

TENTHS AND HUNDREDTHS

On Your Own / Pair and Share / In a Group

SQUARE OFF

Use estimation to choose the box that correctly completes each fact. Circle the correct boxes. Then write the letter in the circled box in the riddle answer below.

1. 45 × [23 T] [65 R] [(87 Y)] = 3,915
2. 66 × [18 M] [(29 O)] [41 P] = 1,914
3. 31 × [(77 U)] [87 S] [97 E] = 2,387
4. [92 R] [61 O] [(34 C)] × 53 = 1,802
5. [14 D] [28 N] [(53 A)] × 19 = 1,007
6. [51 A] [(74 N)] [92 D] × 36 = 2,664
7. 23 × 72 = [726 I] [(1,656 C)] [4,980 K]
8. 61 × 55 = [(3,355 O)] [4,735 A] [8,665 R]
9. 21 × 88 = [(1,848 U)] [2,768 L] [5,018 Y]
10. 82 × [(71 N)] [84 O] [98 T] = 5,822
11. 64 × [32 I] [(48 T)] [57 S] = 3,072
12. 27 × [63 S] [(71 O)] [85 P] = 1,917
13. 14 × 92 = [(1,288 N)] [2,188 E] [3,218 T]
14. 38 × 39 = [1,056 A] [(1,482 M)] [1,927 N]
15. 88 × 65 = [3,720 D] [4,720 R] [(5,720 E)]

What did the calculator say to the student?

Y	O	U	C	A	N	C	O	U	N	T	O	N	M	E!
1	2	3	4	5	6	7	8	9	10	11	12	13	14	15

Macmillan/McGraw-Hill, MATHEMATICS IN ACTION
Grade 4, Chapter 11, Lesson 2, pages 434-435

ENRICHMENT-105

Name

TEMPERATURE

On Your Own / Pair and Share / In a Group

TEMPERATURE'S RISING

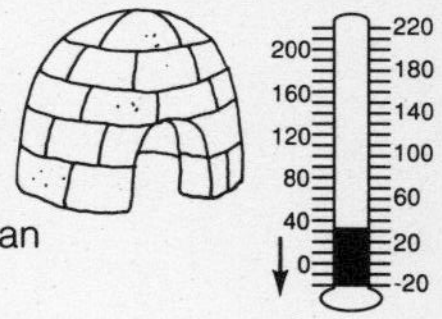

Each of the pictures below suggests a temperature range. On the thermometer next to each picture, draw a band to show a range of possible temperatures. Use an arrow to show temperatures that might be higher (↑) or lower (↓) than those given on the thermometer. Here is an example.

Compare your answers with those of other students. Explain why you think each range is reasonable.

Answers will vary. Possible temperature ranges are given. Accept all reasonable answers.

1. 
75°–100°

2. 
212°–220°

3. 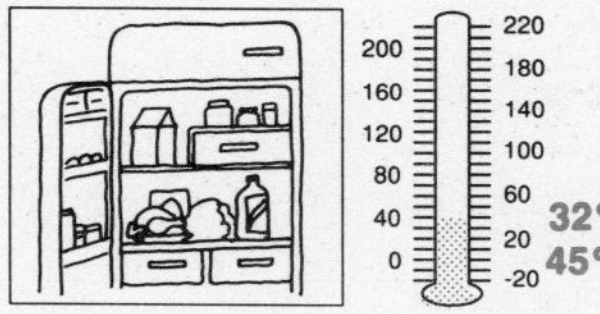
32°–45°

4. 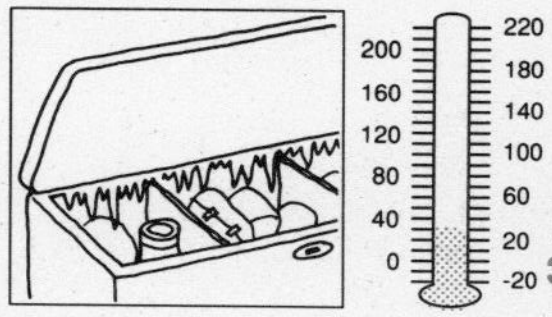
0°–32°

5. 
32°–100°

6. 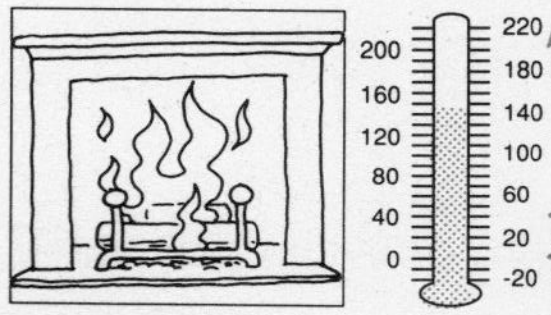
110°–140°

7. 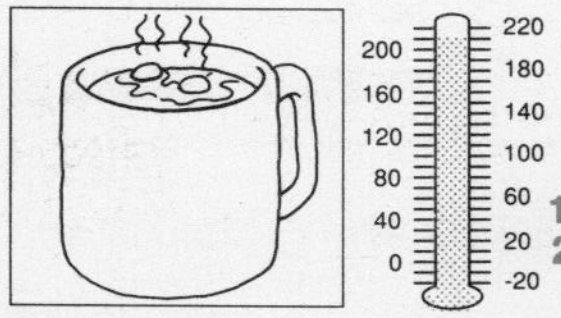
100°–220°

8. 
50°–100°

Macmillan/McGraw-Hill, MATHEMATICS IN ACTION
Grade 4, Chapter 10, Lesson 14, pages 412-413

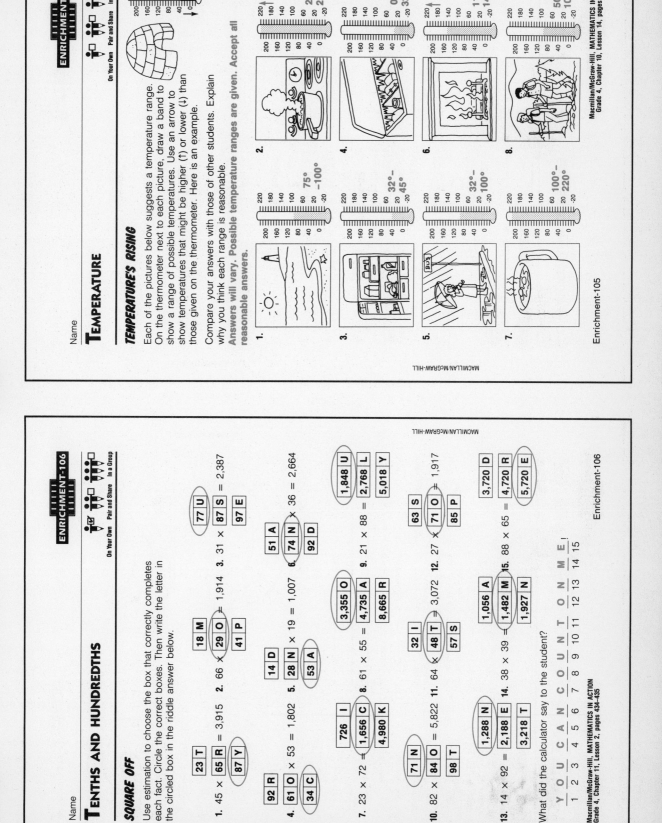

ENRICHMENT-108

On Your Own | Pair and Share | In a Group

Name

PROBLEM SOLVING

TRAIN OF THOUGHT

You and several friends have decided to enter a racetrack contest. The prize goes to the most interesting track for model race cars. The drawings show the sizes you can purchase. You have $15 to spend. How many of each piece of track will you purchase? Write your answer in the blank beneath each piece. Write the total cost of your track in the box at the bottom of the page. What will your train track look like? Work with your group to make a drawing of your final pattern.

Answers will vary.

Straight pieces:

3 inches: 55¢ each

6 inches: 85¢ each

12 inches: $1.50 each

Curves:

half curve: $1.10

full curve: $2.15

Special shapes:

loop: $3.25

zig-zag, 12 inches: $2.95

Total cost of our track: $ ______

Macmillan/McGraw-Hill, MATHEMATICS IN ACTION
Grade 4, Chapter 11, Lesson 4, pages 438–439

ENRICHMENT-107

On Your Own | Pair and Share | In a Group

Name

COMPARING AND ORDERING DECIMALS

MORE NUMBER JUMBLES

Use the digits in the boxes to complete each exercise. Use a calculator to help.

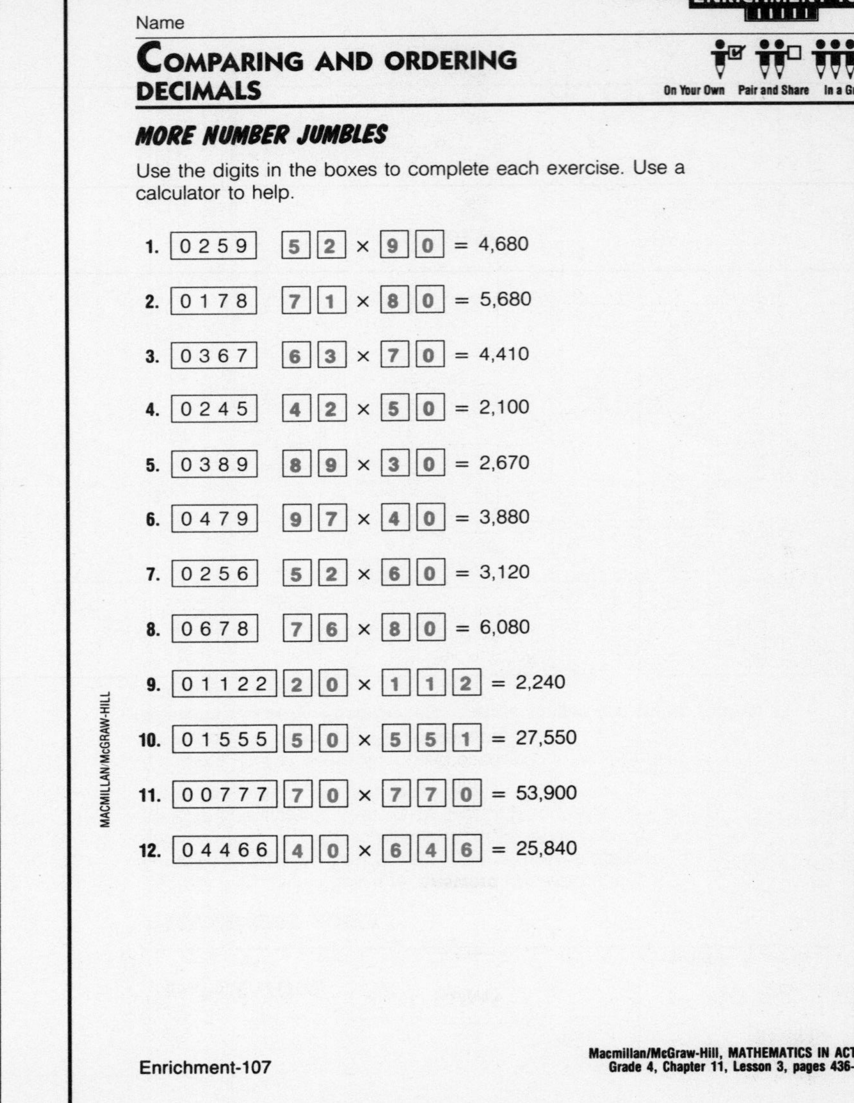

1. 0 2 5 9 — 5 2 × 9 0 = 4,680
2. 0 1 7 8 — 7 1 × 8 0 = 5,680
3. 0 3 6 7 — 6 3 × 7 0 = 4,410
4. 0 2 4 5 — 4 2 × 5 0 = 2,100
5. 0 3 8 9 — 8 9 × 3 0 = 2,670
6. 0 4 7 9 — 9 7 × 4 0 = 3,880
7. 0 2 5 6 — 5 2 × 6 0 = 3,120
8. 0 6 7 8 — 7 6 × 8 0 = 6,080
9. 0 1 1 2 2 — 2 0 × 1 1 2 = 2,240
10. 0 1 5 5 5 — 5 0 × 5 5 1 = 27,550
11. 0 0 7 7 7 — 7 0 × 7 7 0 = 53,900
12. 0 4 4 6 6 — 4 0 × 6 4 6 = 25,840

Macmillan/McGraw-Hill, MATHEMATICS IN ACTION
Grade 4, Chapter 11, Lesson 3, pages 436–437

Name

ENRICHMENT-110

ADDING DECIMALS

On Your Own · Pair and Share · In a Group

IT'S A FACT

Work with a partner. Each set of numbers can be used to make addition facts. Each number in a set should be used exactly once. Can you find all the facts? The first fact has been done for you. When you are finished, use a calculator to check your work.

~~8.21~~	5.74	13.73
7.78	2.28	~~4.75~~
5.50	7.99	~~12.96~~

4.75 + 8.21 = 12.96
5.50 + 2.28 = 7.78
5.74 + 7.99 = 13.73

3.54	1.11	2.21
5.75	14.43	8.55
5.88	8.71	9.82

2.21 + 3.54 = 5.75
5.88 + 8.55 = 14.43
8.71 + 1.11 = 9.82

3.68	6.66	9.98
5.01	8.11	0.89
2.22	8.69	15.85
9.09	4.44	7.74

2.22 + 4.44 = 6.66
5.01 + 3.68 = 8.69
7.74 + 8.11 = 15.85
9.09 + 0.89 = 9.98

The next set is tricky, so be careful.

7.07	8.66	18.40
8.48	8.08	4.24
1.01	3.58	5.25
13.35	9.74	4.24
6.11	9.77	11.36

9.74 + 8.66 = 18.40
1.01 + 7.07 = 8.08
4.24 + 4.24 = 8.48
6.11 + 5.25 = 11.36
9.77 + 3.58 = 13.35

Name

ENRICHMENT-109

ESTIMATING DECIMAL SUMS AND DIFFERENCES

On Your Own · Pair and Share · In a Group

FOUR SCORE

Play this game with a partner. **Answers will vary.**

Part One

Player 1 picks any number in a circle below and writes it in the first box for that round. Player 1 then crosses out the circle. Player 2 picks any number that is not crossed out. Players take turns until each has chosen four numbers. Use estimation to try to pick four numbers that will have a sum close to 15.

Part Two

Players use a calculator to add their numbers. They also find the difference between their sum and 15. The player closest to 15 wins that round. Players go on to the next round.

Round		Numbers				Sum	How close to 15?
1	Player 1						
	Player 2						
2	Player 1						
	Player 2						
3	Player 1						
	Player 2						
4	Player 1						
	Player 2						
5	Player 1						
	Player 2						

4.31	3.38	5.67	1.02	3.56	6.89	8.72	3.54	4.98	2.20
3.10	2.22	7.98	1.15	3.75	3.87	4.96	5.52	4.12	2.78
1.12	8.79	1.82	2.78	4.10	5.22	3.28	4.99	5.14	3.85
3.33	4.44	2.67	3.39	4.29	6.82	7.72	7.21	2.09	0.77

ENRICHMENT-112

Name

PROBLEM SOLVING

On Your Own Pair and Share In a Group

WHAT TIME IS IT?

Do you know how long a minute is? Try this experiment with a partner to find out.

You will need a watch or a clock with a second hand.

For the first experiment, you will try to guess when ten seconds have passed. First close your eyes. Your partner will tell you when to start by saying "Go." When you think ten seconds have passed, say "Stop." Your partner will tell you and write down how much time actually passed. After you have tried three times, switch roles with your partner.

Goal: Ten Seconds
First Try: __________ seconds
Second Try: __________ seconds
Third Try: __________ seconds
Did your guesses grow more accurate or less accurate?

Next, find out how close you can come to estimating one minute. Try this experiment twice.

Goal: One Minute
First Try: __________ seconds
Second Try: __________ seconds

How close did you get? Did you guess too short or too long a time? Compare your results with the rest of your class. Did students who guessed very close to the correct time use any mental tricks? Write your conclusions about this experiment below.

____
____
____
____
____
____
____
____

Macmillan/McGraw-Hill, MATHEMATICS IN ACTION
Grade 4, Chapter 11, Lesson 10, pages 450–451

ENRICHMENT-111

Name

SUBTRACTING DECIMALS

On Your Own Pair and Share In a Group

DIFFERENT TRIANGLES

Work with a partner or small group to solve these puzzles. The numbers in the top row of each triangle tell you how to complete the triangle. Each circle shows the difference between the two numbers directly above it. Look at the first triangle. The difference between 5.43 and 2.21 is 3.22.

Can you finish every triangle? Sometimes there is more than one way. Compare your work with another group. Did you get the same numbers?

Answers may vary. Sample answers are shown.

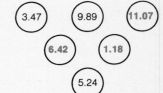

5.43 2.21 1.44
3.22 **0.77**
2.45

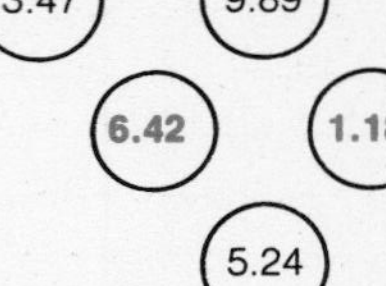

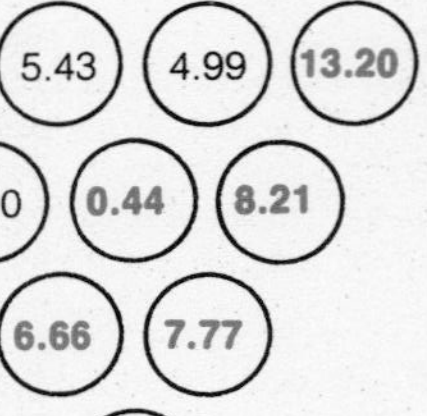

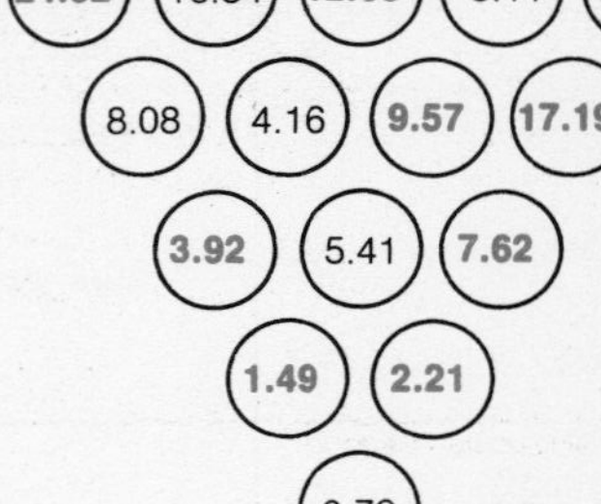

Macmillan/McGraw-Hill, MATHEMATICS IN ACTION
Grade 4, Chapter 11, Lesson 8, pages 446–447

Name

ENRICHMENT-114

PREDICTION

On Your Own Pair and Share In a Group

TAILSPIN

Play this game with a partner. You will need three coins and two markers to play.

Each player places a marker on START. When it is your turn, guess what your toss will be, and then toss the three coins. Move your marker the number of spaces shown below. If your guess was correct, double the number of spaces your marker moves. The first player to reach FINISH wins. Can you find a way to improve your chances of winning?

If you toss . . .	**move . . .**
3 heads	3 spaces forward
2 heads and 1 tail	2 spaces forward
1 head and 2 tails	1 space forward
3 tails	1 space backward

Note: If you ever fall off the gameboard, go back to START.

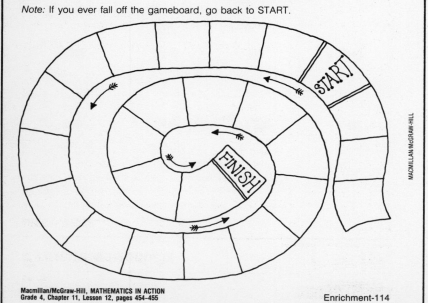

START

FINISH

Name

ENRICHMENT-113

PROBABILITY

On Your Own Pair and Share In a Group

CLEO'S CLUTTERED CLOSET

This is Cleo's closet. Look carefully at the picture. Then answer the questions below.

Cleo's closet contains:
4 shirts
3 pairs of pants
5 hats
1 scarf
2 purses
3 pairs of shoes

Cleo dresses in a hurry. She usually picks clothes from her closet without looking.

1. Cleo picks a shirt. What are the chances she will pick the white shirt? **1 in 4; $\frac{1}{4}$**
2. Next she picks a pair of pants. What are the chances that she will pick the black pants? **1 in 3; $\frac{1}{3}$**
3. If she picks a hat, what are the chances she will pick the flowered one? **1 in 5; $\frac{1}{5}$**
4. What are the chances that she will pick the black purse? **1 in 2; $\frac{1}{2}$**
5. If Cleo picks two shoes from her closet, what are the chances that she will get a matching pair? **3 in 15; $\frac{3}{15}$ or $\frac{1}{5}$**
6. Now suppose that Cleo picks a shirt and a pair of pants. What are the chances that they will match? (*Hint:* draw a tree diagram to help you.) **3 in 12; $\frac{3}{12}$ or $\frac{1}{4}$**
7. Now suppose that Cleo picks a shirt, a pair of pants, and a hat. What are the chances that all three items will match? **3 in 60; $\frac{3}{60}$ or $\frac{1}{20}$**

ENRICHMENT-116

Name

ESTIMATING PRODUCTS

On Your Own · Pair and Share · In a Group

FAMILY AFFAIR

What did the baby volcano say to its mother?

To find the answer, complete each multiplication.
Write the letter for each product in the spaces below.

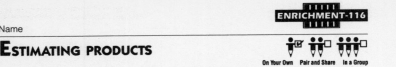

20 × 36 Y 720	47 × 30 T 1,410	60 × 25 O 1,500	20 × 74 S 1,480
65 × 70 L 4,550	56 × 40 D 2,240	22 × 30 I 660	18 × 80 L 1,440
112 × 40 A 4,480	70 × 210 M 14,700	160 × 30 L 4,800	20 × 433 E 8,660
50 × 139 A 6,950	30 × 462 O 13,860	40 × 236 V 9,440	60 × 385 U 23,100

Answer:

D (2,240) O (1,500) Y (720) O (13,860) U (23,100) S (1,480) T (1,410) I (660) L (4,800) L (1,440)

L (4,550) A (6,950) V (9,440) A (4,480) M (14,700) E (8,660) ?

Macmillan/McGraw-Hill, MATHEMATICS IN ACTION
Grade 4, Chapter 12, Lesson 2, pages 476–477

ENRICHMENT-115

Name

MENTAL MATH: MULTIPLY 10s; 100s; 1,000s

On Your Own · Pair and Share · In a Group

MULTIPLICATION RACE

A. This is a game for 2 or more players.

30	40	50	60	70
80	300	400	500	600
700	800	2,400	16,000	25,000
42,000	56,000	180,000		

1. Each player cuts out a set of 18 cards with the numbers shown above. All players start at the same time.
2. Each player works as quickly as he or she can to make 6 correct multiplication sentences using all the cards in the deck exactly once.
3. The first player to finish is the winner. The other players should check the multiplication sentences to make sure they are correct.

80 × 30 = 2,400
40 × 400 = 16,000
50 × 500 = 25,000
60 × 700 = 42,000
70 × 800 = 56,000
300 × 600 = 180,000

B. Work with your friends to create a different set of playing cards. Then exchange cards with another group. Try playing each other's games.

Macmillan/McGraw-Hill, MATHEMATICS IN ACTION
Grade 4, Chapter 12, Lesson 1, pages 474–475

ENRICHMENT-118

Name

PROBLEM SOLVING

On Your Own Pair and Share In a Group

YOU FIND OUT

Each problem below is missing a fact needed to solve it. Work with a partner to decide what fact is missing. Then use a reference book to find the fact. Solve the problem using the fact you found. **Answers will vary slightly depending on reference used.**

1. Mount Rainier in Washington State is 14,410 feet high. The highest mountain in the United States is Mount McKinley in Alaska. How much higher is Mount McKinley than Mount Rainier?

   MISSING FACT **the height of Mount McKinley**

   FACT YOU FOUND **Mount McKinley is 20,320 feet high.**

   ANSWER **5,910 feet higher**

2. The Snake River is in Wyoming. The Wabash River in Ohio is 529 miles long. Which river is longer? How much longer?

   MISSING FACT **the length of the Snake River**

   FACT YOU FOUND **The Snake River is 1,038 miles long.**

   ANSWER **Snake River—509 miles longer**

3. Lake Superior is the longest of the Great Lakes. Lake Ontario is the shortest. It is 193 miles long. How much longer is Lake Superior than Lake Ontario?

   MISSING FACT **the length of Lake Superior**

   FACT YOU FOUND **Lake Superior is 350 miles long.**

   ANSWER **157 miles longer**

4. Illinois became a state in 1818. Nebraska became a state many years later. How many years after Illinois did Nebraska become a state?

   MISSING FACT **the year Nebraska became a state**

   FACT YOU FOUND **Nebraska became a state in 1867.**

   ANSWER **49 years after**

Macmillan/McGraw-Hill, MATHEMATICS IN ACTION
Grade 4, Chapter 12, Lesson 4, pages 480–481

ENRICHMENT-117

Name

MULTIPLYING BY MULTIPLES OF TEN

On Your Own Pair and Share In a Group

TARGET PRACTICE

Work with a partner. Decide which two numbers on each target have a product closest to the given score. Ring the numbers you choose.

1. Targets: 48, 36, 24, 12 — Score 600

3. Targets: 59, 42, 25, 14 — Score 1,000

5. Targets: 88, 72, 65, 49 — Score 6,300

7. Targets: 555, 404, 333, 202, 111 — Score 40,000

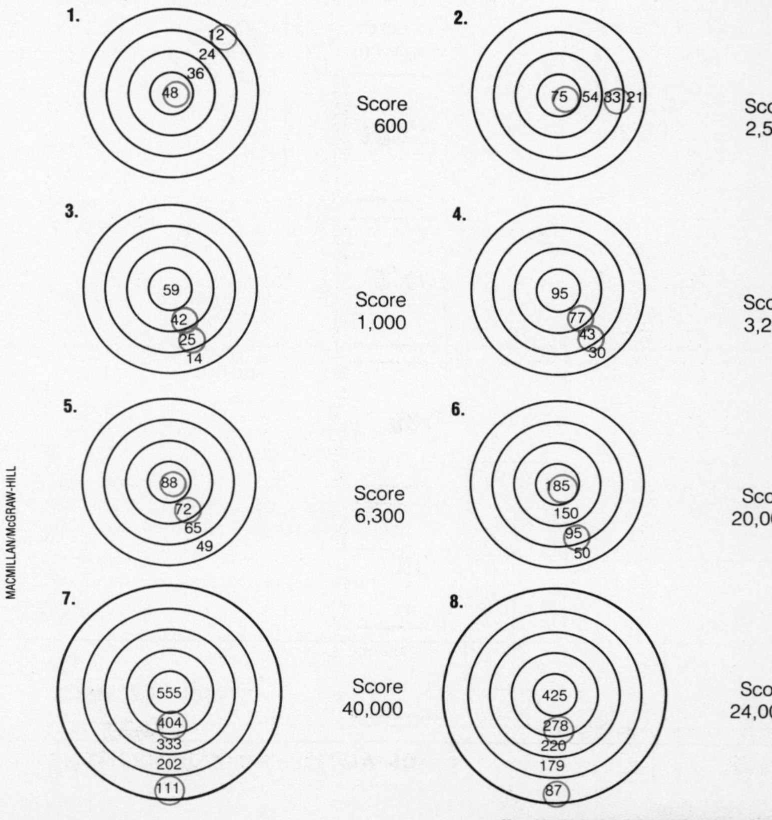

Macmillan/McGraw-Hill, MATHEMATICS IN ACTION
Grade 4, Chapter 12, Lesson 3, pages 478–479

ENRICHMENT-120

Name

More Multiplying 2-Digit Numbers

On Your Own · Pair and Share · In a Group

A-MAZING MULTIPLICATION

Find a path through the maze. Multiply each factor in the bowl by each factor on the spoon. Cross out each product that you find. Then draw a path through the crossed-out boxes to get from START to FINISH.

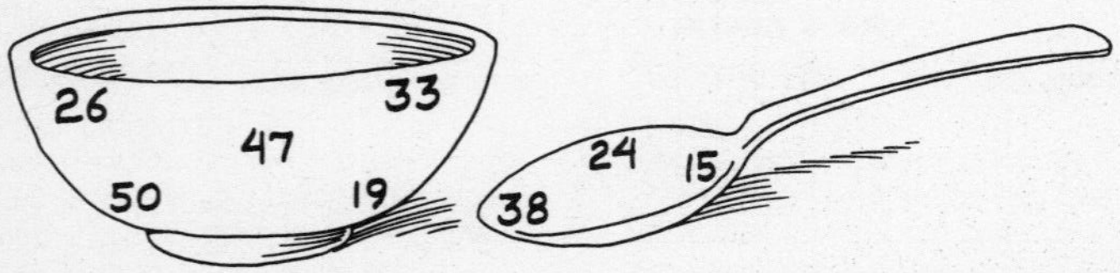

Bowl: 26, 33, 47, 50, 19
Spoon: 38, 24, 15

FINISH

1,355	2,400	1,233	456	390	705
1,880	1,456	943	750	1,254	1,298
824	285	1,786	624	722	1,156
1,050	792	1,900	348	742	1,078
595	1,300	988	782	970	595
1,200	495	1,128	1,558	651	280

START

Macmillan/McGraw-Hill, MATHEMATICS IN ACTION
Grade 4, Chapter 12, Lesson 7, pages 486–487

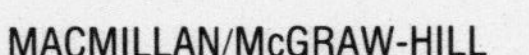

ENRICHMENT-119

Name

Multiplying 2-Digit Numbers

On Your Own · Pair and Share · In a Group

CLIMB THE LADDER

This is an old way of multiplying. You use a square like the one shown at the right.

Suppose you want to find the product of 34 × 26.

Write the first factor (34) across the top and the second factor (26) down the right side.

Fill in the spaces by multiplying each digit of one factor by each digit of the other factor.

Add along the diagonals, starting at the lower right corner. Regroup if necessary.

The product is 884.

4 × 2 = 8

8 + 2 + 8 = 18
Write 8,
regroup 1 ten.

8 8 4

Find each product using the method above. Check each answer using regular multiplication.

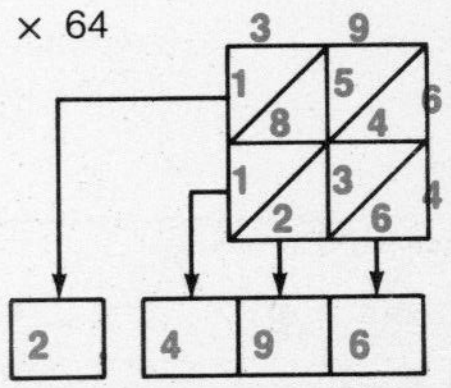

1. 19 × 35 — 6 6 5

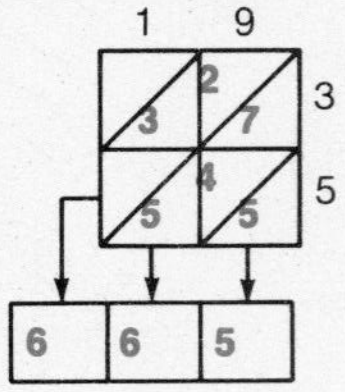

2. 27 × 38 — 1,0 2 6

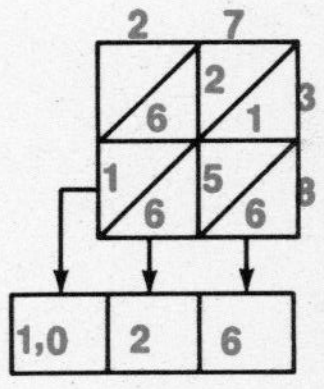

3. 42 × 53 — 2 2 2 6

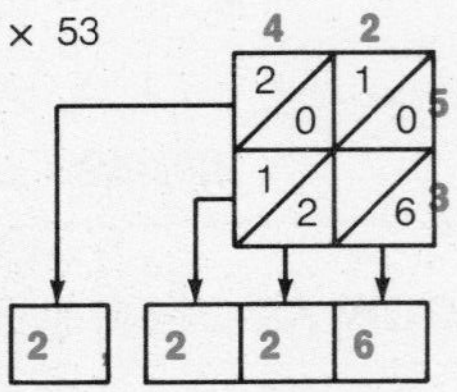

4. 39 × 64 — 2 4 9 6

Macmillan/McGraw-Hill, MATHEMATICS IN ACTION
Grade 4, Chapter 12, Lesson 6, pages 484–485

ENRICHMENT-122

Name

MENTAL MATH: DIVIDE 10s; 100s; 1,000s

On Your Own Pair and Share In a Group

LOOK BOTH WAYS

1. Ring two that are exactly alike and in the same position.

2. Ring the puzzles that do *not* have two or more pieces that are the same. The pieces may be in different positions.

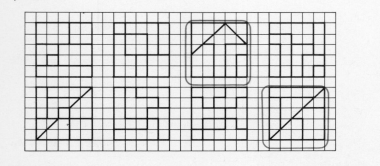

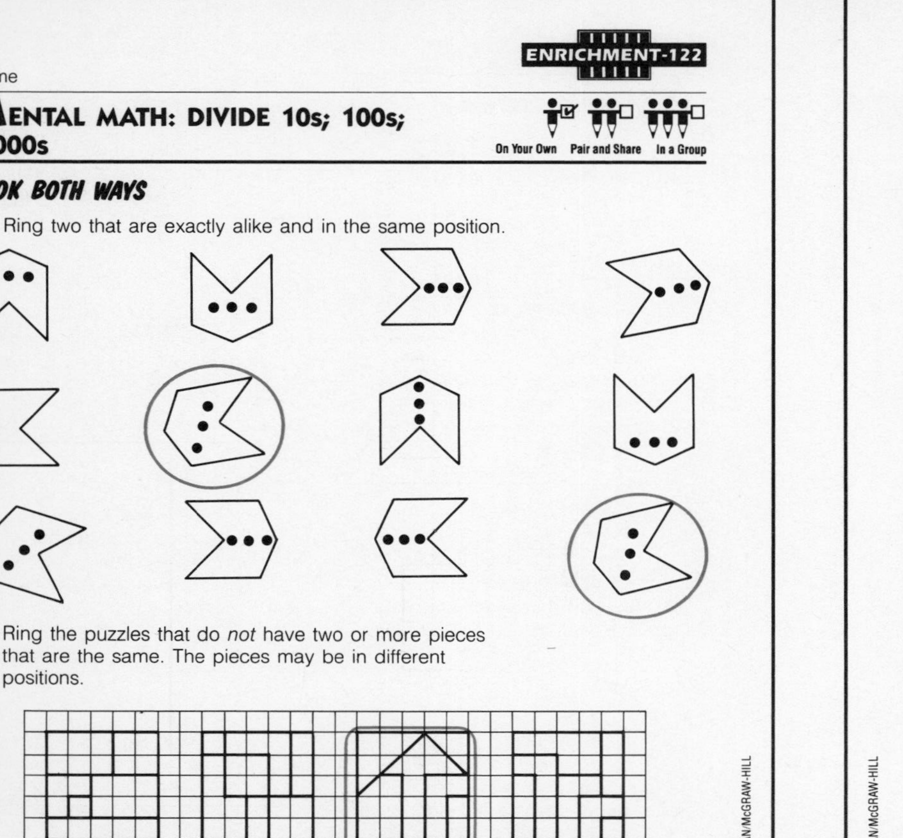

ENRICHMENT-121

Name

MULTIPLYING 3-DIGIT NUMBERS

On Your Own Pair and Share In a Group

WAGES AND HOURS

Here is a game for 2 to 4 players.

- Make the two spinners shown below. (You can cut them out and glue them on cardboard. Use a paper clip for each pointer.)
- Each player takes a turn spinning both spinners. The player then multiplies the hourly wage by the number of hours to find the total earnings for that turn.
- The other players check the multiplication to be sure it is correct. (Calculators may be used only for checking.) A player who multiplies incorrectly receives no earnings for that turn.
- The players record the amounts they earn for each turn on individual score sheets.
- After 5 rounds of play, each player calculates his or her total earnings for the game. (Calculators may be used.) The player who has earned the most money is the winner.

Here is part of a score sheet for a player named Laurie.

Answers will vary. Check students' score sheets.

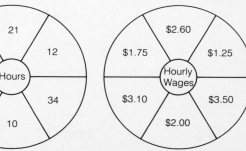

Player: Laurie		
Hours	**Hourly Wage**	**Earnings**
12	\$2.60	12 × \$2.60 = \$31.20
25	\$1.75	25 × \$1.75 = \$43.75

Hours: 21, 12, 34, 10, 25, 16

Hourly Wages: \$2.60, \$1.25, \$3.50, \$2.00, \$3.10, \$1.75

ENRICHMENT-124

Name

PROBLEM SOLVING

On Your Own | Pair and Share | In a Group

DON'T DELAY, RELAY

In each set, use your answer from Problem A to solve Problem B.

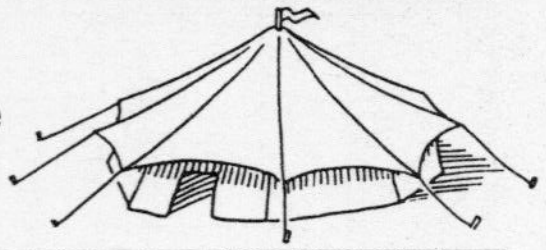

Set 1

A. Last year, a ticket to the circus cost $4.75. This year, a ticket costs $.75 more. How much does a ticket cost this year?

$5.50

B. Neil bought 7 tickets to the circus this year. How much money did he spend for tickets?

$38.50

Set 2

A. On Sunday, 1,238 people came to the circus. On Saturday, 166 fewer people came than on Sunday. How many people were at the circus on Saturday?

1,072 people

B. How many people in all were at the circus over the weekend?

2,310 people

Set 3

A. There are 32 rows of seats in the circus tent. Each row has 26 seats. How many seats are in the tent?

832 seats

B. A circus program is placed on each seat in the tent. There are 80 programs in a bundle. How many bundles will have to be opened?

11 bundles

Set 4

A. The circus is in town for 28 days. The circus owner pays $195 a day to rent the circus grounds. How much rent will the owner pay in all?

$5,460

B. The performers' total wages are twice as much as the total rent. How much are the wages? How much does the owner spend in all?

$10,920; $16,380

ENRICHMENT-123

Name

DIVIDING BY MULTIPLES OF TEN

On Your Own | Pair and Share | In a Group

MODERN MACHINERY

A. The machines below have been given the following instructions:

	Example
INPUT A NUMBER	INPUT 65
DIVIDE BY 20	65 ÷ 20 = 3 R5
MULTIPLY THE REMAINDER BY 40	5 × 40 = 200
DIVIDE BY 10	200 ÷ 10 = 20
OUTPUT THE RESULT	OUTPUT 20

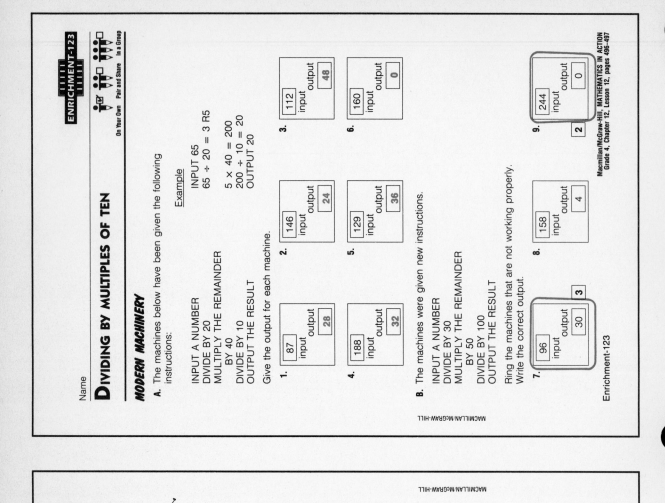

Give the output for each machine.

	input	output
1.	87	**28**
2.	146	**24**
3.	112	**48**
4.	188	**32**
5.	129	**36**
6.	160	**0**

B. The machines were given new instructions.

INPUT A NUMBER
DIVIDE BY 30
MULTIPLY THE REMAINDER
BY 50
DIVIDE BY 100
OUTPUT THE RESULT

Ring the machines that are not working properly. Write the correct output.

	input	output	correct output
7.	96	30	**3**
8.	158	4	
9.	244	0	**2**

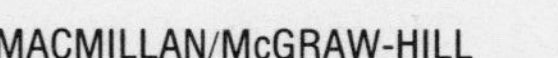